Acclaim for

Amal Naj's
Peppers

"A revelation...*Peppers* reads like the complete biography of a world hero....The story is alive with the characters caught in its pungent thrall, from scientists studying its medicinal powers to cooks seeking the perfect sauce. This is a flavorful tale."
—The New York Times Book Review

"An anecdotal history of the fruit to which so many diners worldwide are addicted. [Naj] is a wonderful pepper journalist, a man who tells terrific stories that happen to have a foodstuff as a central character."
—Los Angeles Times

"As a chile aficionado, I couldn't put this book down. It contains fascinating new aspects of chile lore, and I found myself learning something new in every chapter. If you weren't a chile lover before, this book will certainly convert you. The well-written tales alone take the noble chile out of obscurity and into the forefront of the culinary scene."
—Mark Miller

"Peppered throughout with many amusing anecdotes about this pungent fruit and its devotees, this well-researched book is as entertaining as it is informative."
—Library Journal

Amal Naj
Peppers

Amal Naj was born in India and was educated there and at Queen's University in Belfast, Northern Ireland. He has been on the staff of *The Wall Street Journal* for the last twelve years, and has reported from Pittsburgh and Detroit on the steel and automotive industries. He now covers manufacturing technology and environmental issues from New York City, where he lives.

tepín

tomato pepper

rocoto

Anaheim

piquín

Peppers
A story of hot pursuits

Cayenne

6-4

pasilla

scabel

Amal Naj
Illustrations by the author

Thai green

bell pepper

pimiento

poblano

zol

pepperoncini

de árbol

Vintage Books
A Division of Random House, Inc., New York

co

Big Jim

serrano

First Vintage Books Edition, August 1993

Copyright © 1992 by Amal Naj

All rights reserved under International and Pan-American
Copyright Conventions. Published in the United States by
Vintage Books, a division of Random House, Inc., New York,
and simultaneously in Canada by Random House of Canada
Limited, Toronto. Originally published in hardcover by
Alfred A. Knopf, Inc., New York, in 1992.

Library of Congress Cataloging-in-Publication Data
Naj, Amal.
Peppers: a story of hot pursuits / Amal Naj.—1st Vintage Books ed.
p. cm.
Originally published: New York: Knopf, c1992.
Includes index.
ISBN 0-679-74427-4
1. Hot peppers. 2. Food habits. I. Title.
[SB307.P4N35 1993]
641.3'384—dc20   92-50625   CIP

Book design by Iris Weinstein

Manufactured in the United States of America

10 9 8 7 6 5 4 3 2 1

To my parents,
Anil and Biva Näg

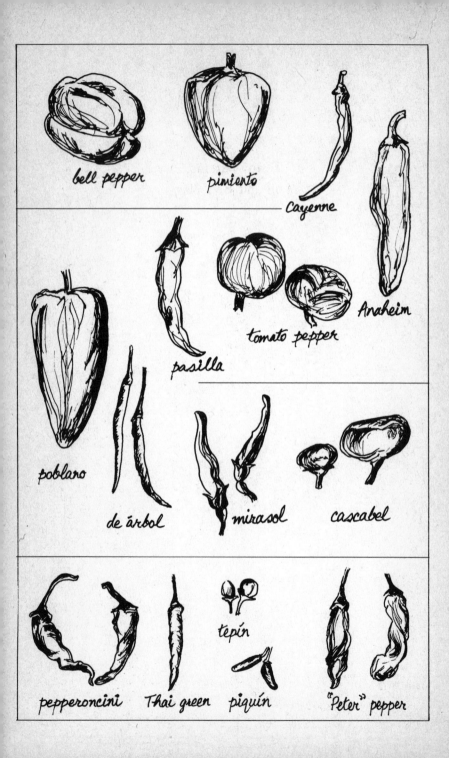

bell pepper

pimiento

Cayenne

pasilla

tomato pepper

Anaheim

poblano

de árbol

mirasol

cascabel

pepperoncini

Thai green

tepín

piquín

"Peter" pepper

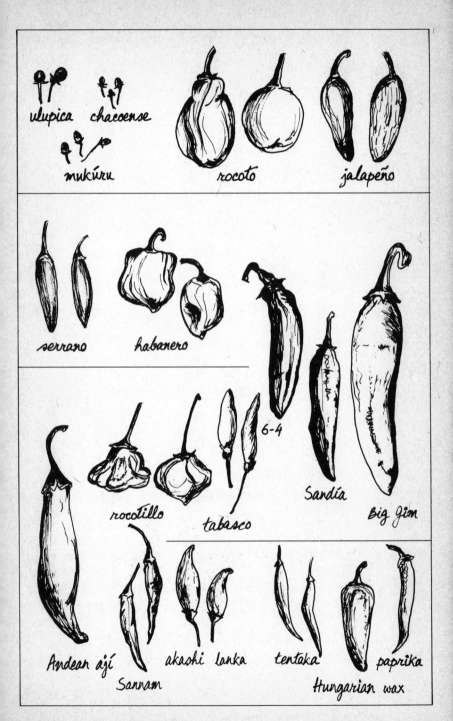

ulupica chacoense

mukúru

rocoto

jalapeño

serrano

habanero

6-4

Sandía

Big Jim

rocotillo

tabasco

Andean ají

Sannam

akashi lanka

tentaka

paprika

Hungarian wax

Contents

Introduction: How the Pepper Got its Bite

My earliest memory of peppers goes back to my child-hood. I was six years old, and living in a remote farming village in Bengal, a northeastern region of India dotted with rice paddies and ponds. Ponds are a big thing in Bengal. When the Bengali looks at his scrap of land, he doesn't wish for a vegetable garden or a lawn. He thinks of fish and digs deep. Year-round the pond holds his main staple. Ours was a big pond, shaded by banana and bamboo trees, and it edged against a row of pepper plants the size of rosebushes. They were the most-tended plants in the garden, and their fruits daily found their way to our dinner table.

On a rainy afternoon, while wandering by the pond, I was approaching the esteemed pepper patch. I heard a hiss and saw a black snake fan its head above its coiled body under a bush. I screamed and scampered back to the kitchen in tears.

"A cobra! A cobra!"

My aunt, unfazed, wiped her hands and sauntered out to investigate, and I followed behind her. The snake had slithered away. With a casual wave of her hand she dismissed my frightening encounter and instructed me to keep away from the pepper bushes, which bore oblong fruits of deep lavender. "Cobras take shelter under pepper plants, and that's how the pepper gets its bite," she declared as we headed back into the house.

Suddenly the pepper became a terrifying symbol for me, a spooky object. I avoided it as if it would leap out and bite me like that cobra under the bush. It wasn't a big sacrifice at the dinner table; I had never liked the thing as food anyway. My first taste of it was as medicine: whenever I caught a cold or flu, my aunt would chop a fresh pod into a bowl of steaming rice and lentils and force-feed me, ignoring my howling cries. After the encounter with the cobra, I now altogether avoided peppers and the backyard bushes.

Many years later I would learn that my aunt's remark was meant to keep me away from the pond and, indeed, away from the cobras, which had adopted as their home a burrow just above the watermark at the pond's far end. The cobras were not to be disturbed, let alone killed, since, according to Hindu mythology and as our surname suggested, we had "descended" from the serpent-god, also known as Näg. By the time I learned all this and figured out why my aunt had made up the story, I already had developed a palate that eschewed the blustery spice. I remained uninfluenced even though the pepper was daily fare not only at my aunt's home but at all dinner tables in the village.

In most dishes the pepper was cooked into the food. But it always made an unmolested appearance with the first course, which usually consisted of fried fish or vegetables served on rice that was lightly scented with clarified butter. A whole green pepper, plucked from the backyard bushes, would be laid next to the rice on each plate. The diner would grip the pod between the thumb and the forefinger and press it against the plate, and the fruit would break into halves with a pop. Pop! Pop! Pop! The muffled sound would arise from all corners of the table. A sharp pop would attest to the freshness of the pod. The pepper would then be bitten off, starting from the broken end, with each mouthful of food. My aunt sometimes would complain mildly if her pepper was unusually hot—"Oh, this is hot!"—and then as quickly resume her amorous skirmishes. If the pepper wasn't up to her expectation, she would call out: "Shomnath, will you get me a good one this time." And the kitchen help would dash off to the pepper bushes. It was one element of the meal, I remember, that was constantly fussed over, even though it was neither the main course nor a side dish. But it seemed the pepper formed the lattice over which the rest of the meal grew, as a smooth and orderly whole.

I somehow managed to evade peppers during my adolescence, even though it was a daily nuisance for the cooks at home: my meals had to be prepared separately, or sometimes my portion would be isolated from a preparation just before hot peppers were added. Sometimes the cooks and the rest of the household weren't willing to be all that cooperative. Since adding hot peppers at the end—as opposed to in the very beginning and in subsequent stages, as required by the recipe—

would have deprived the others of the dish's subtleties, I often was served vegetables and meats that had been cooked to the majority's taste and then washed and reheated.

I forgot about peppers altogether after I went to Northern Ireland for undergraduate studies. But it wasn't for very long: a year of Ireland's monotonous food provoked even my unadventurous palate. My stomach rebelled one late Sunday afternoon in Belfast. I was walking along a long row of attached brownstones, and I smelled through the shuttered windows the dreary waft of boiling starch and burning fat rising from the pans and ovens of one kitchen after another. No scent of tarragon, oregano, basil, or rosemary, let alone garlic, or cumin, or coriander—or the pepper! I pondered my plight.

It was drizzling that Sunday, as it had been the afternoon of my encounter with the cobra at the pond in Bengal. I laughed at the notion of the pepper's getting its bite from the venom of a cobra. The memory for the first time filled me with nostalgia, and curiosity. I longed for a bite of that venom. Later that evening I would elevate my gastronomic condition to critical as I confronted a plate of mashed turnip, mashed potato, mashed carrot, and calf's liver, which, fortunately, had been spared the kitchen masher and instead was sautéed with onion.

There was little one could do during those days in Belfast to mollify a palate craving for flavor, for aroma, for a zing, for any kind of zing. It was the early 1970s, and the beleaguered city, electrified by Bernadette Devlin and Ian Paisley, was the last place on earth that enterprising Chinese and Indian restaurateurs would look upon as suitable for new business opportunity. The grocery shops and supermarkets weren't any help either; when I inquired about dried red peppers—whole or crushed, anything—I received blank stares or crushed black pepper. "I don't think, lad, I ever seen this stuff red. Always black," a corner grocer once insisted as he handed me a small jar of peppercorns.

One day I asked for help from an English friend in London—the second-best place after New Delhi for curry. And it came by post in a box: half a dozen or so plastic packets of spices, ranging in color from brown to yellow to red. And, of course, my friend hadn't forgotten my request for fresh pepper pods. I immediately broke open one of them and held it under my nose at a safe distance. It sent razor-sharp rays piercing into my nostrils, and my tongue, warned of the lurking danger, kept itself safely behind my clenched teeth. That evening, buffered by some precautionary measures, I finally had my tryst with the pepper. Instead of nipping a fresh pod with my teeth—the way I remembered my aunt relishing her fresh pepper—I chopped it into baked beans. Canned red beans piled on toast with sausage and chips (French fries) were a popular dish at the time in Belfast, at least among students. I ate the peppery meal, sniffling and sweating, in the privacy of my room.

Why confine the pepper experiment to beans, and why not let fellow boarders in on my culinary experiments, I thought. So what started out as a playful indulgence in the kitchen gradually became frequent evening sessions with Irish classmates. Slivers of peppers went into shepherd's pie. One weekend someone returned with a pot of lamb stew from home, and whole pods were immediately dropped into it, giving zest to the stew as it was reheated. A popular late-night supper used to be a sandwich of Cheddar cheese and orange marmalade; soon the marmalade was replaced with chopped peppers and the whole sandwich grilled. A classmate one day surprised us all with a bottle of vinegar in which he had soaked hot peppers for several days. Vinegar is standard fare on fish and chips, and that greasy and soggy food was something we all looked forward to when we staggered out of a pub in the wee hours. "No vinegar, thank you," we would tell the street vendor and rush home to our bottle of fiery vinegar. My London friend who had sent the peppers had included this note in the box: "This should last you the rest of your stay in Ulster." He was mistaken.

What struck me about our pepper indulgences was that

after some initial inhibitions we had developed a craving for the biting taste. The otherwise bland Irish dishes seemed tastier when spiced with hot peppers. Some of us one night pondered over a bottle of Bushmills whiskey whether the pepper transformed the food, or was it that it heightened the sensitivity of the mouth and the tongue by piercing open their sensory receptacles. Or was there something in the pepper itself that we all craved. As for me, given how eagerly my Irish friends had taken to the pepper, my sudden attachment to the fruit couldn't be explained away simply as hereditary or cultural.

Our growing addiction, if it was that, was only shyly acknowledged, however. It was seen as an odd predilection, even embarrassing, given the physiological reactions—flaming mouths, tearing eyes, and gasping lungs—peppers brought upon us. The matter would have rested there with me, but years later I would encounter people in the meat-and-potato Western world who quietly admitted to a narcoticlike attachment to the fruit.

Some went to great lengths to procure their favorite types. They sought not just any pepper but one that had a "bouquet," a pepper that had that "pleasant nip," a pepper that displayed its razzmatazz "on the front of the tongue rather than on the back" to satisfy their newly discovered sensory titillation. I would meet aficionados who rhapsodized their pepper infatuations with the flourishes of a sommelier. I would meet an American, an international consultant, who even in Thailand would buy a bag of extremely hot peppers in a local market before showing up in a restaurant, because he wasn't convinced that the Thai chefs took him seriously when he demanded that his dishes be prepared as hot as possible.

What's so extraordinary about hot peppers? I felt I had to find out.

I discovered an underworld of pepper culture, rich in lore and mysteries, dating back to the beginning of recorded history. The pepper was one of the first fruits that the hunter-gatherer cultivated. It was this biting taste that would later spark voyages on uncharted seas, including those through which Columbus would "discover" the New World, where the pepper originated. Columbus, who was trying to reach the Indian subcontinent for black pepper and other spices, thought he had reached his destination when in fact he had dead-ended in the Caribbean. From there he described hot peppers—which are not to be confused with the black pepper. It's because of this bungling that Native Americans are mistakenly called Indians.

Columbus died in obscurity, his hot peppers shunned in his native land. But the fruit traveled on to other parts of the world and not only changed cuisines forever but also broadened the world's taste spectrum to include pungency alongside sweet, sour, bitter, and salty. That peppers didn't exist in India before Columbus horrifies Indians. "What do you mean, we didn't have it first?" they often ask, surprised. They have a right to be astonished at this fact, since most people associate the pepper with the pungent food of Asia and Mexico.

It's somewhat odd that it has taken centuries longer for the appetite for peppers to hit the United States, a stone's throw from the fruit's South American birthplace. I traveled to the Southwestern United States, where an increasing preference for *picante* food is spawning an industry of pepper farms, canners, and botanists. There I met a man known as Dr. Pepper who has nothing to do with the popular drink of the same name. In Hatch, New Mexico, I met farmers who grow tailor-made peppers and introduce them to an eager populace, much as the auto industry in Detroit introduces new models.

I traveled, too, to Louisiana, where one hot pepper has been the subject of drawn-out Cajun court battles—the contest reached all the way to the steps of the U.S. Supreme Court. In Los Angeles I linked up with an eminent physician who's the chief of medicine at the prestigious Olive View Medical Center and whose reputation recently had been enhanced by his advocacy for pepper as a nutrient and as a subject for pharmacological applications. Since ancient times peppers have been an important item in folk medicines of Meso-America, South America, Africa, and Asia. Now peppers' mysterious chemicals are being unraveled, sparking interest among neuroscientists: the fruit, they are finding, holds the potential cure for certain painful human disorders for which there's presently no remedy.

Continuing my pursuit of peppers, I journeyed farther south, to Mexico's Yucatán, where I discovered that the indigenous pepper, the hottest known to exist on earth, was the sweetest thing on the tongues of the Mayas. The pepper's sharp, smooth bite and its aroma make it the most remarkable pepper in the world, and it quickly became my favorite. Then I traveled to Bolivia's highlands, the supposed birthplace of the fruit, with the botanist who has spent three decades researching peppers. When I accompanied the plant hunter, he was in search of the "mother pepper" in his long effort to draw the genealogical tree of peppers, which come in mind-boggling shapes and sizes and coloring.

When I undertook the exploration of the pepper, I was drawn into it mostly by the pepper's comic value, the unrelenting craving it induced in the pepper eater. That side wasn't apparent to me in India, where the pepper was taken for granted. Only in the West did the pepper eater's special relationship to the fruit become evident as I observed acquaintances and friends first violently turn away and then get hooked.

On first consideration, it seems odd that humans should have ever embraced the pepper: it's the only edible fruit on earth that bites back. Such a spiteful reaction normally signals danger, and humans are programmed to instinctively respond by steering clear of the plant or fruit. But the first bite of pepper, once endured, rewards the venturesome with an unmistakable sensation of pleasure, and it's this craving that sends the smitten back for yet another bite—and to be bitten again. By the time I finished my journey, I knew why the pepper, despite its quarrelsome temperament, had cut a wide swath across the culinary landscape from one end of the earth to the other.

Peppers

The Pepper Pod

On the surface of it, the practice of eating peppers appears preposterous, given the menacing uses the fruit has been put to. Incas burned heaps of dried red peppers in the path of the invading Spaniards to temporarily blind them; Mayas thrust mischievous children into pepper smoke and rubbed fresh pepper into the sexual organs of unchaste women. The British rubbed the hot Bahamian pepper into the eyes of mutinous slaves in the West Indies. During Iraq's violent occupation of Kuwait, the invaders, according to news accounts, beat up Kuwaitis and forced them to sit naked on hot sauce. Africans to this day spray water containing hot pepper juice into the eyes of delinquent children. In an account of a robbery, a New Delhi newspaper recently told of burglars throwing a thick dust of powdered red pepper into the eyes of the victims to manage a quick getaway. In a more sophisticated form the U.S. Army considered using pepper's chemical to make a "nonlethal incapacitating" tear gas. In 1640 Sir John Parkinson observed in his *Theatricum Botanica* that dogs detest hot peppers, and this gave birth centuries later to the aerosol sprays that make the

Peppers

rounds in the postman's bag. Members of Liberia's Grebo tribe, in a rite called "peppering the child," smear mashed peppers into every orifice of a baby and place the child in the sun in the belief that it forces the new arrival to fight for life, as a sort of initiation into a difficult world.

Oblivious of these uses, more than a quarter of the world's people eat hot peppers—also known as chiles in many parts of the world—with gusto. In Mexico, where people took to hot peppers eight thousand years ago as hunter-gatherers, many wouldn't eat a meal without them; sometimes the pepper itself is the whole meal, with everything else on the plate a sideshow. The Mayas in the Yucatán peninsula of Mexico snub all peppers but one, the habanero—arguably the world's hottest—which they toast and then drop into a bowl of fresh lime juice, to make a condiment; mashed, the habanero makes a sauce called xnipek—the Maya word for dog's nose—that is indeed hot enough to make the nose moist like a dog's. In Brazil, malagueta is a sought-after inch-long pepper that grows on a weedy plant. The same pepper grows on the Guinea coast of West Africa; there, however, malagueta is a plant that bears pungent seeds called "grains of paradise," which in the West are known as allspice. Hot green chile fried on its own is a popular dish in Guatemala, and the town of San Martin Chile Verde is so named because its residents have a particular affection for chile verde. The Indians in Peru eat the rocoto, a fiery breed that looks like cherries and grows high in the Andes; it's too hot for many, who cut open the pugnacious round fruit, stir it into their soup, and then discard it. In a somewhat reverse approach, the Malay dips his stuffed hot pepper into a steaming pork soup and instead of discarding the pepper eats it with fish paste—the soup serves to cook as well as flavor the pepper, just as the pepper flavors the soup for the Peruvians. When it comes to selecting among their peppers one with a well-balanced dis-position, aficionados marvel at South America's rocotillo, a crispy, crimson red pepper the shape of pattypan squash, which is neither so hot that it sends the mouth tongue-twisting nor so mild that it smacks of cucumber.

In India, cooks are alchemists of peppers. They begin preparation of meals by tossing some dry pods into hot oil. Then, as the dish progresses, they add spoonfuls of the same pepper powdered and then a purée or slivers of fresh pods. As a result, a dish often contains the same pepper in three different forms, each adding its own distinct panache to the whole. Indians generally prize heat more than flavor in the pepper; indeed, as a measure of its value a small purplish-black pepper in Northern India is simply called *ake lota pepper*, meaning a pepper that requires one glass of water to extinguish its heat. Guntur, in southeast India, is the pepper capital of the world. Pepper crops are shipped there from all over India, brokered, and from Guntur dispersed throughout the world. In the warehouse district the air is hazy with pepper dust. Contrary to common perception, the workers never grow immune to the pungent air; sneezing is rife. A popular snack in the region is pepper pods marinated in yogurt and fried crisp, which students carry in their pockets and eat with a spice made—naturally—of powdered hot red pepper.

Thais eat more hot peppers than any other people in the world—an average of five grams per person daily, twice the individual average in India—and they don't even spare their clear soups, which they transform into liquid fires with the extremely pungent green pickeenu pepper. The Koreans, who come close to matching the Thais in hot-pepper consumption, are fond of a fleshy and highly pugnacious dried red pepper that's the main spice in kimchi, the country's staple dish. It's the same biting pungency the people of Szechwan in China crave before any other flavor; they start their day with a breakfast of noodles over which they pour hot-pepper oil or sauce.

The Japanese are known for preferring food that's untainted by spice, but they nevertheless crave pungency, which they seek in the mild-tempered green horseradish, or wasabi, that unfailingly accompanies their sushi. Ironically, the country produces small quantities of two very hot peppers, the long and slender santaka and hontaka. Because the cost of growing them in the land-starved country is high, Japan also has farmers in China grow the same peppers to meet a rising domestic demand. The santaka and hontaka grown under contract in Tianjin, southeast of Beijing, return to Japan as tentaka. These peppers are dried and turned into powder for sprinkling on soupy dishes, but some sushi chefs find the beautiful, three-to-four-inch-long, vermilion-red pods irresistible. They skin a whole daikon and pierce four holes across the radish's entire length, and then jam the pepper pods into the holes, end to end. They then grate it by hand. The resulting condiment, which they call "grated autumn leaves," brings to a delicate fish soup an autumnal play of contrasts, coolness, and heat.

Pepper sauce rather than the fresh pod itself is preferred to spice foods in Africa. The practice may have started with folk-medicine men, who, deft at concocting mixtures with esoteric herbs, found the pepper a mysterious and effective ingredient to embellish their preparations. The berbere sauce, which distinguishes Ethiopian cuisine, is made of wine, ground red pepper, and nearly a dozen other spices. West Indians combine their hottest peppers with herbs and spices to make condiments they believe promote general well-being; the simplest of these is a paste of crushed scotch bonnet peppers, fresh orange juice, and honey. In space many U.S. astronauts like hot sauce on their foods and it's automatically included in their "kits," but astronaut William Lenoir also took a jalapeño with him in 1982. The world's most famous pepper sauce is the Tabasco, manufactured on Avery Island in Louisiana in accordance with an 1870 recipe of a New Orleans banker. In the 1920s—the Age of Jazz—Fernand Petiot combined tomato juice, lime juice, Worcestershire sauce, salt, vodka, and a dash of Tabasco. In Paris it was called the Bucket of Blood and then the Red Snapper, and when Petiot brought the recipe to New York in the 1930s, the cocktail became the Bloody Mary. Now vodka itself is sold spiked and aged with the pepper; chilled, it delights the palate with fire and ice all at once. In 1989 Pabst Brewing Co. in Milwaukee bottled a peppery beer for a big distributor who grew up eating hot in Louisiana and wanted to market the brew himself, but the Cajun beer didn't find many takers. While these attempts to inflame a drink with hot peppers are relatively recent, the practice dates back to the Aztecs, who soaked maize in water and then drank the broth with the pepper to start their day.

Of all the pepper centers in the world, Hatch, New Mexico, stands out. Its plant breeders and botanists create tailor-made peppers, which are introduced to the locals like new car models. During harvesttime, the region comes alive with mountains of shiny pods in roadside stands, and before long the pods end up on backyard grills and in adobe ovens, filling the evening sky with the unmistakable aroma of roasted peppers. Neighbors walk across their fences to compare the flavor of one another's roasted peppers. Texans, on the other hand, find the heat of the pepper more interesting, and with regular pepper-eating contests abhorrently equate human tolerance of the incendiary with machismo. But hot peppers are still a novelty in the eastern United States, where people mistakenly call all hot peppers jalapeños.

That suggests a notable geographic-culinary pattern world-wide. People in the south eat hotter food than those in the north. The rule applies in the context of continent and country. Inhabitants of the southern parts of the Americas eat hotter food than those of the northern parts; the food of southern Mexico is hotter than that of northern Mexico; people in South Texas eat more fiery food than their northern counterparts. In New Mexico people say that by tasting the pods they can often tell whether the peppers came from the north or south side of Interstate 40, formerly U.S. Route 66, which runs from east to west. The rule also holds for South Korea and North Korea, southern and northern Italy, southern and northern India. Peru is an exception.

On an economic-culinary pattern, the poor eat more hot than those who are well-off. In India and Mexico hot peppers help peasants and ordinary laborers face the monotony of starchy rice and tortillas daily. In Liberia, when some people can't afford even a plain morsel, they chew tiny hot cayenne pods between their back teeth to stimulate saliva, which trickles down to suppress their hunger pains.

Incas called the pungent fruit ají, Aztecs called it chilli, and the Spanish changed it to chile. Those names have stuck in South America and Mexico. But in the rest of the world the fruit—incidentally, it isn't a vegetable botanically—has come to be known as pepper, more precisely green or red pepper. The name pepper has stuck from the initial confusion in the West that it was a cousin of the black pepper, which is also pungent but is a berry and belongs to a different genus. To distinguish the pepper pod from the peppercorn, Greek spice merchants in the sixteenth century called it chilli pepper; Hungarians changed the name to paprika; Italians called it peperone. It was red pepper in England; in Germany, Indianifcher pfeffer; poivre de l'Inde to the French, who still continue to link this pepper with India; and mircha in India. Frenchman Joseph Pitton de Tournefort (1656–1708) gave it the Latin name *Capsicum*, which some think comes from the word *capsa*, Latin for box. Others believe the origin of the name is the Greek root *kapto*, meaning "I bite," which describes the fruit appropriately.

But with rising appreciation for the pepper, the bite has come to be associated with something pleasant, and amorous. "Hot chile" is used to describe an attractive young woman. In the Punjab, India, Khalsa warriors under the command of Guru Nanak, the founder of the Sikh religion, called hot pepper "a quarrelsome dame" and carried it with them even to battlefields. A pleasant character in Hungarian puppet shows is

Jancsi Paprika. Lombok, the Indonesian island across the strait from Bali, gets its name from the Javanese word for long red pepper. The country Chile, however, isn't named after pepper but represents the call of an indigenous bird; some say it was also the name of a native chieftain.

Physiologists theorize that the pepper is truly addictive, like nicotine or cocaine. Indians of India travel with doughlike spicy balls made principally of hot pepper; it isn't uncommon to find South Americans carrying their own chiles; some Texans carry tiny hot peppers, called piquín, in pillboxes. There may be something to this thing about addiction, for many pepper eaters admit to getting high eating it or experiencing from it a subtle euphoria.

Pepper might induce deeper changes, according to some beliefs. In 1970, following a string of sexual offenses in prisons, the Peruvian government banned hot pepper sauces in prison food, contending that they aroused sexual desires and thus were not "appropriate for men forced to live in a limited lifestyle." The principles of *brahmacharya,* the attainment of purity of soul and body, forbade India's young Brahmans from consuming hot peppers. The prohibition was based on the belief that the pepper produces "too much heat in the system," which "makes blood and sexual fluids watery and the mind restless. . . ." That peppers can induce heat in the veins was also believed by South American Indians and even by the learned Turks, who concocted love potions with crushed red pepper, wine, and spices. David Livingstone, the nineteenth-century Scottish medical missionary and explorer, wrote of native African women bathing in water in which pepper's juices had been dissolved, to "intensify their attractiveness."

The connection between pungency and amorousness goes back to medieval India (from A.D. 600 to A.D. 1526) when, according to a study on Indian eroticism, one of the spicy potions employed to bring orgasm in women came with the instruction: "The man who rubs his penis with pepper leaves and raisins together with long pepper mixed with pure honey will succeed in bringing a very old woman to the right frame of mind for love." The pepper itself, because of its shape and the heat it induces, is associated with the male sexual organ. In Swahili, Pili Pili is a hot pepper and is also slang for penis; in Louisiana and Texas a particularly pungent variety of the annuum species bears such an unmistakable resemblance that it's called "penis" or "Peter" pepper.

The source of pepper-induced "euphoria" resides in the inside wall of the pod and is concentrated at the stem end. It's a chemical called capsaicin, which is odorless and tasteless. The amount of this chemical, controlled by a single gene, determines the pepper's pungency, and this varies from pepper to pepper. The Aztecs categorized pungency into six grades, which in their Nahuatl language were: *coco* (hot), *cocopatic* (very hot), *cocopetz-patic* (very, very hot), *cocopetztic* (brilliant hot), *cocopetzquauitl* (extremely hot), and *cocopalatic* (runaway hot). That's how most people today describe their pain when they bite into a hot pepper, without knowing they are using the Aztec scale.

In 1912 Wilbur L. Scoville, a pharmacist at the Detroit-based Parke, Davis & Co., which now is part of the pharmaceutical concern Warner-Lambert Company, devised the first modern technique for measuring pepper's bite. The measure is used to this day by spice companies and sauce manufacturers. If all known peppers are put to this measuring technique, their scale of pungency would range from 0 Scoville units, for the bell pepper, to 350,000, for the Mexican habanero.

Seemingly without realizing the reason, people have prescribed peppers as a cure for cold and flu and other respiratory ailments for centuries. Some medicine men in the eighteenth century were even confident about the fruit's effectiveness against malaria and arthritis. That the pepper has health-sustaining properties was confirmed by Hungarian scientist Albert Szent-Györgyi, who found in it a rich source of vitamin C while out of curiosity examining the dinner of peppers his wife had prepared. For discovering this white crystalline substance he won a Nobel Prize in 1937, which *Time* magazine called the "Paprika Prize."

The pepper serves to convey the appearance of health in other ways, albeit superficially. The brilliant red pigment of the sweet red pepper goes into women's blush and lipstick, and it colors sausages and cold meats. Chickens are fed a mash of dried pepper powder to turn their feet bright yellow and the yolks of their eggs orange-red. The colors used to develop naturally in chickens when they roamed freely and thus had access to vegetation and a stress-free existence, but cooped up in mass production they lost the natural colors. While "free range" chickens are rare and fetch a premium price today, paprika is fed to their caged cousins to create the illusion that they've lived a healthy life.

The pepper's other enigmatic characteristics now are coming under study. Claims are already being made in prestigious medical journals about hot pepper's ability to reduce the risk of heart attack, prevent cancer, and avert obesity. In a major breakthrough in the treatment of the nerve disorder shingles, researchers have developed a medicine using the pepper's chemical; it is now the only effective treatment for this pain, which afflicts tens of thousands of people each year and drives many to suicide. This property of the pepper's active chemical, capsaicin, was cited in the Dublin Medical Press long ago, in 1850. The medical journal said that a drop or two of hot-pepper extract applied to a sore tooth brought instant relief for toothache. It works this way: capsaicin, rubbed on the skin, selectively attracts the body's pain messengers and then zaps the neurons that carry the pain message to the brain. This discriminating ability of capsaicin is singular among all chemicals.

Contrary to popular belief, the pepper didn't come from India or China. It originated in South America, and the precise birthplace—the subject of considerable research and some controversy among botanists—is believed to be central Bolivia. But the misconception that the pepper was native to India is fundamental to one of history's biggest bunglings and is compounded by the enthusiasm with which Indians embraced this pepper. Native to India, more exactly its Malabar coast, was the peppercorn, or black pepper, piper nigrum. From Calicut and Quinlon on that western coast, the tiny black pepper reached the Greeks and the Romans through Arab traders. So valued were these peppercorns by the Portuguese, the Spanish, the Italians, the Dutch, and the English that these Europeans took to uncharted seas in a fierce race to establish a spice-trade monopoly. Columbus sailed westward, in 1492, and dead-ended in the Caribbean. But he was certain he had reached his destination, India, and he spoke of smelling the river Ganges. His physician and knowledgeable botanist, Diego Chanca, equally eager to discover the Orient, described a native as wearing "around his neck" ginger-root, which is not indigenous to South America at all but is an Asiatic plant.

Columbus called the natives "Indians." His ship surgeon wrote to Spain's royal court about discovering the native "Indian pepper." Later Columbus himself reported: "The land was found to produce much ají, which is the pepper of the inhabitants, and more valuable than the common sort [the black peppercorn]; they deem it very wholesome and eat nothing without it. Fifty caravels might be loaded every year with this commodity at Espanola." But the peppers Columbus brought back didn't impress the Catholic majesties and remained unnoticed in Europe — as the Genoese adventurer himself would later — for a long time.

The Portuguese, meanwhile, had sailed south on a circuitous route and stumbled upon the pepper at their trading posts in Pernambuco, on the east coast of Brazil. As the journey continued, the pepper traveled with tobacco and cotton on Portuguese carracks and galleons to the next trading post on the west coast of Africa. The pepper then rounded the Cape of Good Hope to Goa, on India's west coast — where it came to be known as Pernambuco pepper — and then from Goa it sailed to Malacca, through the straits between the Malay peninsula and Sumatra, to Macao in South China, then to Nagasaki, Japan, and then south to the Philippines. From there it continued its sail across the Pacific to the Spice Islands, whence it journeyed home to North America with African slaves on Dutch and English ships — circumnavigating the world in less than fifty years. (It took as long for the potato and tomato, two other New World crops, to even gain acceptance in Europe, where physicians pronounced that the potato — which Linnaeus called "devil's herb" — could cause leprosy and syphilis and that the tomato was poisonous and could induce fits of insanity.)

Even fifty years after the pepper arrived from the New World, it mistakenly remained connected with the India of the East. In his magnificent illustrations of pepper plants, which were widely reprinted in botanical and medical journals in the sixteenth century, Leonard Fuchs, a professor of medicine at the University of Tübingen, Germany, described the fruits as Calicut peppers. Calicut was the port in India where peppers — by now widely cultivated in India—were put on the ship to Germany, where the earliest recorded shipments arrived in 1542. George Eberhard Rumphius, a German-born Dutch naturalist and one of the greatest of botanical authors of his time, was emphatic that the pepper was cultivated in India in ancient times, centuries before Columbus found it in the New World. Rumphius asserted himself as an authority on the issue because he had the unique opportunity of observing peppers on both continents—in Brazil, where he was in 1646 with the Dutch West India Company, and later in Batavia, Java, where he joined the Dutch East India Company in 1653. The botanist spent the rest of his life on the island of Amboina, where he wrote six volumes on Malayan botany in which he offered one of the earliest classifications of the pepper species as well as his opinion on the origin of the fruit.

"The Capsicum today is believed to have come from Brazil, West Indies and the East Indies," Rumphius wrote. "Actually it came from the East Indies from where it was gradually brought to Europe and the Americas. I can see, however, that today the Capsicum that comes to our region is chiefly from the Americas." But there is no written evidence to substantiate Rumphius's claim: there is no reference to Capsicum in Sanskrit, Roman, Greek, Hebrew, or Arabic literature.

Eventually it would be the Turks who would bring wide attention to the pepper as an item of food in Europe. It started with the Turkish invasion of India. The Turks of the Ottoman Empire besieged the Portuguese colony of Diu, near Calicut, and brought back the "Calicut" pepper, which eventually went north with Ottoman soldiers to their conquered territories in Hungary. It was there—and not in Spain or Portugal, the two countries that first brought the pepper from the New World— that it found its warmest reception, permanently altering the cuisine of Hungary.

Legend has it that if it hadn't been for a young Hungarian

peasant girl, the pepper, which can be petulant in the climates outside the tropics, never would have found a home in that country. The girl had been forced into the harem of the pasha of Buda, and there she saw how the palace gardeners grew paprika. It interested her. After Hungarians successfully stormed the palace, she was liberated; back in her village she showed farmers how to cultivate paprika. The pepper, more pugnacious than the expensive black pepper, quickly became the spice of the poor. "This capsicum, or Indian pepper, is painstakingly grown in Castilia both by gardeners and by housewives," Charles de l'Ecluse, who had been the court botanist of Emperor Maximilian, wrote while traveling on the Iberian peninsula in 1593.

Napoleon's sea blockade, which cut off the trade in black pepper and other spices, eventually forced the upper class to grudgingly take to pepper pods as well, and it was quickly won over. Traveling in Hungary in 1793, Count Hoffmannsegg wrote to his sister: "Here . . . the most pleasant thing for me was . . . meat with paprika, which I liked very much. It must have been wholesome, for, although I had eaten quite a lot at night, it did not do me any harm whatever. . . . Eating paprika is nothing but a habit, but one finds it quite agreeable. If there is time for it, plant some paprika in flower pots, I should like to use it in winter." According to a Hungarian saying, "One man may yearn for fame, another for wealth, but everyone yearns for a paprika goulash."

But the Hungarians over the years fell in love more with the flavor than with the pepper's pungency. At harvest hundreds of women would sit in front of piles of pepper and remove the inside veins of the pods to kill the fruit's temper. Then in 1945 Erno Obermayer, an agricultural researcher, after twenty-five years of selecting and interbreeding, developed a paprika that was genetically mild mannered, launching Hungary's now famous paprika industry. Today the sweet and brilliant red pepper grows mostly in Szeged, on the river Tisza in southern Hungary, and in Kalocsa, on the Danube. These two regions have become the centers of paprika cultivation because of a "particularly felicitous coincidence of circumstances," according to one Hungarian botanical account of early cultivation in the country. In a perfect "rhythmical alternation" of warmth, sunshine, and rain, the total of daily average temperatures consistently adds up to 2,900° C in Szeged and Kalocsa at the end of the five-month growing season. Those climatic combinations aren't reached anywhere else; a total less than 2,700° C produces a mediocre crop at best.

Most of Hungary's pepper output is dried and turned into powder, also called paprika, and this is what gives Hungary's fish soup and goulash its national character. This mild pepper used for flavoring and coloring is also produced by Spain, Portugal, Yugoslavia, Morocco, Bulgaria, Romania, Italy, and Greece. But the Hungarian variety, especially the "rose" variety, known for its sweet aroma and its brilliant color, is most prized by gourmets. To protect their industry, Hungarian agricultural authorities jealously guard their paprika seeds, and it is said that an outsider trying to lay hands on the seeds risks committing an offense that ranks with stealing government classified information. "If they catch you near a paprika field they would probably shoot you," says Bob Heisey of Asgrow Seed Co. of Kalamazoo, Michigan. Eager as he is to procure some seeds, he has thus confined his attempts to the official channels, but has had little success. "They gave me fresh market samples. They gave me a Bulgarian variety. They gave me a Russian variety. Not the Hungarian I wanted. It's restricted, they said."

Some paprika seeds did find their way to the United States. A U.S. agricultural news bulletin of October 10, 1941, gleefully announced that "several emigrants had succeeded in bringing with them a small supply of seeds." The seeds were planted in the Yakima Valley in Washington, and in St. James Parish, Louisiana. But climatic requirements for growing paprika are so rigorous that neither the U.S. nor any other country in the world has been able to make so much as a dent in the well-organized Hungarian pepper industry. As a result, the rest of the world concentrates on the pungent version of this red powder, called cayenne. Cayenne powder comes not from Cayenne, French Guiana, but from India, Africa, Mexico, China, Japan, and Louisiana.

With paprika earning precious foreign exchange for Hungary, it is not surprising that twice as many acres in the country are planted with peppers as with tomatoes. In 1989 it produced 62,000 tons of peppers. During the same year, India, the world's largest producer, harvested 800,000 tons, and consumed 95 percent of the output right at home. The chile-growing world as a whole—which also includes China, Pakistan, Mexico, Sri Lanka, Nigeria, Ethiopia, Thailand, and Japan—produced about four million tons of hot peppers in 1989. For the same year the worldwide production of black pepper, which is what Columbus was after when he stumbled onto chiles, amounted to less than 200,000 tons.

The pepper has evolved into a bewildering number of distinct species and varieties, taking on a new shape and pungency, depending upon the local soil, rainfall, and temperature as it has circumnavigated the world. Today peppers range from the pea-shaped chili piquín, the cherry-shaped cherry pepper, the lantern-shaped habanero, the dumpy and pointed jalapeño, the pattypan-shaped rocotillo, and the most common long and thin Anaheim. The flavors, too, differ from variety to variety. Peppers grow on bushy plants, most about two to three feet tall. Wild varieties grow on plants as tall as ten feet; and one of them, in Bolivia, has been measured spanning sixty feet. All peppers redden as they ripen. But unripe, some are light green, some dark green, some bluish green or brownish green; yet others are yellow or whitish yellow, or dark green with a lavender hue, or purplish black. Even among peppers of the same size and shape, pungency can vary sharply within the same growing plot. That's why those who are familiar with the pepper's fickle personality aren't taken in by appearance, and often, at the vegetable stand, break open several pods to steal a bite or two before buying. Generally, peppers that grow in a hot climate are hotter than those that grow in a cool climate; in terms of shape, pungent pods usually are thin, with sharply tapering shoulders and pointed ends.

At least two peppers, each in a different part of the world, are named the same for like behavior: Mirasol, which means "looking at the sun" in Spanish, is so called because the lanky pungent pepper popular in Mexico curves itself up from the branch to peek at the sun; and for adopting the same posture, an inch-and-a-half-long dumpy and chisel-pointed pepper in Bengal, India, bears the names akashi lanka (looking at the sky) and surjamukhi (looking at the sun). But the pepper's propensity to assume different personalities has misled people into giving different names to pods even though the seemingly different strains might belong to the same variety. This has created a mind-boggling number of names. As long ago as 1902, the U.S. Agriculture Department noted that "there is such an indiscriminate use of epithets as to make the distinctions in varieties very bewildering." The United Nations' agricultural committee had to intervene in 1976 to devise a nomenclature so that pepper botanists and farmers around the globe could identify whether they all were speaking of the same pepper or an entirely new kind. According to the latest classification, varieties that fall within one species or another total sixteen hundred. Only about two hundred of them are grown commercially, and a great bulk of those belong to just one species, Capsicum annuum, which is a grouping based on the fact that these varieties must be replanted every year to bear fruit.

Mexico cultivates the greatest number of distinctive varieties, and as a result its pepper markets are eye-catching. Of the 53,000 tons of peppers it produces annually, only a tiny portion is the nonpungent bell pepper—and nearly all of that crop is exported to the United States. The bell—which with its prominent lobes at the tapered end looks like an apple, but was also called a mango pepper at the beginning of the century—is used exclusively as a vegetable. It represents 60 percent of the 687,000 tons of all peppers the United States produces, and this sweet variety has taken on a staggering number of commercial names, often reflecting the place of origin or the breeder's fancy: Lady Bell, Yolo Wonder, Keystone Resistant Giant, Canape, Green Boy, Big Bertha, E. Calwonder, Shamrock, Big Jim, Ruby King, and California Wonder, among others.

The other major nonpungent pepper in the world is the pimiento, and next to the bell this is the largest variety cultivated in the United States. The heart-shaped pimiento is fleshy and resembles a meaty tomato when it comes out of the can. The first American pimiento was grown in Spalding County, Georgia, in 1911, by farmer S. D. Riegel and his son George. Out of curiosity they had purchased some pepper seeds from a Philadelphia seed company and planted them in the family garden. The fruits resembled the canned Spanish pimientos that were just beginning to arrive in Georgia from Spain, but the Riegels' peppers were quite inferior. So they had their district congressman take up the matter with the American consul in Spain. Soon the Riegels had seeds shipped from Spain. Plants from these seeds produced pimientos that were "very fine specimens," and the Riegels were pleased by the pods' perfect size. That was the start of the now well known "Perfect Pimiento."

One of the earliest Americans to grow extremely hot peppers was George Washington, who on June 13, 1785, planted two rows of "bird peppers" and one row of cayenne peppers in his botanical garden in Mount Vernon, Virginia. Washington must have planted them out of simple curiosity, because the pungent pepper isn't incorporated in any of the recipes in Martha Washington's *Book of Cookery*.

Some better-known varieties of pungent chiles are: cayenne, serrano, cascabel, jalapeño, habanero, rocoto, tabasco, Sandía, birdeye, piquín, Japanese santaka and hontaka, ancho, Du chili,

Coral Gem, Devil, Louisiana Sport, chiltepins, Sannam, Mundu, Coimbatore, Bombay cherries, and tianjin from China. They vary widely in size, shape, color, flavor, and pungency. Most of the Mexican, African, and Louisiana varieties—as well as the wild hot species—are less than an inch and a half long and highly pungent. Those from California and New Mexico are considerably larger—over four inches long—and are redder and not as hot.

Jalapeño now has established itself as the hot pepper of the United States. The stout dark green pepper is meaty, with a level of pungency that Americans find neither too hot nor too mild. Its increasing presence, pickled, on nachos and hot dogs at ballparks makes it the all-American hot pepper. But nearly 90 percent of this fruit is imported from Mexico, where it was domesticated thousands of years ago and where it accounts for nearly one fifth of all varieties produced, mostly in the region from which it gets its name, Jalapa, in the state of Veracruz. Despite the strong demand, farmers in the United States haven't been able to get the pepper to grow well.

The hot variety that does grow widely in the United States is a long, curved green pepper—ranging from three to eight inches long—that bears different names depending upon type. It's believed that the ancestral seeds were brought to New Mexico in 1597 by General Juan de Oñate, who colonized the state. But this claim is disputed by archaeologists who have discovered pepper remnants along the well-established trade routes that linked New Mexico and central Mexico thousands of years ago. The offspring of this pepper today are known as Anaheim, cayenne, and Sandía, among others.

In 1896 rancher Emilio Ortega, who raised cattle and alfalfa in New Mexico, moved back to the family adobe on the west bank of the Ventura River in Ventura, California, and took with him some pepper seeds to try a new business. In a few years he had started a bustling pepper-canning industry in Santa Ana—and the pepper he used soon came to be known as Anaheim, which is now the most widely grown pepper in California. The pepper brought Ortega local renown. The Ventura *Daily Democrat,* in its issue of August 1, 1902, described him as "the gentleman of green chili fame."

The development of modern varieties of pungent peppers that now are a staple of pepper eaters in California and the Southwest owes a lot to Fabian Garcia, a horticulturist at the New Mexico College of Agriculture and Mechanic Arts, now New Mexico State University. Finding hodgepodge appearance of peppers in his Las Cruces neighborhood unappealing, in 1907 he collected peppers of all shapes and sizes, and through a tedious process of interbreeding he developed "the most ideal pod"—which would later beget generations of new and equally distinguished varieties. In valley after valley farmers cleared their fields of whatever they were growing and switched to Garcia's peppers. And for decades, pepper eaters in New Mexico would tell their grocers and waiters: "Give me some Fabian Garcia."

The Scoville Heat

At the height of the summer pepper growing season, I traveled to the South and Southwest of the United States, where booming demand is spawning an industry of pepper breeders, farmers, canners, and chefs with a bent for the piquant. When I asked people in the industry to suggest a starting point for my exploration of the peppers, they immediately mentioned Benigno Villalon, a plant pathologist at Texas A&M University's agriculture experiment station in Weslaco, Texas, who was noted for his work on pepper viruses and breeding programs. To emphasize Villalon's prominence in the pepper industry, they told me he was also fondly known as Dr. Pepper. He was sort of a universal pepper man.

When I arrived at the small airport in Weslaco, William Warfield was there to drive me to the agriculture station. The wiry young man with flowing blond hair explained that he was Villalon's assistant in the pepper program and that Villalon was visiting farmers that morning. I climbed into his blue pickup, and although it was only ten in the morning the sun was scorching; I had to quickly roll the window down to let in cool air.

I would later learn that summers in the area are just too hot for many varieties of peppers to grow and that some of those that do grow have developed a more scorching temperament than elsewhere. As we took off, Warfield said he was more a lepidopterist than a pepper man. What had lured him from Wisconsin to the scrubby South Texas valley on the Rio Grande were the surrounding dense mountains.

"There are all kinds of vegetation right across the river, and that attracts a lot of species." Pepper was far from his mind, I learned quickly; it was butterflies and moths that excited him. He talked about them with passion, and during our drive nothing—neither the red traffic lights and stop signs nor the occasional traffic jam—interrupted his narrative. "I probably have three thousand butterflies and moths in my collection," he said. He told me of his regular trips to the forest at sunset to collect moths and butterflies and other insects in his ethyl acetate "killing jar." Just as I was contemplating Warfield's weird interest, he told me, for the first time steering to the subject of peppers, "I think eating those doggone hot peppers is weird."

Villalon hadn't returned yet when we arrived at the experiment station, a complex of low-lying buildings and rows of nurseries. Warfield suggested we have lunch and invited a Mexican assistant to come along. We went to a local eatery, where even hamburger came with a side dish of pickled jalapeños. After all, we were almost at the border with Mexico, so it sort of made sense. When our meals arrived, the Wisconsinite, ignoring his hamburger, reached for a strip of jalapeño. "I would say it's about six, maybe even seven," Warfield said, chewing and squinting his eyes as if straining to read a thermometer inside his brain.

The Mexican assistant looked at Warfield, and then he himself reached for a piece. "Maybe five," he said, chewing his piece.

They were judging the pepper's heat level, on a scale of one to ten. The disagreement, although small, led to another trial and a new set of readings. They reached for several more pieces, in succession, for a moment forgetting why they were there. Then, without further fuss, they began to eat their lunch.

Warfield said they habitually evoke that scale of heat when a pepper, raw or pickled, on a plate or on a vine stares them in the face. "I taste peppers for a living," he said. "I never thought growing up on a diet of meat and potatoes that I'd have to eat pepper for a living."

The peppers that are developed by the Weslaco agricultural station for release to farmers are rigorously tested for their pungency. The pungency has to be of certain levels, which the pepper breeders select based on their perception of what they think a certain consumer group would tolerate in a certain pepper. Moreover, the pepper, when replanted, must year after year produce the same level of pungency. When these aspects of the pepper are scrutinized in the laboratory of the agricultural station, the scale deployed to measure and designate hotness is a formal one. It's the Scoville Organoleptic Test devised by Wilbur Scoville. In conducting his studies on pharmacological uses of peppers the pharmacist was frustrated that the peppers he would acquire were unpredictable in pungency. "The pharmacist cannot, by specifying a certain species of Capsicum, be sure thereby of securing the most active medicinally," he complained in the *Journal of the American Pharmaceutical Association* in 1912. Scoville felt it would be judicious to specify heat levels when ordering peppers, instead of just specifying the type, since peppers within the same type vary considerably in pungency.

It is worth deviating slightly to show how Scoville developed his technique and what impact it has had on the hot-pepper industry. The pharmacist tried first to measure pungency by studying how pepper's extract reacted with other chemicals but concluded that none was sensitive enough to offer readings with any degree of precision. He found that the tongue, on the other hand, was far more sensitive, capable of detecting capsaicin dissolved in a solution a million times its volume; no laboratory test could detect such a low concentration. He chose the tongue, which later brought sneers from his peers. What can be more subjective than the tongue, they cried out. Scoville was unfazed: "Physiological tests are tabooed in some quarters, yet when the tongue is sensitive to less than a millionth of a grain, it certainly has an advantage."

Scoville's method was simple. He obtained the leading commercial pepper varieties of the time that were known for pungency—the Japan, Zanzibar, and Mombasa chiles—and soaked each separately overnight in alcohol. Because capsaicin is soluble in alcohol, the soaking extracted the pungent chemical from the pods. Then the pharmacist took a precise measure of the extract and to it added sweetened water in definite proportions until the mixture's distinct but weak pungency was barely perceptible on his tongue. In the case of Japan chiles, it took sweetened water in volumes between 20,000 and 30,000 times the pepper extract before the pungency was barely discernible. He thus rated the Japan chiles 20,000 to 30,000 Scoville Heat Units. Zanzibar chiles he rated 40,000 to 50,000 and Mombasa chiles 50,000 to 100,000. Thus the Mombasa chiles were the hottest, followed by Zanzibar and Japan chiles. (Scoville couldn't resist passing judgment on the peppers' flavor. Capsaicin, which resides in the crosswall, doesn't itself have any flavor. The flavor is borne by the outer wall. He found the Japan chiles to have "a very rich and full flavor" and the Mombasa to be "the poorest in flavor.")

Scoville's name has since become closely associated with the measure of pungency, but the oral test is now being slowly displaced by a modern machine that's as sensitive as the human tongue. Called High Pressure Liquid Chromatograph, or HPLC, the $30,000 instrument looks like a hi-fi system, with its components straitjacketed into a rectangular metal box, which has a lot of gauges and needles and knobs, and a computer. In the center of the box is a six-inch tube packed with a spongy and porous carbon material. The pepper's chemical extracted into ethanol is forced, under high pressure, through the tube. It separates the pungent chemical, or the capsaicin, from other compounds in the pepper, such as pigments and acids. Capsaicin, which fluoresces, is then exposed to a light beam. A detector measures the fluorescence of the chemical—the greater the fluorescence, the higher the pungency of the chemical—and the radiation is measured electronically into a graph, which resembles a seismogram, with peaks and valleys. It turns out that capsaicin is composed of several individual compounds—each representing a unique type of pungency— and thus the HPLC readings are in the form of several rising and falling lines. The peaks of all the curves are added to designate the pepper's pungency.

I once asked James Woodbury, technical director at Cal-Compack Foods Co. in Santa Ana, California, if the instrument has made much difference to his firm, which makes spices and salsas. "A very positive development," he said. He told me that his company once had a permanent panel of five people who did nothing but sample products as they came off the production line. Their job was to make sure that the product met preset levels of pungency, which were "recorded" in the minds of the panelists; a hot sauce that's too hot or too mild would alienate the consumer. Each member would taste a sample and write down what he or she thought was the Scoville unit. No two tongues would ever agree. So the panelists' estimates would be averaged, and that number determined if the production line was deviating from established standards. There was another problem with Scoville's organoleptic test: it limited the number of tests a panelist could do in a day. Because the tongue would temporarily get used to a given level of pungency, it had to be given rest to cool down before resuming the task. "In an eight-hour period, you couldn't run more than six samples through the panel," Woodbury said. "The machine has now replaced the tasting panel, and we're able to measure thirty samples in eight hours. What's more, we don't have to worry about accuracy."

Accuracy is important to spice and condiment companies as buyers of heat. Like Scoville, they want their money's worth when ordering Capsicum. "We buy and sell heat, not flavor or color," an official of McCormick and Company told me. "The cost is linked to the heat. Higher the heat, the greater it costs us." The spice company's concern is obvious: it buys peppers in tons from nearly a dozen countries—mainly India, Pakistan, and China—which produce peppers with varying and unpredictable levels of pungency. "Accuracy in measuring heat level is critical for another reason," the official added. "We sell red pepper powder, sauce mix, seasoning mix. You don't want to sell a product that will blow away the consumer."

The American Spice Trade Association, an industry trade group, is a strong proponent of the machine. And HPLC measurements are expressed in ASTA units, after the acronym of the group. But Scoville's name is so well established that the association has had as much success in making people adopt the scale as the U.S. has in adopting the metric system. The companies that do employ the modern instrument use a conversion scale to express ASTA units in the familiar Scoville units. Such is Scoville's legacy.

Back at the agriculture station, Warfield led me into the low white building that houses Texas A&M's plant researchers. On the way through the hallway we passed a group of men in high boots and cowboy hats who were sitting on benches and chairs in a scene that looked like the waiting room in the emergency ward of a hospital. In place of a nameplate, a wreath of dry Anaheim peppers was hanging on Ben Villalon's door. Courteous and energetic, Villalon was wearing short sleeves and an out-of-style wide tie the likes of which tailors' magazine ads offer to narrow at cut-rate prices. He said he had just returned from visiting farmers. One of his goals as a pepper man was to make Texas the country's leading pepper producer. "These farmers are going broke. Why don't they grow chiles? They should diversify. Then they won't have to compete with farmers in Iowa or Illinois; their only competition will be across the border, in Mexico. These farmers are growing corn and sorghum and losing all this money. Banks here would love farmers to switch to peppers."

Farmers are beginning to listen. He said that some of the farmers I had passed in the hallway were actually waiting to see him about growing peppers. Peppers being imported from across the border were fetching high prices in Texas and that was finally stimulating interest among local farmers, who had long dismissed peppers as an exotic staple of poor immigrant communities. He said the state's canning and sauce industries were expanding processing and marketing facilities, and an organization called the Texas Pepper Foundation—consisting of growers, processors, and researchers—had recently been formed with the goal of making Texas "the number one pepper producing state." Villalon showed me some calculations on the economics of pepper growing and compared them with those of other crops. "Next to marijuana, it is the highest-profit cash crop," he said.

I had heard similar claims from others. The one that was often repeated was made by Jean Andrews, a Texas artist who has both painted pepper plants and written about them as well as hunted for them in fields and wild swamps. On a radio program she said that farmers could earn $10,000 an acre by growing chiltepins, a fiery little pepper the size of a pea that sells for $64 a pound. The pepper grows wild in the desert mountain ranges from Arizona to northern South America and collecting it from scattered and bushy plants requires much time and tedious effort. After Andrews's appearance on the radio, the phones at the station and at her home rang for weeks with calls from farmers and gardeners who wanted to know how they could get hold of some seeds. Villalon said Andrews wasn't exaggerating.

To induce farmers to grow peppers, Villalon directs most of his research work at the agricultural station toward developing varieties that can flourish in Texas heat and survive assaults from indigenous viruses and insects. One reason farmers here haven't been keen on pepper is that the crop has had a long history of succumbing to these attacks. "Farmers have been known to walk away two months after planting their crops," he said.

Villalon, who studied agronomy at Texas A&M and earned a doctorate in plant virology, founded Texas A&M's virology-breeding program in 1971, the year he joined the university's Weslaco experimental station. To launch his pepper "clinic" he obtained pepper seeds from collections at the University of California at Davis, University of Florida at Gainesville and at Belle Glade, Auburn University, Michigan State University, and from food and seed companies. By crossbreeding plants grown from these seeds, his greenhouse has released several varieties that thrive well in the Texas climate.

Villalon and I walked over to his greenhouse. It was a large one-story glass structure, fitted with monitoring devices, pipes, and air conditioners. Inside, on the floor and on picnic tables, sat knee-high plants, bearing pods of different colors and shapes. "This is what we call the isolation chamber. We do all the development work here, and once we think we have created the type with the traits we are looking for we plant their seeds on our trial plots outside," he said.

I learned that one of the challenges of conferring disease resistance to a pepper is keeping the fruit's original shape and size in the process. When the pepper is crossed with another type that's resistant to disease, the siblings take on different shapes and sizes. More often than not the progeny that looks like the original pepper—the one that's to be made disease-resistant—hasn't yet managed to inherit the gene. The one that does doesn't look anything like the original pepper. Villalon said that consumers get used to a shape and size and refuse to accept any variation even though taste and flavor mightn't have changed at all. He showed me a long, red and wrinkly cayenne used in Louisiana hot sauce. "I think it's the ugliest-looking pepper around, and you would think people would demand to improve its appearance, but this is what they are used to in Louisiana," Villalon said. "I have to make it disease-resistant without changing its ugly shape; otherwise farmers won't be able to sell it." The breeder has to keep on crossing till he hits upon the right combination. The whole process can take six or seven years or longer. Sometimes the trial-and-error method doesn't bring the desired results, and the effort goes to waste.

In some cases, farmers do request a change in the pepper's shape. That usually reflects some particular trend in the market place. Villalon showed me a bell pepper he's crossing with a number of other varieties to create a bell that can not only withstand Texas plant diseases but also possesses four identical lobes. He said the source of the demand was fast-food restaurants that had now diversified into salad bars to give their business a healthy touch. To enhance the looks of their salads, they wanted not just any crooked-shaped bell pepper rings but perfectly symmetrical ones.

When I was there, Villalon was handling another strange request. He showed me a row of potted tabasco pepper plants, which have become highly susceptible to a number of plant diseases. He said he was crossing them with serrano and other peppers to make the tabasco pod not only withstand disease but grow pendant—it's one of the rare types that grow upright—so that the fruit could be harvested by machine.

The feat that has made Villalon a darling of farmers and canners, however, is something else: tempering peppers' pungency. He has permanently altered, for instance, the character of the jalapeño—the dumpy dark green pepper that was once synonymous in the United States with hot peppers—by developing a very mild variety. Before him jalapeños were uniformly hot, period; a mild jalapeño wasn't known to exist.

This foray was inadvertent. He was trying to develop a virus-resistant bell pepper by crossing it with a serrano, a two-inch stringy pod. Since the serrano hasn't been domesticated as widely as the other common varieties of peppers, it still contains a lot of primitive genes. So the union between the bell, a Rio Grande 66, and the serrano begot a carnival of pepper plants: some sprouted big bells, some little bells, some sweet bells, some pungent bells, some sweet pimientos, some hot pimientos, some little serranos, some big serranos, some dark jalapeños, some light jalapeños, and some pods that couldn't be put into one variety or another. "When genes mix, there is no telling what is going to come out. Each variety of pepper has literally hundreds of thousands of genes," Villalon told me.

Since Villalon had blinders on to develop a new virus-resistant bell, he didn't pay much attention to the other types that emerged from the union. He just isolated all the plants that were sprouting pods that looked close to the bull-nosed, bulby bell pepper. He propagated them, by crossing and recrossing their siblings, till he came up with a bell that not only resembled the original fruit but was resistant to all Texan viruses. But the anxious Texas farmers who were visiting Villalon's greenhouse to watch the progress on the bell were getting more interested in a progeny of the original union: a fruit that looked a lot like the jalapeño. The attraction of this jalapeño was that it wasn't hot. Visiting farmers noticed that Villalon, during the course of giving a tour of the greenhouse, would casually pluck this mild jalapeño and nibble away at it. He never stopped to think much about this progeny, but a visiting canner from San Antonio was quite taken by it—and by its potential—and told him: "If I could grow genetically mild jalapeños I would become a millionaire. I could sell it to McDonald's and all the other fast-food chains." Villalon, who's accustomed to eating only the very hot peppers, told me he didn't realize at that time that this "weird mild jalapeño would go over big."

Word of the mild jalapeño spread quickly. Farmers and canners from across the country clamored for a peek at it. They were sighing with relief that finally there was a jalapeño for the uninitiated. At their urging Villalon bred the mild jalapeño through several generations to ensure that it would continue to maintain a mild disposition as well as resist pepper diseases, a process that took more than five years. In 1981 he released that perfect mild sibling to farmers as TAM Mild Jalapeño-1. One cannery was so impressed—and thankful for the business it was generating—that it sent him a picture of a syringe with effusive scrawlings, a gesture presumably holding Villalon among men of modern medicine for his ability to "cure," in this case the temperament of the jalapeño, which by birth is pugnacious. This latest feat brought Villalon the nickname Dr. Pepper. (The drink Dr Pepper, incidentally, has nothing to do with peppers. It's named after Dr. Charles Pepper, a Virginia doctor. A pharmacist who worked with Dr. Pepper and later went into the soft drinks business in Texas named the syrup Dr Pepper in 1885 in an unsuccessful bid to win the doctor's consent to marry his daughter.)

The tempered pepper became an instant hit from northeastern Texas all the way to Maine. It's now grown in Texas, Arizona, Florida, and California. It is even growing in Wisconsin—the home state of Villalon's lepidopterist assistant, William Warfield—in Warshara and Dodge counties; the big Wisconsin cheese manufacturers blend the mild jalapeños into their Monterey Jack and other brands to produce peppered cheeses. In fact, these spicy cheeses have become so popular that some cheese companies now have their own jalapeño farms. The mild jalapeño also has made it to fried-chicken and pizza outlets and to stadiums around the country.

"A Civilized Jalapeño," heralded the Milwaukee *Journal*, which reprinted an account of Villalon's feat from the Houston *Chronicle*. "It may strike some Mexican-food purists on both sides of the Rio Grande as a breach of frontier tradition, something like forcing Pancho Villa to doff his sombrero and serape for a bowler and pin stripes. . . . But flavor with less fire makes it pleasing to the palate."

Encouraged by this reception, in 1986 Villalon released two

other varieties that were cured of their sharp dispositions: the Hidalgo, a mild serrano pepper, and TAM Mild Chile-2, a mildly pungent stringy and long pepper.

I wasn't sure what to make of Villalon's stunt. As a seasoned pepper eater—or at least someone who was rapidly becoming one—I could suddenly see myself at a produce market or a supermarket, fumbling with peppers one pod at a time, trying to pick out the real ones from among the bland impostors. It is bad enough that one cannot always be sure peppers from the same batch will be uniformly hot, without human tinkering. I mentioned to Villalon that there was something strange, something incongruous, about calling a jalapeño mild. Jalapeño by definition is hot. When the pepper eater wants a jalapeño, he has in mind an established measure of pungency; it states the person's preference for heat.

Perhaps Villalon should have called these impotent peppers something else. I would later tell a regular pepper eater the story behind the mild jalapeño. "Christ, why didn't he call it by some other name. I bought some the other day and when I sat down at the table I realized it wasn't hot at all. It ruined my dinner," he reacted.

I sympathized. I remember being frustrated myself while shopping in supermarkets in the Midwest and Northeast. I would break open jalapeño after jalapeño and then, unable to find pods true to their character, I would leave a dozen or so halves as a score of my anguish—not knowing then that its cause was none other than Villalon himself. I predicted to the venerable Dr. Pepper that the practice of breaking peppers in half, which is a normal habit of the pepper customer anyway, would only intensify now that the names previously synonymous with certain levels of pungency could no longer be trusted. "But the hot-pepper lover has something already," Villalon said in consolation, pointing out that there still exists a large variety of peppers that are quite pungent.

It would be unfair, however, to say Villalon was ignoring the hot-pepper lover. In his greenhouse, among the hot varieties was the notorious habanero pepper. He said he initially planted "this silly thing" out of curiosity but now he was experimenting with it to see if the pepper that grows well in the Yucatán could be cultivated in Texas. The segment of the pepper-eating crowd that likes it hot is asking for more heat, he said. The habanero is extremely hot. He plucked a pod and took out a pocket knife and, holding the fruit carefully between his fingers, shaved off thin slices. He put a piece into his mouth and gave one to Warfield and one to me.

"I would say it's about twenty thousand," Villalon said to Warfield. But unsure of his assessment, he chewed it a few more times.

"Hmm," Warfield said, and then nodded.

"I would say it's certainly no more than thirty thousand. This would mature to become two hundred thousand to three

hundred thousand Scoville units," Villalon told me. The imma-
ture pod was already so hot that the stillness of the greenhouse
was quickly broken with coughing and sniffling, as if we all had
been suddenly struck by a severe case of flu. I asked Warfield
how he would describe the pepper's bite. Still squirming from
the heat of the pepper, he summoned a scale from music. "It has
a high pitch," he said. "I would say sharp." Villalon passed
around a roll of spearmint.

The habanero is an extreme case of pungency. Even the
jalapeño, which ranges between 3,500 and 4,500 Scoville units,
is too hot for many Americans. Villalon, who still follows
Scoville's tongue-squirming method for pronouncing pungency, showed me his chart of heat levels for a number of peppers:
bell and pimientos, 0 Scoville units; the long green Anaheim,
between 250 and 1,400; the Hungarian Yellow, 4,000 units;
poblano, about 3,000; the serrano, between 7,000 and 25,000;
chile de arbol, between 15,000 and 30,000; the tabasco, between 30,000 and 50,000; the Japanese santaka, between
50,000 and 60,000; the Mexican tabiche, about 100,000; cayenne, between 100,000 and 105,000; birdeye from India, between 100,000 and 125,000; the Japanese kumataka, between
125,000 and 150,000; habanero, 300,000.

The chemical responsible for the pepper's pungency was
first isolated by an Englishman in India in 1877 and later was
identified as 8-methyl-N-vanillyl-6-nonenamide. Other mysteries behind the pepper's heat are now being unraveled. It has
been found, for instance, that the pungency level doesn't de-
pend on the amount of capsaicin present in the pepper but on its
chemical structure. The longer the acid chains in the structure,
the lower the heat in the pepper, and vice versa. Peppers vary in
more than pungency: the nature of their bites also differs. A
pepper that is extraordinarily hot on the Scoville scale can in
fact be more agreeable to the tongue than another whose heat is
very low. The habanero, for instance, offers a sharp and violent
bite but then as quickly it disappears, leaving behind a soothing
and aromatic sensation; and the pepper eater, basking in that

mild euphoria, hardly remembers that he had been savagely mauled just seconds earlier. Other peppers, like the thin and small types from Thailand and India as well as the dumpy jalapeños from Mexico, have bites that linger in the mouth and send even the most adept pepper eater reaching for a drink. There are other variations, too, in the way peppers of practically the same pungency make themselves known in the mouth: some produce irritation more toward the back of the mouth than in the front, some burn the lips more than the tongue, and some leave their mark smack in the middle of the tongue.

These quirky variations result from the fact that the chemical capsaicin itself is made up of elemental parts—called capsaicinoids—that vary in their chemical structures; thus the composition of capsaicin is usually different in different peppers, each lending its own peculiar bite. This trait of the pungent chemical is now coming under close scrutiny from pepper researchers, especially canners and spice merchants. What interests the food people in all this is obvious: if a pepper could be bred to produce only the capsaicin of the type that does its job on the tongue and then swiftly vanishes, it would boost pepper consumption—and profits for the companies and farmers alike.

But not much is known yet of how peppers acquire pungency or how some manage to acquire none at all. What is known, however, is what affects the level of pungency once a pepper already has the gene for it: heat and sunlight intensify it and thus determine the range. California's coastal valley, for instance, is about ten degrees cooler than its central valley. Thus the best mild peppers for powdered red pepper, or paprika, grow in the coastal region. But pepper diseases in the cooler valley are pushing growers to move into the central valley, and they are discovering that their paprika is getting hotter and hotter. In the foothills of the Alps near Turin—the home of Asti Spumante—the local Giallo Quadrato di Asti, or the "yellow square pepper," is meaty and nonpungent and is delicious roasted and served in strips with olive oil. The same pepper in the south, in Sicily, is considerably hotter. Breeders in the United States have been trying to grow the nonpungent strains from the Asti region, but the same plant in the hotter American climate ends up producing on its branches both sweet and hot pods—the hotter pods growing on the side that gets the most sun. A breeder at Asgrow Seed's operation in California, which tried to grow the pepper in the United States, told me, "There are a lot of things about peppers we don't understand yet, but there is no question that environment affects pungency. In peppers, the sun transforms itself into heat." More specifically, another pepper man told me, what matters is not simply the overall temperature of the day but the night temperature. "Longer evenings with warm temperatures raise the heat level even more."

Villalon helped found the National Pepper Conference, which held its first international gathering in 1973 and was attended by plant pathologists, breeders, horticulturists, geneticists, physiologists, virologists, botanists, sauce makers, picklers, and wholesalers and retailers. They came from California, Florida, Louisiana, Pennsylvania, Texas, and from Mexico, Honduras, Colombia, and Venezuela. The idea of an international get-together on pepper seemed at once absurd and intriguing. I wondered what weighty issues they discussed, and I considered the comic undertones in an assembly of pepper-eating people. I had heard that at one such gathering, the pepper theme was taken to such extremes that the opening reception featured exclusively pepper foods—stuffed bell, pickled jalapeños, stuffed jalapeños, serranos tossed on nachos, desserts complemented with sweet peppers—all accompanied by a pepper wine manufactured by a California winery.

The ninth National Pepper Conference was held in North Carolina in June 1988. When I arrived at the North Raleigh Hilton, where the three-day conference was being held, the lobby was overrun by conventioneers in summer slacks and short-sleeved shirts and T-shirts. I inquired at the reception desk where the National Pepper Conference people were gathering that evening.

"Sorry?" said a good-looking brunette at the counter, straining to understand my query.

"The National Pepper Conference."

"You mean pepper as in bell pepper?" she asked, looking puzzled, then gave out a small laugh, amused by the nature of such a gathering.

"That's close," I said. I wasn't sure if she believed me.

She moved to a nearby folder, ran her eyes over a schedule, and said, "We have a national postmasters' conference and a national contractors' conference. . . . But . . . Aha! There it is. Pepper conference. Sorry about that."

I went to the suite, where a reception was in progress with more than 175 people in attendance. And I worked the crowd. José Ivan Ortiz Monasterio Rosas, a *profesor investigador* at a technical institute in Querétaro, in Mexico, told me his specialty is the jalapeño. He said Mexico is very strict about the quality of jalapeños exported to the United States. "They have to be seven centimeters long and of thick flesh," he said. "Veracruz is the biggest producer of jalapeños, and the Veracruz type is preferred because it has thick walls and a good heat level." The state of Chihuahua has been trying to catch up with Veracruz, in terms of production, he told me. But instead of planting more acres, farmers there had taken a short cut: for replanting they had selected year after year from their crops only those plants that produced more than their normal output. The result of this pressure on productivity is that while the Chihuahua plant now produces substantially more fruits than its cousin in Veracruz, it has spread itself too thin: it sprouts jalapeños whose walls are much thinner and which contain too much juice. Thin-walled jalapeños, which are a bit on the mushy side, don't sell well in America, so the Chihuahua jalapeños are now being consumed almost exclusively at home—mostly in thin strips, called *carrerros*. So Chihuahua, far from beating Veracruz, is losing the profitable export market.

Hugo Restrepo is a big tabasco pepper farmer from Bogotá, Colombia, who has the country singer Willie Nelson's face and the actor Orson Welles's body. He told me about a researcher from the Colombian agriculture department who had gone deep into the Amazon jungle in Orinoguia, in the region called Mitu, to study the eating habits of an Indian tribe and found that members smoked a tiny native pepper called pajarito, or "little bird"—so called because it looks like a bird's beak. "They actually smoke it," Restrepo repeated for effect. "The Colombian agriculture department is investigating this."

One attendee nearby was showing another man Polaroid pictures of shriveled peppers, and both were speculating what virus might be attacking the plants. Another, Ted Winsberg, a Boynton Beach, Florida, farmer, said that while he grew bell peppers for commercial reasons, his own preference was for really hot peppers. "I am addicted to them," he said. Hot pepper was indispensable to his wife too. "My wife, at the suggestion of a holistic health expert, takes a half teaspoon of cayenne powder daily to promote good health."

I also ran into Sam Meiner, an attorney, who said he had opened a hot-food restaurant in Orlando, Florida. "I am in search of hotter peppers," he told me, his reason for coming to the conference. "I haven't found a hot pepper that I have had to spit out. I want it real hot. I have been buying peppers from India, China, and Mexico, but there's no consistency in the shipments as far as pungency is concerned. I am real frustrated." Chris Schlesinger, a chef who has opened a "hot" food grill in Cambridge, Massachusetts, was also there. He said, "I can't make my food hot enough for my customers." Schlesinger said he had recently branched out into marketing his own bottled hot sauce, made with peppers from Jamaica. "It's very, very hot. It's called Inner Beauty."

A leaflet detailing the conference agenda said:

We have a memorable meeting planned for you. There will be an opportunity to see some of the North Carolina pepper industry, visit with your friends and colleagues, and hear about the latest research on peppers. We will see elements of the North Carolina pepper industry, which will include a pepper canning plant, a vegetable research station with a variety of breeding line trials, a farm producing three hundred acres of pepper with plastic mulch and drip irrigation, a farm growing six kinds of peppers, and topped by a visit to a pepper-pickling plant. The day will end with a Spring House Dust Chaser at our hotel in Raleigh.

The Pepper Improvement Committee was in session over breakfast, at seven the next morning. One member suggested that efforts be doubled to collect pepper seeds from around the world, especially from South America, to infuse new genes into America's commercial varieties. "I think that should be our priority," the chairman of the committee declared.

For two days researchers at the conference presented technical papers and slides under such titles as "Genetic Control of Six Viruses in Capsicums," "Flower Drop in Bell Peppers: Causes and Control Measures," "Update on Mechanical Harvesting of Peppers," "Effect of Ethephon on the Yield and Color of Mature, Mildly Pungent, Long, Green Chile," "Cherry Pepper Production in Delaware," "Critical Periods of Weed Competition in Chile Pepper," "Pepper Weevil: A Threat to Georgia's Pepper Industry," "What's New in Pepper Products," and "Breeding Toward Ideotypes in Chile Peppers."

Although the topics of these technical papers didn't reflect it, one theme that was loud and clear in private conversations among these pepper men was that American taste is changing. The consumers who hadn't gone anywhere near hot peppers now were slowly approaching them, and those already initiated were demanding hotter ones. Judging from the conversations, it seemed the rising demand for *picante* had caught the country's pepper men by surprise. They frequently mentioned that there wasn't a large enough supply of hot peppers, and that message frustrated Michael G. Natali, who came to the conference to find new sources of supplies. His small company in Melrose Park, Illinois, packages large cans of serranos, jalapeños, and a mixture of pickled vegetables and hot peppers. "I am having a lot of problems getting peppers," he told me as we were being bused to a pepper field to see the mechanical harvesting of pepper. "I am a little guy. The big guys jump in and buy up everything and the farmer doesn't want to sell to the little guy like me. But I must find more peppers. Every hot dog in Chicago now has at least two slices of 'sport' [a long serrano] pepper. I buy it from Mississippi. But I can't get enough. I have searched Jamaica, Costa Rica, and Tahiti." A short, stocky man exuding a lot of anxiety, Natali gave the impression that his business survival depended upon finding more hot peppers. I had seen him often darting around the crowd and pumping hands. "I have been taking suppliers to breakfasts, lunches, and dinners. I came in a day early, so that I could meet with all the big suppliers as they came in. I even carried Arturo Jurado's bags when I found out who he was." Jurado is one of the biggest pepper producers in New Mexico, and his cayenne goes into Louisiana hot sauces.

I ran into Natali again at nearly eleven o'clock that night in the hotel lobby. He was standing near the entrance to the hotel disco. Young men and women in evening dress were drawn into the lobby like moths, and rock 'n' roll blasted out of the dance floor every time the doors opened. Conventioneers were heading into the disco, but Natali was standing at the entrance like a bouncer, alone.

"Any luck?" I asked.

Anyone else hearing that question might have taken it to mean something else, given the number of young women making their way in and out of the disco.

"No, but I haven't given up," he said.

"I figured most of the guys from the pepper conference

would follow the girls into the disco and I would buttonhole them again," he continued. "There are some guys I haven't met yet. This may be the best location to catch them on the last night. I wouldn't go in there myself; it would be a slap in the face for my wife. She is about to give birth, probably tomorrow."

He was clutching a fistful of business cards.

3

Big Jim

In New Mexico, No. 6 is number one. Some years ago No. 9 was number one. And lately a number of others have been vying for the number one position: Española, Sandía, NuMex R Naky, NuMex Joe Parker, Rio Grande 21—and Big Jim, a relatively new contestant that's rapidly winning people over.

Welcome to Hatch, where farmers produce "designer chiles" and christen them with alluring names. It's the Fashion Avenue of peppers.

In Hatch, just off Interstate 25, along the Rio Grande, is Jim Lytle, Jr.'s, Hatch Chile Express. Standing in front of his store, Lytle is staring at his neatly lined bins and open sacks filled with just one product, chile. But at first glance his stand looks like a green market with all kinds of produce on display, so diverse are the shapes and sizes and colors of his chiles. Of all the types he carries, Lytle declares his personal preference: the Big Jim. This pepper is so big that from a distance it can be mistaken for a green banana, except that it's flat and pointed like a chisel. "I think it's one mighty beautiful chi'le," Lytle says, with one eye

poised adoringly on his peppers and the other on the steady
stream of cars pulling up in front of his store.

Nearby, a huge wiry cylinder is rotating against a battery of
hissing gas burners, tumbling pepper pods inside it. Lytle says
that's a roaster. People who buy his peppers, usually in big sacks,
make their next stop at that tumbling contraption. The air is
heavy with a mildly pungent smoke that smells like burning
molasses. Crates of peppers arrive on the back of pickups from
the three hundred acres he has planted in the valley this year.

The peppers leave his store as fast as they arrive—three workers are loading a semitrailer with gunnysacks tagged with colored labels: green (mild), yellow (medium hot), orange (hot), and red (very hot).

"Headed for R'zona and Cl'rado," Lytle says.

Lytle is a busy man this time of year. It is late August—harvesttime. He is clutching a Motorola mobile phone in his left hand. His right hand is free, which is just as well: he's so conscious of his long mustache angling skyward that he constantly rubs it down. Lytle, forty-seven years old, is built solid, except at the middle, where he soars forth. In a straw cowboy hat and dark glasses, he looks more like a sheriff than Hatch Valley's most prominent chile producer. Big Jim, the pepper, is named after his father, Jim Lytle, Sr. It's his biggest seller.

In Hatch and its surrounding valleys, when people go to a produce market or a roadside stand to buy peppers, they don't simply ask for peppers. They ask for New Mexico 6, or NuMex 6, or just 6. Some ask for 6-4, which is a later version of the No. 6; hence some farmers call the 6-4 the New Improved Six. Those who prefer something more pungent ask for Sandía. To the untrained eye the Sandía may not look different from No. 6, but those who favor one or the other know the difference well. Lytle says his customers are discriminating, prone to fussing over the thickness of the pod, its color and smoothness, its level of pungency. Customers return whole sacks if the peppers get mixed with an unwanted variety—"a picker's mixup," Lytle says—and Lytle then not only offers new sacks of the right kind but also returns the customer's money.

Lytle tells me stories of his customers' loyalties to one chile or another. One time a customer thought she'd bought a bag of Big Jim, but she claimed that the pepper sold to her was too hot to be Big Jim. It was as hot as the Española, she claimed. Lytle took a look at the pods and said there was no way the pepper was Española. The customer insisted. Lytle, who claims he can recognize a pepper from fifty feet, was visibly irritated. He grabbed a pod out of the customer's sack, took a bite out of it,

and realized the customer was right. He says he knew exactly
what had happened. The peppers were Big Jim all right, as he
had insisted, but they came from plants that had been
"stressed." When pepper plants come under stress, they respond by intensifying the heat in their fruit; it's the pepper's
built-in mechanism to deter predators that try to dine on the
plant's leaves.

In this case—and Lytle says he knew exactly which plants
the fruits came from—it wasn't a predator that had stressed the
plants. "The peppers came out of the corner of a field that was
really sandy and suffered from lack of water, which stressed the
plants. That's what happened," he says. "I gave her another bag
of Big Jim and I went to the cash register and gave her money
back. I have a reputation to uphold."

People drive as many as fifty miles to Hatch to buy Lytle's
chiles. Lytle is among the more than a dozen chile farmers who
dominate the town with their chile farms and roadside outlets.
During the harvest the town seems to sell nothing but chiles.
Right now the town, which has proclaimed itself "the chile
capital of the world," is hosting its annual Hatch Chile Festival,
which coincides with the peak of the harvesttime. The whole
town is swirling in chilemania. I visit a huge tent where, amid
banjo- and fiddle-playing bands, the town fathers and local
horticulturists are poring over fourteen different varieties of
chiles—ranging from tiny pearl shapes to monstrous pods over
a foot long—entered in a contest by local farmers. Stores, even
gas stations, are decked with ristras, long strands of red peppers, which are green peppers that have been allowed to ripen
on the vine. A local credit union is holding its grand opening,
and I see town dignitaries, scissors in hand, lined up behind a
ten-foot garland of chiles.

Menus are peppered with chiles. Chiles appear promi-
nently in rellenos (stuffed peppers) and salsas. Chiles end up in
strips on pizzas and eggs. They go into dishes of squash and

corn and into the folds of warm tortillas. They are stewed with pork and beef or are sliced and diced and sprinkled on hamburgers and hot dogs. At more esoteric eateries, wild buffalo and rattlesnake are stewed with chiles. Sometimes a whole meaty pod is grilled and served as a side dish. Some prominent restaurants as far away as Santa Fe offer Hatch Chile Soup.

Because the harvest season lasts less than two months, the rush to buy starts as soon as chiles begin arriving in the market, and it turns into a frenzy as the season nears its end at about Labor Day, with people trying to store enough chiles to get through the winter. I saw families making getaways with fifty-pound sacks in their car trunks.

The pods are roasted to prepare them for freezing. In fact, the roasting of pepper is as much a part of chile harvest here as the picking itself. For decades mounds of chiles ended up popping and crackling on the backyard grills that are fixtures behind the adobe homes prevalent in the area. More recently, the locals have invented the pepper version of the modern roaster, a spinning drum that tumbles pepper pods against the jets of gas burners—the machine I first saw in front of Lytle's Hatch Chile Express. This implement has given rise to a breed of vendors who travel with the roaster from pepper farm to pepper farm or simply plant themselves in front of stores and supermarkets in wait for the sack-carrying customer. As a result, during harvest season the Hatch and Mesilla valleys take on a distinct aroma from the smoke that is perpetually suspended in the sky.

The moment after the peppers are roasted they are shut tight in big plastic bags. That keeps the pods hot, and as the moisture inside the pods rises it loosens their cellophanelike skin, making them ready for disrobing. The glistening green flesh underneath has the slippery consistency of a fresh oyster. Sprinkled with garlic salt, the meaty pepper wrapped inside a warm tortilla is a delectable snack. More traditionally, it's stuffed and coated with batter, and fried crisp in searing oil.

Peppers are also stored for the winter in ristras weighing

thirty to forty pounds, which are hung on the patios or on the outside walls of adobe homes to dry. The lengths of these ristras aren't random. In a long-established rule of thumb for estimating the amount of chiles a household would need till the next season, each ristra corresponds to twice the height of each family member. Once dried, the ristras are hung in the kitchen for easy reach and the dried peppers are generously used in the preparation of sauces.

In Hatch chiles are also available in nonedible forms: chile-shaped earrings; chiles imprinted on T-shirts, socks, pillow-cases, bed sheets, and place mats; and pots and pans adorned with chiles. In the nearby town of Mesilla, where Billy the Kid settled scores as a hired gun, the chile isn't so much a symbol of machismo as an icon of arts and crafts. The name of one knickknack store on the town's main square, for instance, is Chiletos. Chilpepe is another. The locals say chile is like the cartoon character Garfield—it evokes a warm and fuzzy feeling.

How chile came to the valley is a subject of some controversy among the locals. The story that has been perpetuated is that in 1598 conquistador Don Juan de Oñate brought it to New Mexico. The local Indians have disputed that claim, and in my visit to Hatch I heard one Native American remark, "Why is it that when it comes to good things we automatically assume the Europeans brought them?" Archaeologists recently uncovered evidence that once a busy trade route existed between New Mexico and Central America, suggesting that more than likely chile had become part of the Pueblo Indians' diet long before Oñate's arrival in the state. (This discovery came too late to prevent a local variety from being named the Conquistador in Oñate's honor.)

Whoever brought the pepper, once it arrived it found a nurturing home in the dry climate and natural irrigation of the Rio Grande Valley. Today miles of canals shoot off at ninety-degree angles from the Rio Grande, and acre upon acre of farms flanking the river languidly sip while basking in the sun. The Hatch Valley, in the southern part of the state, with its warm days and nights and longer growing season, produces hotter varieties than does the north, near Albuquerque. Some aficionados consider the northern varieties more flavorful. These northern types, bred at a higher altitude, are about half the size of those in the south, and are cultivated in small farms under extraordinary care, and are known as Chimayo, Dixon, Velardes, and San Juan after the names of the isolated valleys they grow in. These chiles are in so much demand that "you have to practically know the farmer to be able to get any supply," Peter Raub, the resident chef at the Santa Fe School of Cooking, told me. "The purchase contracts are signed and sealed even before the peppers are planted."

I had called Raub after I learned that the culinary school had enlisted a pepper botanist recently to give students a primer on the botany of peppers—more specifically, on the varieties of peppers, their flavor, and their pungency. (I don't know if any Italian cooking school ever deployed a tomato botanist. And the tomato certainly has many distinctive varieties—I have tasted as many as five in a single Southwestern salad, which is twice as many varieties as I have had in my entire experience with Italian cuisine.) The idea of cooks picking a pepper botanist's brain suggested how seriously this spice was being pursued for adoption into American cuisine.

Raub said chefs and would-be chefs from around the country had been packing his classes on Southwestern cuisine, and the ingredient that had caught their imagination the most was the pepper. The hot pepper was ending up, in one form or another, in salad dressing, in sauces for glazing fish, even in certain desserts. And not only the students at the school but chefs all over the Southwest, he said, were exploring which pepper would complement what—which to use in a creamy sauce, which would go with pork, which with poultry, for instance—and what peppers were out there that hadn't yet made their way into mainstream Southwestern cooking. It's safe to assume that until now these eager cooks probably had relied entirely on garlic, black pepper, and a limited number of herbs to animate their dishes. Now they had discovered in hot peppers a major tool, like a new set of colors, to lend depth and breadth to their dishes.

Not that Southwestern dishes don't already employ hot peppers. Most do. But a myriad of new dishes are being created in the Southwest by marrying America's European cuisine with the techniques and ingredients taken from Native American, Mexican, and Caribbean foods.

One man who has been engaged in this amalgamation more than anyone else I encountered was Mark Miller, the chef-owner of Coyote Cafe in Santa Fe, north of Hatch. I asked him why Southwestern cuisine had suddenly inflamed the American palate. Obviously, Miller told me, social and demographic factors are playing a big role; immigrants from Mexico and South America as well as from other "spicy" countries in Southeast Asia are finally being accepted as part of the American social fabric. Whether it's the influence of the new immigrants or simply the nationalism of the Reagan era that has prodded Americans of European descent into acknowledging America's ethnic roots, there is clearly a new awareness and curiosity at the table—from New York to San Francisco. No longer does a dish have to be Italian or French to be chic.

The popularity of Italian and French dishes—which I have found not so vastly better than the Irish food I once dreaded and which finally sent me exploring the pepper—has always puzzled me. What's so extraordinary about cold mozzarella on sliced tomatoes, or grilled eggplant and radicchio swimming in olive oil? And what's so extraordinary about pasta—which Miller sarcastically describes as nothing but plain dry wheat—whose distinction lies more in the myriad shapes it comes in than in its flavor?

How about French? My own experience is quite limited, and so I defer the question to Miller, one of America's foremost chefs. "In terms of mouth experience, French food is at a higher level than Italian, but not much," he told me. "It has a great tradition, but Southwestern food has a lot more flavors and uses a lot more techniques in its preparation. Also, French and Italian aren't rooted in the earth itself the way Southwestern cuisine is. When you taste Southwestern cuisine—its smokiness, its herbaceousness, its bursting flavors—it creates sensations that aren't confined to the mouth alone. You see rugged mountains and deep, green valleys, and you smell the creosote bushes after the rain in the desert. Southwestern food, with the sweat and tears it induces, offers a much more active experience in the mouth. It isn't flat like the European foods. The difference between the two is the difference between a chamber music ensemble and a mariachi band, the latter being the discordant European cuisine."

The new breed of diners are seeking the full symphonic experience, Miller said, and hence the increasing fascination with "new" herbs and spices that had long been available right in America's backyard. "In the 1970s we discovered balsamic vinegar, raspberry, green peppercorns, mozzarella, prosciutto, radicchio; and in the 1980s, wild mushrooms and truffles," he said. "Now people are discovering cactus, different types of corn, quinoa, amaranth, Mexican cinnamon, and chiles. People are also discovering different cooking techniques: slow roasting of garlic; blackening of tomatoes; adding citrus, because why restrict sweet to dessert only?"

But, of course, the thing that gives Southwestern cuisine its main character is the chiles. Miller told me that two-thirds of his dishes rely on chiles. For example: a two-color chile soup (one side is made with green chiles, the other with red); lobster folded into a crepe of smoked corn with roasted poblano and habanero chiles; marinated venison served in a sauce of ancho chiles and cherry; grilled beef tenderloin with a sauce of serrano chiles and blackened tomato; a rib-eye steak with jalapeño mustard glaze; chutney made with Mexican hot green peppers, apples, and pine nuts. Chile is the first thing the diner tastes in these dishes, and then as the pepper's subtleties are progressively revealed other items in the dish make their entrances on the palate, leading up to the scene where all major and minor players harmoniously come together to complete the act.

"Without chiles Southwestern food couldn't exist," said Miller, an anthropologist by training who once taught at the University of California at Berkeley. When he talks about food, he doesn't describe the form—as almost all food critics in America tend to do—but rather recounts his sensory experience, often evoking musical references. "Chiles give rhythm to the food, each acting on a different part of the palate, like each musical section of the orchestra contributes its own musical notes, the highs and lows, to the symphony." Miller said he has tasted ninety different peppers and defined the flavor and pungency of each, the way a wine expert classifies wines in terms of their bouquet and weight and mouth feel. "Peppers are like grapes."

New Mexico produced 46,780 dry tons of chiles—after discounting for water weight—in 1990, double the 23,410 tons the state grew in 1980. It is the country's largest chile-growing state, and the Rio Grande Valley accounts for most of the production. In terms of tonnage, the state produces more chiles than any other single fruit or vegetable. While the chile lags behind hay and cotton in acreage planted, it produces a profit of $1,600 per acre compared with $300 for hay, which is the state's biggest revenue-producing crop. So important is the chile crop that the state's fish and game department has given farmers special permission to shoot at the deer—which also seem to have developed a taste for peppers—that come salivating into their fields.

Before the chile, Hatch's only distinction was its Fort Santa Barbara, which stood on the east bank of the Rio Grande and was under the command of U.S. Army general Edward Hatch between 1880 and 1895. The scrubby and dusty patch of the valley was called Hatch's Station and later Hatch's Ranch. Located midway between Las Cruces and Truth or Consequences, Hatch is a tiny speck on the vast plain and from Interstate 25 it is easy to miss in a blink at the wrong moment. It's home to some three thousand souls, but during the chile season the population temporarily swells to ten times that. Banners announcing the chile festival go up on roads leading to Hatch. The nearest airport is in El Paso, Texas; from there it's seventy miles north to Hatch.

On the plane to El Paso, the young woman sitting to my right was also heading for Hatch. Jedre Wilker was coming in from Des Moines, Iowa, where she is a hospital medical researcher, but she had lived in New Mexico for many years. "In Des Moines I used to send for chile by mail, but the quality was never reliable. After I roasted and peeled it, there was hardly anything left to eat," she said. "Now I come down myself, and see friends and return with a fifty-pound sack."

Wilker is blond, blue-eyed, and a bit on the mischievous side. She quickly gives the impression that chiles are what keeps her going during the frigid Iowa winter. "For a while I imported dried whole chiles from Hatch," she said. "I don't bother with it anymore. The Iowa weather is so moist that the chiles get covered with a fungus in my kitchen," she said. "In Iowa if you stand still your hair grows moss." Wilker and I agreed to look for each other in the chile festival the next day.

Lytle takes me on a ride to show me his chile fields, which are scattered in parcels of ten to a hundred acres in a twelve-mile area. The fields are deliberately dispersed, he says: If an unexpected hailstorm whips the valley, the damage will be minimized, whereas if all his acreage is in one area the entire crop could be destroyed by such a storm.

The dispersal also allows him to isolate one variety of pepper from another. It maintains the purity of each variety. Peppers pollinate each other easily, and an unwanted genetic intrusion from the next field can influence the shape, flavor, and pungency of his future crop. So before he plants he goes around asking his neighbors what type they were planning to plant. "If they are planting NuMex six near my field, then I plant NuMex six. If they are planting Sandía, I plant Sandía." Lytle is polite; usually others defer to whatever he's planting. Still, he says, cross-pollination is becoming a problem, as increasing numbers of farmers take to growing peppers and as their fields close in on each other. Bees are carrying pollen between fields even as far apart as a quarter mile, he says. As a result, his fields increasingly are sprouting strange-looking pods here and there— "rogues," he calls them. Lytle and his farmhands periodically wade through the fields uprooting the undesirable plants. Lytle says he has built his reputation on the quality his peppers guarantee, and for that assurance his customers willingly pay a little more; he says he's a dollar higher than his competitors on each bag.

The most striking thing about the row upon row of pepper plants in his field is the size of the fruit in relation to the plant. The plants, spread into a dense canopy at the top, are about two feet tall, and the pods that hang from the branches are ten to twelve inches long, about half as tall as the plant. Each plant bears fifteen to twenty pods on average. That the plant can stand upright under that burden is astonishing.

"In the beginning of time chile was a small pod," Lytle says, as he holds a glistening fourteen-incher against the sunlight.

At first glance, the pod seems odd, somewhat unnatural, because of its disproportionately large size. It gave me the same uneasy feeling I have when I'm served "dwarf" vegetables on oversize plates at haute cuisine restaurants. Or, for that matter, when I'm confronted in supermarkets with rows of uniformly shaped and sized tomatoes, or potatoes, or asparagus, or apples, or oranges—all selected solely for appearance and commercial convenience. In contrast, I have found the markets in Bolivia or Mexico or India seductive for their genetically unexpunged harvests—untamed nature laid out in all its variations. No symmetry there in the overflowing racks and bins. No whole-saler or canner to impose geometry. To close one's hands around the varied shapes is to feel the sensation of touching the earth itself. But when I'm choosing from the symmetrical stock in my local supermarkets, I only see images of packinghouses and canning factories and the robotic sleights of hand that sweep identical tomatoes or bell peppers into standardized cartons and cans. And now, standing in the pepper fields with Lytle, I couldn't help but imagine a commercial agenda in the uncomely size of the peppers, which seemed more appropriate fruit for tall trees, at least the height of a banana tree, and not for a knee-high bush.

Lytle is proud of the size, brought about by genetic tinker-ing. "Bigger the pod, higher the yield," he says. That means that in terms of weight more would be picked for the same amount of effort, since it's no more time-consuming to pick a big pod than to pick a small one. In fact, there's constant pressure on the farm to push the bigness to its limit: at the end of each week he and his wife award a five-dollar bonus to the picker who's found the biggest pod. The seeds from the largest pods are planted the next year in the drive to increase yield.

The record for picking the biggest pod, however, is held not by one of his farmhands but by Lytle's mother, June. She entered the *Guinness Book of World Records* in 1988 for grow-ing a thirteen-and-a-half-inch Big Jim. "Ha'eck, I've since grown some that are seventeen inches," she said when I met her during my visit. In Hatch she's a kind of celebrity, thanks to the fertilizer ads in which she appears. "For two years I've been in commercials. On the radio. On TV. I'm considered, what do you call them people in the movies . . . ah, movie stars. I've been inducted into the Actors Guild."

As we walk through Lytle's fields, he picks samples to make this or that point about peppers. "Perfect chi'le," he exclaims at a fruit, and reaches for it. When we finish stomping, both Lytle and I find ourselves holding heaps of pods in our hands. He lays them down on the trunk of his car. I had by now forgotten which belonged to which variety, and most were indistinguishable to my untrained eyes anyway. "You can take ten different varieties of chiles and throw them in a bag and shake 'em up and I can go through them and tell you what each one is," he says. He randomly picks half a dozen and lines them up next to one another. He goes over one at a time. "Big Jim will be a heavier pod next to all others, smooth and real wide. Sandía has square shoulders and comes to a point much more sharply than Big Jim. NuMex looks a lot like Big Jim, but has darker skin and sloping shoulders. Española is the lightest of all, and the smallest of all."

When Lytle was a little boy he used to tag along with his father in the pepper fields. He came to own his first chile field when he was still in high school. "I always looked forward to the fall. My dad and I would compete over who picked the prettiest chi'le."

I asked him how he defined a "perfect chi'le."

"To me a perfect chi'le would be a large pod, ten to fourteen inches long, all the way smooth, real pretty sloping shoulder with a real pretty point on it. With a perfect chi'le, you would be able to put it in the roaster and be able to expect the garden hose to peel the skin right off. That's ideal. Not a chi'le that you have to take your fingernail and have to scrape the skin off. You should be able to plant five hundred acres with the seeds of perfect chi'les and expect that every plant that grows out of them is the same size, has the same leaf shape, the same load of fruits shaded by a beautiful canopy of leaves. That's a perfect chi'le."

Sloping shoulders, so that water won't sit on the pod and rot the fruit. Pointed end, so the skin peels right off the end of the pod. Large size, so each picking yields the greatest possible load. The right plant height—three feet, including the one-foot-high ridge on which it grows—so the field worker can snare the pod from the plant without having to bend into awkward positions. Perfection and beauty defined by convenience. I wondered if Big Jim would go the same way as the high-yield tomato (rock solid and juiceless), cucumber (leathery), and strawberry (dry and bland), to name a few.

The trend for developing the "perfect" pepper—rather, a uniform pepper based on the perception of what the consumer would prefer—was started by Fabian Garcia, the pepper breeder who introduced, in February 1921, what became the chile growers' staple for decades: the No. 9.

Garcia saw little value in the myriad shapes and sizes of peppers that were then growing in New Mexico. "The varieties now being grown produce pods that are irregular in form, more or less wrinkled, with thin flesh, and with a deep shoulder at the stem end," he wrote in an agricultural bulletin. "All of these are considered undesirable characteristics of the pod, and are a drawback, to a certain extent, to the canning industry, inasmuch as a fleshy, smooth, tapering, and shoulderless pod can be easily and more economically peeled. Since all of the canned chile has to be roasted and then hand peeled, the faster this can be done, the cheaper it can be put on the market. The speed in peeling the green chile pods can be materially increased by having a smooth, tapering, and shoulderless pod." The large chiles used for canning have to be peeled to get rid of their cellophanelike shiny skin.

In order to create an ideal chile, Garcia collected chiles from neighbors' backyards and got to work in the spring of 1907. In an undertaking that would last eleven years, Garcia crossed these varieties with one another and continued the process with their progeny until, in a tug-of-war with nature, he was able to yank out of the peppers' genetic makeup traits that he thought were commercially desirable. Garcia started with twelve different types of a long, stringy pepper called pasilla, as well as one that was known as "black chile" and another called "red chile." He numbered each, one to fourteen, and planted them in January 1908 in a greenhouse and then in April transplanted them to the field. But a chile wilt disease attacked in July and

August, killing most of the population. In 1909 he selected the best of the surviving plants. The wilt again killed most of them, and the surviving plants were replanted in 1910. Each year through 1912, most of the plants succumbed to the disease. In 1913 Garcia finally had a healthy population that withstood the disease.

Progeny of Nos. 2, 9, 11, and 13 set fruits that were closest to the "ideal" pod Garcia had in mind—their shoulders sloped smoothly. But No. 2 was a little too narrow and thin-fleshed. No. 11 was a bit short. No. 13 was a little sunken in the middle. No. 9, however, didn't have any of these blemishes. In 1914 Garcia discarded all but Nos. 9 and 11 and distributed their seeds to a number of farmer-collaborators to evaluate how the varieties would grow in different areas and under different environmental conditions in the state. After evaluating the results, he dropped No. 11 and in 1916 planted 5,455 small hills of No. 9 on an acre: two plants in each hill, with the rows three and a half feet apart. This time 198 hills were blighted by the wilt disease.

In 1917 Garcia planted another acre from the seeds of the 1916 harvest and found that "there continued to be a number of hills that would still produce wrinkled pods with a sunken shoulder at the stem end." The rogues were uprooted and seeds from the remainder replanted in 1918. It was that crop, Garcia felt, that met his criteria for "a larger, smoother, fleshier, more tapering, and shoulderless pod for canning purposes," and he officially released the variety three years later.

"The plant No. 9 has a tendency to grow quite tall, varying in height from two to three feet. It is very vigorous and quite prolific," he declared in his agricultural bulletin study.

A number of farmers and home gardeners were pleased, and they wrote to Garcia.

I planted four varieties of chile in the same plot of ground. There were two from the College (No. 9), one from California, and one of the seeds from last year's, grown on my ranch. The chile from the College grew tall and bore more heavily and had larger pods than the native. In fact, it was the best chile I ever saw raised here. . . .

Hugh A. Teel
Teel, N.Mex.

As I am gardening in a small way I want some chile seed like you sent Mr. Watts two years ago. It was the finest chile I ever saw grow.

G. T. Davis
Roswell,
N.Mex.

We have grown your chile No. 9 for four years. During the last two years we have grown no other kind.

Percy W. Barker
Mesilla Park,
N.Mex.

Garcia's No. 9 was the first "scientifically" developed chile, and it ruled the palate in New Mexico for thirty years, until 1951, when it was supplanted by No. 6.

The No. 6, a pepper about six inches long also known as NuMex 6, was created exclusively with the canning industry in mind, specifically the standard four-and-a-half-inch-tall can. My curiosity about the canning industry's influence on peppers' shape and flavor led me to call upon Paul Bosland, a horticulture professor at New Mexico State University. "The reason NuMex six evolved into that size is very interesting," he told me. "The canneries wanted a pepper that could be chopped off at the stem end, which is where the seed core is, and be left with just enough length to fit into the standard can, top to bottom. You needed to start with a six-inch pepper."

The development of No. 6 was spearheaded by Roy Harper,

also a horticulturist at what was then the New Mexico College of Agriculture and Mechanic Arts. His starting material was a number of chiles of "undetermined origin" from the state, and the long-established No. 9. That the six-inch-long pepper came to be called No. 6 has nothing to do with its length. It was the sixth group of Harper's trial plants that ended up producing a progeny that was not only six inches long but yielded the most and had the ideal shape. The No. 6 became an instant success with farmers and canners also because it was only 50 to 60 percent as pungent as No. 9, which helped win over the uninitiated consumers, especially Anglos.

Bosland told me that while No. 6 became a big hit with canneries, Big Jim, a recent introduction, didn't. It failed because of an ironic twist. Big Jim was a made-to-order pepper commissioned by a cannery in the Mesilla Valley, which wanted a big pepper that would be compatible with a high-tech processing operation the factory was contemplating; the goal was to slash labor costs. One of the biggest costs in pepper canning is the laborious task of "de-coring" each pod—which is done by a knife-wielding worker—before sending it off on a conveyor belt for further processing. The cannery was experimenting with an automatic machine that lopped off the stem end of each pepper as it passed beneath the machine's blade on a conveyer belt, thus eliminating the tedium of removing the seed core by hand. The company asked Roy Nakayama, who was then a professor of horticulture at New Mexico State University, to develop a chile that could accept the beheading—which took off a sizable chunk of the pod—and still have something substantial left to offer in a can to the consumer. Nakayama went to work with his closest friend, farmer Jim Lytle, Sr., who provided him with land for developing the chile. One thing was clear to them: the pepper had to be huge—not six inches like the No. 6, but at least nine inches.

Nakayama, who died a few years ago, was devoted to the interests of the pepper farmers, because, as he told me before his death, hot peppers not only spiced his otherwise bland diet but also provided important nutrients during the Depression. Born in the United States of Japanese parents, and a soldier at the Battle of the Bulge, Nakayama was an experienced chile breeder. He had worked with Harper on No. 6 and later created a new strain of that pepper—"the Son of Six"—called the NuMex 64, or simply the 6-4, and several minor varieties designed to flourish in local soil and climatic conditions. Nakayama, who was called Mr. Chile by farmers and canners, did for chile what Steven Jobs, with the Apple, did for computers: he brought it to the masses. Founder in 1973 of the International Connoisseurs of Green and Red Chile in nearby Las Cruces, Nakayama directed his efforts to creating milder varieties so a larger number of people, including those new to its pungency, could venture to eat hot pepper. "If it wasn't for the milder chiles there wouldn't be any Taco Bells and Old El Paso brands," he told me. Years later, another man, Dr. Villalon of Texas, would continue in that direction by developing a mild jalapeño, stirring up considerable controversy.

Nakayama finally developed the "huge, big mild chile" the high-tech cannery wanted and named it Big Jim for Jim Lytle, Sr., who never lived to see the final product: he died of cancer in 1970. Nakayama's Big Jim was shipped to the cannery in 1975, seven years after he had begun work on it.

But the cannery discovered something it hadn't thought of before. As much as 40 percent of the shipments was wasted—the result of automatic beheading. The losses outweighed the benefit of mechanization. The cannery backed off.

That riles Jim Lytle, Jr., who remembers hovering around his father and Nakayama when the pepper was being developed. "We spent a lot of time developing the chi'le," he says. "The canneries said we can't use it because we are throwing too much tonnage away. So from the cannery point of view, Big Jim fell by the wayside," he says. Three years ago, Lytle decided to resurrect Big Jim for the retail market. "I knew Big Jim was a fresh-market chi'le superior to anything else there was. I started to plant it, and pretty soon people started to notice it.

The word spread in the valley. Big Jim. Big Jim. And now it has caught on. It is the prettiest chi'le to look at. No other chi'le catches more attention."

In New Mexico, Big Jim is the biggest seller after NuMex 6 and Sandía. Sought for its thick flesh, Big Jim has one problem, however: Although medium hot, its heat level is unpredictable and can vary from plant to plant. That has given rise to a tradition at dining tables in the Mesilla and Hatch valleys: whenever a dish in which Big Jim is the main item is served, people pass their plates around so that everyone eats from everyone else's plate and thus everyone ends up with the same amount of heat. "Pass the plates around; tonight we're eating Big Jim," they kid each other.

NuMex R Naky, a big pepper named after Roy Nakayama, is uniformly low in heat; NuMex 6, uniformly medium hot; Sandía, uniformly hot; and Española, uniformly very hot. But Big Jim can be mild as well as medium hot. "We never fixed the heat level in Big Jim," says Lytle, declaring that his next objective. "We have Sandía, which is uniformly hot, but the walls are thin. Big Jim is a heavy chile, real meaty, and it would be nice to have a chile that has real meat and also real heat. There is nothing like that in the market today," he says. "We have to get some help from the university."

New Mexico State University, based in nearby Las Cruces, works closely with chile farmers in the state. In gratitude for that kinship the farmers recently chipped in $20,000 to establish a scholarship at the university in the name of Joseph E. Parker, who was a respected field man for a cannery and whose name is on a fleshy pepper called NuMex Joe Parker. The university is the nation's hotbed for pepper breeders, or more appropriately, pepper designers. In addition to Paul Bosland, who concentrates on breeding new varieties, there are twenty-four people there who work on chiles. Plant pathologists concentrate on disease control; physiologists work on postharvest concerns, such as how to improve chile shelf life and prevent bacterial contamination; molecular biologists are mapping the genes that give pungency; and food experts are studying fiber quality and nutritional values of pepper and are exploring new uses, such as in snack foods.

"We are not a condiment industry. We are a big industry and we want to get a little more respect," says Bosland, who is trying to shake the notion that chile is some minor spice. The university is creating the country's first "chile institute," he says. It will offer scholarships for the study of chile, invite chile breeders and botanists from around the world to present papers, take on research and promotion for the industry, and also maintain seed banks for all species of peppers.

Bosland is already working toward creating marketable varieties of chiles from such exotic types as piquíns and mirasols. Piquíns are the elongated version of the tiny oval and round tepíns, all of which grow in the wild and are prized by American Indians; mirasols are the pungent peppers valued in Mexico. Bosland says new varieties that his department develops will be targeted at specific markets—one that's specifically for the fresh market, another that's specifically for canneries, and another that's specifically for use as dried red pepper. That hasn't been the case in the past. The NuMex Joe Parker released to farmers in 1990, for instance, is a "dual purpose" chile. It serves the green as well as the dry red markets: when enough is harvested for the fresh market the green pods are left on the plants to turn red and then sold as dried whole red or ground paprika. The pepper, as a result, is just thick enough for the fresh market consumption when green, and it's also just thin enough so that it dries easily. Ideally, the pepper should be fleshier for fresh market consumption, but it would be prone to spoilage if left on the plant to dry. "It is not perfect for the green market now, and not perfect for the red," says Bosland. He says it will be the last of his department's "dual purpose" chiles.

Bosland says his next project is to endow the New Mexico chiles with a skin that's as thin as that of the bell pepper. That would mean canneries won't have to bother with skinning chiles anymore, which would be a considerable cost saving for them.

The genetic manipulation to achieve that may take five to seven years, at a cost of $20,000 a year, he says.

Bosland doesn't agree that bowing to commercial concerns means that taste and flavor prized by the fresh-market consumer are being overlooked. He says growers and canners are invited every year to a serious all-day conference on chiles at the university. It is an occasion for consumers to voice ideas— suggestions as well as complaints. "If people have complaints, we hear about them," he says. "For instance, some people have complained that Sandía's walls are thin. That's why we are working on making a thicker-walled Sandía."

Some consumer complaints aren't justified, Bosland says. "We learned from some people that they liked NuMex R Naky but the skin didn't peel off as easy as No. 6," a complaint that's common to some New Mexico peppers, all of which have to be peeled by roasting or other means to get to their flesh. "Well, that may be terrible for the home industry. But the fact is that R Naky was developed for the red chile industry to be a highly red chile and not a green chile. The processors use a steam peeling method in which the steam pressure pops the skin open. They haven't had any problem with R Naky," he says. "I don't think we will modify R Naky. Usually, if we have a serious problem, we reach a middle ground."

Before leaving Hatch, I stopped to inquire after the friend who had traveled all the way from Iowa to Hatch to buy fresh chiles. She wasn't feeling all that well, her host told me on the phone. When I arrived at the house, Jedre Wilker led me into the kitchen to show me the cause of her ailment. In the sink lay a plastic bag of roasted Big Jim. She said she was sick with a bout of pepper-induced stomach cramps. "These things are addictive," she laughed.

4

The Hunt for the Mother Pepper

An hour into the hike, Hardy Eshbaugh frets that this afternoon's search in the Andean foothills of central Bolivia is turning into a wild-goose chase. But he continues to stride from bush to bush. One moment he is atop a mound, the next he is straddling an incline or sliding down a ravine. We are hiking on this particular ridge in this scorched and jagged land because from the dusty road he had spotted some Prosopis trees and cacti. "Indicator species," he calls them. They indicate the presence of his quarry: a wild pepper, a tiny round berry called ulupica.

This isn't the first time he has come to comb this part of the Andean sierras for peppers; it's his fifth foray in twenty years. When he isn't rummaging like this through Bolivia, he is in Peru or Ecuador or the U.S. Virgin Islands. This professor of botany at Miami University in Oxford, Ohio, has studied peppers—and only peppers—for three decades. Lately he has been preoccupied with collecting ulupica.

Ulupica may hold clues to the earliest stages of peppers' evolution. It's one of the most primitive of the peppers that's widely distributed in Bolivia, and Eshbaugh thinks it spread from the central part of the country southeast into Paraguay and northwest into Peru. As it fanned out from its point of origin, it branched into distinct species over hundreds of thousands of years. By charting the variations of ulupicas, Eshbaugh hopes to decipher how the large number of different species and subspecies of peppers—the domesticated peppers alone number over three hundred different types—are related to one another and thus describe the evolution of pepper, the "family tree" of pepper genealogy.

But this afternoon in the Andes we've been tramping through the bushes for over two hours and we haven't even glimpsed an ulupica. Eshbaugh patiently plows on. In his khaki trousers with oversize pockets, a plaid shirt, a khaki Army-Navy hat, and a plastic water bottle strapped around his waist, he looks like a man on a safari. To keep me engaged, he points out this plant and that shrub—"That's an acacia, and it's all over the African desert"—but when he catches the scent of his quarry, in the form of more "indicator species," he falls silent. When he suspects in the distance a bush might be hiding an ulupica plant, he strides up to it and peers into the vegetation. When he doesn't find one, he just as quickly moves on. If the setting were a suburban backyard in an American town, he would look like a grown-up playing hide-and-seek.

When Eshbaugh is about to give up, he suddenly catches a whiff of moisture in the otherwise parched earth, and it fills him with expectation. He stops his running commentary on the flora. The only sounds are those made by our lungs increasingly rebellious at eight thousand feet above sea level. Eshbaugh strides toward the greenish hue under a tall Prosopis and then dashes into the jumble of thorny bushes. Here it is—the ancient pepper.

The four-foot plant, with its long, indolent branches, is poised at the edge of a steep, dry watercourse, where it obviously enjoys extra moisture when it's raining. It also catches whatever shade it can from the scraggly Prosopis that shelters it.

"As you can see, they are very opportunistic," Eshbaugh says. He runs his hand over the narrow, pointed leaves and fondles the flowing branches. The world's leading authority on wild peppers practically embraces the pepper plant.

"You may find it slightly ridiculous that I find these plants so beautiful," he says. He breaks a couple of branches off to take with him.

Eshbaugh tries to justify the chase that has yielded only one pepper plant. "You can see, I am not entirely crazy. I had a strong feeling they were around." On our way down the hill we encounter an Aymara Indian woman who is herding sheep and goats. Eshbaugh waves the branches at her. "Ulupica," the woman says. She nods and raises both hands in the direction of nearby hills and valleys, as if saying, "They're all over."

• • •

To see how peppers have sustained Eshbaugh's career, I joined the fifty-six-year-old botanist on this collecting trip. The Andes mountain range, the humpback of this landlocked country, is his living laboratory. He thinks this is where evolutionary forces conspired to create the blistery fruit. More precisely, he estimates, the place of origin is central Bolivia, and thus this is where all the ancestral relatives are likely to be congregated. The flowers, the fruits, and the plain stems he collects here return with him to Miami University in Ohio. These items and the detailed notes he makes on each specimen become part of his ever expanding herbarium at the university. Eventually he grows the seeds out in his greenhouses and fields. He might compare the fruits collected from different locations and find that the peppers that start out as distinct types all lose their variations in Ohio and in successive plantings converge into a homogeneous population. That tells him how climatic conditions influence the shape and color of peppers. If the fruits retain their distinct appearance, Eshbaugh forces them into a crossing frenzy to see whether they are really distinct species; if they interbreed, then they aren't. He might cross a commercial variety with a wild pepper; if they interbreed, it indicates an evolutionary connection between the two, as well as whether the ancestral variety has desirable genes.

The exercise is more than academic. Wild species of peppers have genes that can be transferred into the cultivated types to improve them. A large number of commercial varieties grown in Asia, Europe, and North America are increasingly succumbing to various plant diseases because these peppers have lost genetic diversity. That's the result of man's selecting them for commercially valuable characteristics and in the process losing genes that ensure the pepper's overall vitality. Hot peppers, for instance, have been selected for certain heat levels, thickness, and color. The perfectly shaped four-lobed sweet peppers all appear to have come out of a factory mold, because over the years they have been carefully selected for visually appealing shape and size. These commercial peppers, as a result, possess just a small part of the genetic variations found in their ancestral species. The European sweet peppers have even less genetic diversity than their American counterparts because the European types were developed from a relatively small number of varieties that arrived in Spain during the early days of European botanizing in the New World.

When the genetic base of a crop is narrow it has a limited arsenal to fight off a virus or fungus epidemic. That's what happened to the potato in 1845, when an airborne fungus devastated crops from Ireland to the Ukraine in the scourge known today as the Irish Potato Famine. In 1970 a corn leaf blight wiped out about 15 percent of America's corn crop because man in his eagerness to selectively breed corn plants that grew faster and faster unknowingly excluded in the process a number of genes that helped protect corn against diseases. Such catastrophes have been limited by the vast armory of chemical pesticides usually trained at the attackers. But plant viruses and insects increasingly are growing immune to the chemicals—many of which are also being banned by the U.S. Environmental Protection Agency because they are environmentally unsafe—and crop destruction from diseases and insects are on the rise. In peppers the problem has become acute, as any pepper farmer in Texas, New Mexico, or Honduras will tell, and researchers are thus looking to the pepper's birthplace for an infusion of new genes.

The search for wild ancestors is urgent for another reason: the ancient plants are in danger of disappearing. Their habitats in South America are fast diminishing; farmers are clearing forests and scrublands for agriculture, and loggers are felling trees to meet a rising worldwide appetite for lumber. The deforestation, of course, is a problem affecting not just peppers; potatoes, tomatoes, and lima beans are among other well-known crops that originated in South America. In fact, when Eshbaugh is charging through bushes in the Andean foothills it is not unusual for him to collide head-on with tomato or potato collectors from Britain, the Netherlands, and the United States. On a collecting trip in 1977 Eshbaugh left his wife alone in the hotel and strayed deep into the Andes for three nights. A group of "potato people" from England were staying in the same hotel, and they kept his wife company. Pepper and potato belong to the same botanical family, the Solanaceae. "We're a family," a Dutch potato collector told Eshbaugh's wife as he welcomed her into the group.

Concerned that some wild species may be nearing extinction, the International Board for Plant Genetic Resources in 1979 proposed Capsicum, the pepper, "as a crop rating high global priority" for scientific collection. The scientific body, under the aegis of the Food and Agriculture Organization of the United Nations, called for "a global plan of action." Later, in a 1983 report, it identified regions where plant geneticists should start collecting seeds and plants. It also designated three central "seed banks"—in Costa Rica, the Netherlands, and India—to store the genetic material. These would act as a savings account from which mankind could draw to revive pepper crops.

The pursuit of peppers now engages nearly a dozen well-known botanists from South America, Europe, and the United States. So far they have documented twenty distinct wild species, in Peru, Brazil, Argentina, and Bolivia. But Eshbaugh believes that instead of collecting peppers randomly, it makes more sense to first learn which wild species have the desired traits and can also pass them on to the commercially cultivated types, since not all wild peppers meet those conditions. Indiscriminate collecting could result in a lot of wasted effort and perhaps not even a single useful species. That's where Eshbaugh comes in: his genealogical pepper "tree" may answer a lot of questions about kinship among peppers.

I asked Eshbaugh how he happened to get into peppers. I thought it was an unusual subject for a Midwestern botanist to pursue, let alone make a career of. He said peppers weren't his choice when he enrolled as a doctoral student at Indiana University in 1959. He was thinking of studying the blueberry family. But he was nudged into peppers by the man who was going to supervise his work at Indiana. This was Charles Heiser, the head of the botany department, who himself had been smitten by peppers. As a student at the University of California at Davis, Heiser was lured into peppers by the "joys and trials of botanizing in the tropics," and he made his first trip to South America in 1953. When he moved to Indiana to teach, he brought along his large collection of South American peppers that hadn't yet been "described." He would later choose promising new students to identify the species, their general habitats, and their relationship to others in the genus—a task botanists call "describing."

Eshbaugh was given a collection of long, pungent peppers—the Andean ají—and Heiser's field notes to investigate how they were related to other species of the genus. Before Eshbaugh arrived, Heiser had recruited another student, Barbara Pickersgill, who had come from Reading University in England to study for a Ph.D.; she was given another group of Andean peppers. Since finishing their doctoral studies, both Pickersgill and Eshbaugh have continued to study Capsicum, Pickersgill back at Reading. With genetic and anthropological studies, they often reinforce each other's findings on pepper taxonomy and the fruit's migratory paths, and sometimes they refute each other. A number of other botanists are also exploring the question of how peppers should be categorized, but most of them are studying one or two species to help fit little pieces into the bigger puzzle. One of the most exhaustive taxonomic studies being done, Eshbaugh told me, is by Armando Hunziker, a noted Argentine botanist at the University of Córdoba and a former Guggenheim fellow at Harvard University. Field collectors have for years been sending him wild peppers from all over South America.

All this work, it is hoped, will bring some order to the

chaotic world of pepper taxonomy. Since the arrival of the pepper in the West, botanists haven't been in agreement even over the simple question of how many peppers there are.

Frenchman Joseph Pitton de Tournefort, who practiced medicine in London and who chose the word Capsicum to describe the genus, classified all peppers into twenty-seven varieties in his *Institutiones rei herbariae,* published in 1700. The Swedish botanist Carolus Linnaeus in 1753 divided all peppers into two simple species: Capsicum annuum, for plants that require annual replanting; and Capsicum frutescens, for the shrubby perennial. (Carolus Linnaeus [1707–78], the founder of modern botanical nomenclature, later recognized four more distinct species.) In 1832 K. A. Fingerhurth, in his magnificently illustrated *Monographia generis capsici,* designated twenty-five species and noted that seven others required further investigation. Felix Dunal, in 1852, divided peppers into fifty different designations, each representing a distinct species. These classifications by early botanists, of course, were based on fruit shape and size, calyx and peduncle types, and other morphological characteristics. Eshbaugh calls the taxonomic approach "clerical speciation."

As pepper became popular as food in the early part of this century, the seed companies and farmers added to the taxonomic confusion by inventing names of their own to distinguish their peppers. A pepper might have belonged to the same variety but by virtue of variations in appearance took on different names from farmer to farmer. The nonpungent bell pepper alone assumed a mind-boggling number of names: Coral Gem, Little Gem, Kaleidoscope, Celestial, Red Wrinkled, Yellow Wrinkled, Etna, Prince of Wales, Ivory Tusk, County Fair, Cardinal, Elephant's Trunk, Oxheart, Emperor, and Giant Emperor. In 1867 a rather grotesque-looking pepper arrived in the United States from France and immediately drew the attention of farmers and pickling companies, who liked its taste and the fact that the plant was a prolific producer. The pepper was very wrinkly and lobed, three to six inches long, dark red, and slightly pungent. In France it was called Piment monstrueux; in England Grossum; in Germany Sehr grosser milder monströser; then somehow years after arriving in the United States what was initially called Monstrous became Crimson Queen, and then simply Sweet Spanish.

Horticulturists and botanists subsequently added their own Latinized flourish to these fruits: Capsicum siliquis longis recurvis, Pipe Calecuticum, Capsicum nigrum, Capsicum violaceum, Capsicum Quitense, Capsicum Narunca, Piment rouge long ordinaire, Capsicum Longum, and Capsicum grossum monstrosum.

This freewheeling baptism eventually raised eyebrows among botanists and horticulturists, who didn't see any botanical basis for such distinctions. Some of them complained to Edward Lewis Sturtevant, a naturalist and leading figure in agricultural science at the New York Botanical Garden. Dr. H. H. Rusby, for instance, wrote to Sturtevant on April 9, 1888: "I have seen a good deal of the genus in South America and have observed a great tendency to variation. I have seen but few well distinguished forms and about these are grouped hosts, presenting every share of variation in size, color, form, and surfaceplanes of fruit. There are corresponding differences in pungency and flavor, in detecting which the natives are expert. Each man will have some cherished plant that to him is very distinct, and far superior to anything that his neighbors can boast."

And in 1892 J. H. Hart, the superintendent of the botanical department of the Royal Botanical Gardens at Trinidad, wrote to F. W. Dewart, a botanical assistant at the Missouri Botanical Garden in St. Louis: "We do not make any specific distinction between the Capsicums from here for the simple reason that they degenerate so quickly to a simple form under cultivation that we cannot refer to them as more than a single species. Some of the finest will in four or five generations be nothing more than 'Bird-pepper' of which the forms are as many as the days of the year."

What these botanists were pointing out, of course, was that peppers can easily cross with each other and assume new physical characteristics as well as levels of pungency. Peppers are also easily influenced by local environment. That doesn't make them inherently different peppers. Pressure mounted to straighten out the names so that farmers and seed companies and consumers could communicate without confusion.

In 1892 Sturtevant gave all his herbarium pepper specimens, notes, and color plates to H. C. Irish, a botanist at the Missouri Botanical Garden, on the condition that the genus would be given a thorough going-over by taxonomists and that the scientific classification would be published in a monograph. The result was Irish's *A Revision of the Genus Capsicum,* published in 1898. Irish ended up accepting Linnaeus's initial classification—that there were only two types of species, Capsicum annuum and Capsicum frutescens. Irish placed all commercial varieties of the time under Capsicum annuum, because the plants weren't shrubby and woody. The few with that appearance were placed under the frutescens category. Annuum, of course, refers to plants that have to be grown annually to bear fruit; frutescens are perennial plants. That important study did little to end the taxonomical controversy, however. L. H. Bailey of Cornell University, for instance, argued in his *Gentes Herbarium* in 1923 that annuum plants weren't woody and shrubby because in the short growing season in the North the plant is killed by frost before it fully matures. If the annuum of the North was planted in the tropics or in a greenhouse, he argued, it would grow perennially and become woody after some years. Bailey thus reduced all previous classifications to just one species: Capsicum frutescens. Pepper botany was back to square one.

These early attempts to identify which peppers were distinct species and which subspecies weren't driven by economic urgency, as such attempts are today. The botanists were interested in establishing a reliable taxonomy so that they could see the genetic landscape of peppers. Without such classification, botanists can't relate to their plants. I once asked a botanist at the New York Botanical Garden why his ilk spent so much time identifying, or "describing," species. He drew the analogy of a man staring at traffic; he said when he stares at a mass of green, he wants to see the same details as he sees facing traffic in New York City—not just cars, but Chevrolets, BMWs, Mercedeses, Cadillacs. In botany, classification sets order, with species forming the basic units and subspecies constituting varieties. Without that botanical equivalent of the periodic table in chemistry, botanists are lost; they don't know where to begin.

The first scientific classification of cultivated peppers was done at the University of California at Davis in the 1950s by Charles Heiser, the man who later became Hardy Eshbaugh's instructor at Indiana, and Paul Smith. Based on extensive crossbreeding of peppers and morphological studies, they classified all cultivated peppers into five species: most of the common peppers were placed in the annuum species, which covers a broad range from the nonpungent bell to the pungent jalapeño; the frutescens, which is represented mainly by the pungent tabasco pepper; the chinense, which includes the most pungent of all peppers, the habanero in Mexico and scotch bonnet in Jamaica; the pubescens, which has the Andean rocoto as its prototype; and the baccatum, which includes mainly the Peruvian and Bolivian ají.

What Eshbaugh is doing is taking this taxonomic study to the next stage—actually backward, genealogically—to the evolutionary stage, identifying these cultivated species' ancestors. Eshbaugh, along with his chemistry colleagues at Miami University, published the first major work on the question of evolution in a series of papers between 1981 and 1983. The distinction of their seven-year study was that it analyzed peppers' relationships to each other at the genetic level. Using sophisticated chemical techniques they measured "genetic distances" among 1,010 wild and domesticated pepper plants belonging to different species. The group concluded: one ancestral species gave rise to a group of wild species that, in turn, branched out into three different directions. One of them gave rise to three of the cultivated species that dominate the world outside of South America; the other two produced two distinct species cultivated mainly in Peru and Bolivia. Into this evolutionary model Eshbaugh now rigorously subjects the wild species he collects to test its validity.

"We still don't know a whole lot about peppers at the molecular level. We have to do a lot of collecting, and move the study to the next level of science, the DNA analysis," Eshbaugh says.

On the way to Bolivia, I met up with Eshbaugh in Ohio. The first thing I learned—to my surprise—was that a man so involved with peppers doesn't much care for them as food. In fact, he totally avoids them. "I don't know whether I enjoy the sensation or not," he told me sheepishly. "Clearly some people do. But I wouldn't eat it by choice. I think pepper masks the natural essence of food. I am very strange in the sense that it is extraordinarily rare for me to put even salt in food. I think I am much more sensitive to the tastes of food than most people and so I have never felt the need for certain kinds of flavors." I attributed this aversion to his German ancestry. Descended from European stock, he represents a vast number of Midwestern Americans who have remained untouched by the "heat" wave spreading through the rest of the country.

That evening in Oxford, Ohio, I had searched out a Chinese restaurant where, thinking that it probably was geared to serve the common palate of a university town, I had requested that my dishes be cooked with whole red peppers. (The dishes, incidentally, arrived with whole red pods not in the food, but separately in a bowl—and they were uncooked, to boot. My special request must have thoroughly baffled the waiter, a young Waspish man.) "I suspect I wouldn't have gone to a Chinese restaurant in the first place, let alone suggest that they add more heat," Eshbaugh told me with a grin.

His aversion to pepper in food obviously hasn't dampened his enthusiasm for the plant. In a corridor of the botany department, around the corner from his office, he showed me a ceiling-high cold-storage room. The steel doors were locked. A gauge showed that the temperature inside was 32.9° F and the relative humidity 25 to 30 percent. Eshbaugh unlocked and threw open the doors. On the shelves were stacked plastic boxes, which he said contain 2,200 different collections of pepper seeds. The boxes are labeled: Iltis, Gentry, Ochoa, Smith, Heiser, Csillery, Timen . . . They are noted plant collectors, and although many of them aren't pepper collectors, they send to Eshbaugh any peppers they encounter while rummaging for their own plants. "What you are looking at is the collection of my lifetime and the seeds I have received from others, from Florida all the way south to Argentina."

Eshbaugh has perhaps one of the largest greenhouses devoted to peppers at any university. (He told me that he demanded and got a third of the botany department's greenhouse, as a condition for joining the university. "That was pretty audacious. Some in the faculty were not happy. They were growing this fern or that," he said.) He guided me through his greenhouse, actually a series of glassed-in rooms crammed with potted plants, about four feet high. They sit on rows of benches: Capsicum annuum aviculare, the "bird pepper"; Capsicum baccatum, variety pendulum; Capsicum baccatum, variety baccatum; a marble-size pepper, a hybrid of the tiny wild ulupica or Capsicum eximium and the bulbous Capsicum pubescens . . . They are meticulously tagged with letters and numbers and dates.

Eshbaugh plants 150 different collections at a time—a single collection consists of seeds from a group of plants in the same location. When these plants bear fruits in the greenhouse, Eshbaugh replants the seeds, and keeps following this routine with successive generations. Some plants have been under study for as many as nine years and have yet to yield answers to his questions. Eshbaugh pointed at two plants. "The dispute

over whether this Capsicum praetermissum is a variety of
Capsicum baccatum or whether they are two separate species
hasn't been resolved yet," he said. Capsicum praetermissum,
from Brazil, had tiny round fruits; the other, from Bolivia,
dangled long pods resembling string beans.

"This pepper is the subject of great debate," he said,
stopping in front of a plant he called Capsicum ciliatum. It had
three marble-size green berries. "The flower of this plant
doesn't look like a pepper flower, but the fruit looks like a
pepper. But the fruit isn't hot. That's a problem—whether hot
should be used to distinguish pepper. Bell pepper is not hot
because it has originated from a simple recessive gene, that is,
the gene for hotness is not expressed in it. So peppers don't
have to be hot, but hot is one important way people have
chosen to characterize them. Some botanists, including myself, have said that one way we could define the genus
Capsicum is by saying that it is a genus that has capsaicin, the
pungent chemical. In any case, ciliatum may be rejected as a
pepper, even though it has been described as a Capsicum,
because its chromosome number is thirteen. Peppers, including the nonpungent bell, all have twelve."

At the time of my visit Eshbaugh was investigating a species
that, in the 1960s, caused the whole genus to be redefined.
Called the Capsicum cardenasii, it has bell-shaped flowers;
previously Capsicum wasn't known to have flowers of that
shape. Even more intriguing is that cardenasii doesn't self-
pollinate like all other peppers. The pollen has to come from
another plant, carried by insects. In the greenhouse the plants
looked like miniature Lombardy poplars; they rose straight into
a point. In the wild they can reach eight feet. The fruit was first
collected in 1956 in a local market in La Paz, Bolivia, by Martín
Cárdenas, a Bolivian botanist and scholar of the Quechua Indians. Since then Eshbaugh has hunted for the pepper in the
only place it has been found, in remote valleys about eighty-five
miles south of La Paz. "Most pepper botanists don't have any
idea what this plant is," Eshbaugh said. "I'm trying to learn how

did it arrive, how did it break away from the norm, and what its real range is."

Back in the botany department, Eshbaugh led me into a room next to his office. It's his pepper herbarium, where tall filing cabinets contain more than five thousand specimen sheets—dried stems bearing fruits and leaves, pressed between cloth sheets. They represent two dozen different species.

"People say, 'How can you continue to work on peppers all these years?'" Eshbaugh responded to the question I also had asked him earlier. He opened a drawer. "Take this material. All the data are here: the flower color, leaf measure, the name, where it occurred, fruit color, seed color, the collector's name, pedicels per axil, fruit shape at peduncle attachment, and so on. But I am reluctant to describe it. This is simply unknown and unnamed at this time. . . . Here are some fruits someone sent me. They look like peppers but I am going to send them back and say these are not peppers . . . and here I have three or four things collected from Peru but I don't have any idea what they are."

In the world of peppers he has attained the stature of a forensic expert. When anyone—from the scholar to the week-end hiker—finds a wild pepper in a Florida swamp or in a Texas field or in the hills of Bhutan, they send the fruit to Eshbaugh for identification. And he takes each request seriously. Lately specimens have arrived from university herbaria, where pepper collections had been sitting "undescribed" for years for lack of expertise or time. "I have specimens sitting here from the University of Wisconsin, Harvard University, and Indiana University, to name a few. I have to identify them. . . . Right now I am having a horrendous problem. There is a worker in Peru who found what he thought was a new species of pepper and he sent it to the Field Museum of Natural History in Chicago, and the Field Museum sent it to me. But I don't remember ever receiving the material. It would be a tragedy if it is a new species and it has disappeared," Eshbaugh said.

As if he didn't have enough work sitting in his herbarium, he himself seeks out herbaria that might not be even aware that they are housing inaccurately described pepper collections. After all, only relatively recently have peppers been properly classified, and some collections at those institutions are as much as one hundred years old. So in his travels he routinely takes detours, to Kew Gardens and the British Museum, for example, which has specimens of wild Andean peppers collected in 1812. Eshbaugh once stopped by to correct Linnaeus, the father of modern botany. He had spotted the error in a microfiche film of a Linnaeus specimen, which was identified as a Capsicum annuum, variety aviculary—known generically as "bird pepper," which is found in the wild from the Florida coast to Central America. Eshbaugh felt the pepper was actually a Capsicum baccatum. "I could see in the film these peaks coming off at the base of the fruit, and that indicated to me that it was a baccatum."

After presenting his arguments in a paper published in 1968, Eshbaugh showed up at the Linnaeus Society in London. "When I went to the Linnaeus Society to see the specimen in the flesh, I was nervous because I was about to face the moment of truth," Eshbaugh said. "In moments like this, you hope you are right. Well, I was right. I annotated it. It was rather exciting to sit there and do it. In the Linnaeus Society, you just don't pull open a drawer. You call a day in advance and a guy brings the specimen and sits there and watches you. The curator and a couple of other people from the Linnaeus Society sat down with me and watched as I made the change."

Eshbaugh now wishes he had never discovered the error, because whenever he is at a herbarium the thought of its housing Capsicum baccatum specimens that are mislabeled as the "bird pepper" puts him in an annotating mood. "I could keep busy by just going around the country and straightening out other people's collections."

Eshbaugh has lectured on peppers at Canton and Jainan universities in China. He has presented scientific papers at conferences in South Africa, England, France, West Germany,

Australia, the Netherlands, Canada, and Costa Rica. In 1988, when he addressed the Botanical Society of America at Davis, California, as the president-elect, his talk, naturally, was all about hot peppers. He said that when he began his address to the five hundred or so botanists at the black-tie dinner, some waiters and waitresses stopped clearing tables and plopped themselves in empty chairs in the back of the hall. When the talk was over, several botanists who didn't know anything about peppers came to the lectern and asked for a copy of the presentation. (He didn't have any because he had spoken from rough notes.) A waitress came over and said she hadn't known the pepper was "so interesting."

"The pepper has been very good to me," Eshbaugh told me with a smile.

But many who meet him and learn what he does for a living are easily befuddled. A local newspaper columnist belittled Eshbaugh's pursuit—why was money being wasted on this, the columnist asked—when the botanist received a big grant from the National Science Foundation. I asked Barbara, Eshbaugh's wife, what she thought of her husband's vocation. "My friends laugh when they hear what my husband does," she said. "But you know, a friend of ours, a geologist, gave a talk the other day at the seniors' center on outhouses, how they are becoming a thing of the past. There's a national registry for outhouses. Did you know that? It was the funniest thing I've ever heard, but at that moment I thought, and it was a terrible thought, that it could have been outhouses instead of chile peppers."

When Eshbaugh and I arrived in Santa Cruz, Bolivia, en route to Cochabamba, he and a fellow passenger struck up a conversation in the lounge while waiting for a local flight. The plane had been delayed by several hours. The man was an engineer for General Electric and was traveling to Cochabamba in connection with a power-generating plant he said GE was planning to build there.

"So what brings you here?" the man in cropped hair and horn-rimmed glasses asked Eshbaugh.

"Peppers. I study chile peppers."

"You've got to be kidding. Huh, really?"

"In fact, I collected some wild peppers right here, at this very site, in 1971," Eshbaugh said, pointing at the green pasture outside. "This airport then was just a ramshackle building."

At dawn, the sun appears quickly from behind the Tunari mountain range on the eastern slope of the Andes. Cochabamba, nestled in the foothills below, is lit up like a ballpark. Eshbaugh sets out south. A botanist named Mario Crespo from the Bolivian Agriculture Research Center joins us with his four-wheel-drive truck; he has accompanied Eshbaugh on pepper-collecting trips before. This morning Eshbaugh is interested in the general area where a potato collector from the Royal Botanical Garden in Denmark had come across ulupica plants; he'd mailed their pods to Eshbaugh. Plant collectors do this sort of thing routinely. The idea behind it is that the favor will be returned one day; chance is very much part of plant collecting. "I didn't know there were ulupica there," Eshbaugh said.

Ulupica, a round fruit eight to twelve millimeters in diameter, is the most widely dispersed of the primitive peppers. It also seems genetically closest to the most primitive of all peppers, the chacoense. That's a tinier round pepper, also pungent, and found in the dry lowlands of southern Bolivia, near its border with Paraguay and Argentina. Chacoense, says Eshbaugh, might be the "mother" pepper, the progenitor of all peppers. This pepper has certain enzymes that are "in primitive states" compared to the same enzymes found in other pepper species. "So we suggest that it had to have come first," Eshbaugh argues.

Eshbaugh has gone as far as pinpointing the location of chacoense's birth: an area bounded by Aquile, Comarapa, and Villa Montes. That's the zone where the primitive expressions of that enzyme are found in the general vegetation. "That's how we were able to triangulate it," Eshbaugh says. "We might be wrong, if our suggestion turns out to be based on inadequate collections, but that's what we are proposing."

Most pepper botanists haven't advanced so far in their research—or simply aren't interested in pursuing it this far—to have a scientific opinion on the precise point of the pepper's origin. Barbara Pickersgill, however, the English botanist who is Eshbaugh's former classmate, is one of the few who have considered that question. When I called her, she said she didn't agree with Eshbaugh's thesis that there was enough evidence to suggest that central Bolivia was the chile's birthplace, let alone which wild pepper was the first to burst out of the earth. What's more, she said, peppers might have even originated from another, as-yet-unidentified berry.

"I don't think we know enough about the neorelative of the genus, and I don't think we know enough about some of the species on the boundary between Capsicum and some species of the related genera. There has been quite a bit of collecting work that has been done in 1986 and 1987 in the old highlands of southern Brazil, and I think they got some very interesting species which haven't been studied in living collections and that may change our view of the origin of the genus quite a lot," she said. "If you find some wild species with an intermediate between Capsicum and related genera living in the mountains of southern Brazil, and if you had nothing intermediate between Capsicum and related genera in Bolivia, then Brazil might be the place of origin."

Pickersgill, who was preparing for a major collecting trip in Brazil when I spoke with her, said that there exist some berrylike fruits in Brazil, pulpy and not hollow like peppers, that have moved backward and forward between Capsicum and other species in the same genus.

When I mention this to Eshbaugh, who has seen more wild peppers in their habitats than any other botanist today, he dismisses it. "I think Brazil might have been an important secondary center at one point in the development and dispersal of peppers." According to his model, ulupicas were the first wave of peppers to evolve from chacoense, hence his relentless collecting of this wild pepper. He figures he has collected ulupica in an area bounded by Cochabamba on the northwest and Villa Grande in the northeast and all the way south to Tarija. That triangle, he estimates, covers about 80 percent of the fifty-square-mile area he thinks is ulupica's habitat. It's a census more exhaustive than the U.S. Census Bureau's.

The idea of covering so much ground for a wild pepper seems preposterous. But without such a census, he says, he wouldn't have a good idea of the range of the pepper and of the changes it has undergone—changes that have led to the emergence of various species of peppers—as it migrated. Moreover, he says, genetic characteristics vary from population to population, so it wouldn't suffice, as far as he is concerned, to collect ulupicas from just one location in Bolivia. A desirable trait—if wild peppers are also to be collected for useful genes that can be transferred into the cultivated types—might exist in only a small number of them. "In a thousand collections we might find only a few individuals that have the genes we are looking for. I have collected four hundred plants of chacoense, and I have found only one that's not hot. For some reason a few developed that way. Now if you want to breed certain disease-resistant genes into the bell pepper without passing on the genes for pungency, that's the chacoense you would use."

Before Eshbaugh sets out, he has a general idea of where he might find his quarry. Maps and elevation measures are his primary guides. He has fifteen maps. One of them is so large that it is in eight sections. This big map gives a detailed layout of the vegetation of the country. Still, as soon as he arrived in Cochabamba, he ran into a bookstore and bought two more maps, just in case they contained updated information. Most of the old maps, he said, show incorrect elevations. And accurate elevation measures are important to him because they indicate where he might find which wild peppers. "There's no point looking past twenty-eight hundred meters," he said, surveying one of his maps before he set out this morning. That's the upper limit of elevation for ulupica, which starts to appear at fifteen hundred meters, about forty-nine hundred feet.

As we drive on this narrow road flanked by mountain ranges, Eshbaugh every now and then points to the rapidly changing geography and climate and says, "Too wet for ulupica."

Mario Crespo, maneuvering the four-wheel-drive truck, nods in agreement. He's a thirty-six-year-old botanist who seems quite excited about the outing because he has been busy with other local plants in recent years. After nearly two hours of driving over cobblestones and dusty roads and over gullies and dry riverbeds and knee-deep streams, Crespo finally pulls up in front of a cluster of adobe houses in a village called Anzaldo. He checks his altimeter, which gives an elevation of 10,216 feet. Still too high for ulupica. Crespo asks a group of young men congregating near the houses if they know of ulupica plants in the valley. They nod and point in the direction we are headed. An elderly man who overhears our inquiry saunters up to Crespo and asks all of us to follow him. He leads the group into his house. Through a maze of doorless rooms we emerge into a courtyard. Against a high wall stands a seven-foot plant. The manicured ground around it suggests that this ulupica plant is well cared for. Desiderio Flores, a Quechua Indian with several front teeth missing, says he planted six ulupica plants but only one survived. "In the winter I prefer ulupica, but you can't find it in the market." Eshbaugh takes pictures, notes the unusual elevation at which the plant is growing, the plant's location, the name of the village, the province, and the name of the owner.

Locations are important details in charting peppers' evolution, so Eshbaugh habitually takes detailed field notes. He showed me some typical entries from previous collecting trips: "Capsicum baccatum var. baccatum, or arivivi, from the home of J. Rivero, in Chuquisaca, in the province of Azero, elevation

1,050 meters, 50 meters from Anna Gonzaleas's house; Capsicum tomentosum, in the town of El-Sauce, 1,730 meters west of Samipata, in the field of Agusto Martinez, north side of the road, unusual tomentosum form, many fruits on a single plant."

It's very rare to find an ulupica plant that has been "domesticated," let alone at that elevation, Eshbaugh says. He wonders whether ulupica is adapting to slightly moist conditions. The size of Desiderio Flores's plant impresses Eshbaugh, although, he tells me, on a trip in 1971 he and his wife measured an ulupica plant that was growing along the road to the Yungus Valley on the eastern section of the Cordillera Real mountain. It was "sixty feet from one end to the other," he says. "That's nobody's concept of a pepper plant."

Crespo hires two of the young men from the village to help scout for ulupica in the hills. They initially demanded payment in dollars, but change their minds after some haggling and climb into the back of the truck. We continue our drive.

The road in front giddily plunges and rises and twists in unpredictable degrees. The geology and climate shift rapidly. The color of the soil changes from pink to red to sandy. The air turns from cool to dry and hot. Cactus and spiky-leaved agave and Prosopis appear on the landscape. "Indicator species," Eshbaugh calls out, staring at a ridge in the distance. "It doesn't mean ulupicas will always be there, but this increases the probability."

We've been traveling for more than two hours and have covered hardly eighteen miles. In that short distance, however, the landscape has undergone drastic changes. This is typical of the Andes. As its eastern slopes descend into the Amazon jungles, temperature, moisture, and soil condition can vary over distances as short as a hundred yards. So many "microclimates," cramped in a country twice the size of Spain, induce a startling diversity in plants. "More indicator species," Eshbaugh calls out, as he sees a denser population of cacti and Prosopis in the fields along the dusty road. A sign announces the name of the town: Chogona, elevation 7,380 feet.

Crespo pulls up in front of a lone hut. A man and a child come out to investigate, and then they lead us all to a steep ravine behind the house, and sliding and slipping past cacti and thorny Prosopis we find ourselves before a group of ulupica plants. "They are so different," Eshbaugh exclaims at the shape of the leaves. I strain to see the plants' uniqueness, which hadn't quite presented itself to me. "The leaves are very narrow, narrower than what I have seen in my previous collecting trips. It's this kind of variation I am interested in. Why are the ulupica leaves in this area longer and narrower?" Eshbaugh clicks his camera while he circles around the plants, as if he is photographing a traffic accident. He wrestles some stalks from the plants. "Let me tell you I am so very excited about these plants. The leaves are so different." The distinction still escapes me, but I attribute it to my untrained eye.

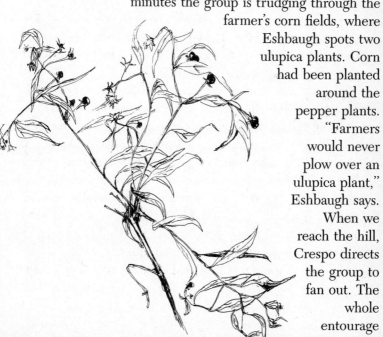

Perhaps seeing Eshbaugh's enthusiasm, the farmer can't resist pointing to the ridge beyond his house. Within minutes the group is trudging through the farmer's corn fields, where Eshbaugh spots two ulupica plants. Corn had been planted around the pepper plants. "Farmers would never plow over an ulupica plant," Eshbaugh says. When we reach the hill, Crespo directs the group to fan out. The whole entourage disappears behind the thicket of tall and scruffy bushes. Soon, the stillness of the hot afternoon is broken by shouts and screams. "Ulupica!" *"Está ulupica!* [It's ulupica!]" "Ulupica!" From the bottom of the ridge, Eshbaugh can be seen darting from bush to bush, crouched.

Plant hunting today is a tame affair compared with the pioneering days. Leonhardt Rauwolf, a German physician who traveled in the Mediterranean in 1573 to view certain medicinal plants in "their proper and native places," had to disguise himself in native costumes but still got robbed and attacked and was constantly on the run. Edinburgh Botanic Garden's James Tweedie, who collected an immense number of plants in South America starting with his first trip in 1832, covered hundreds of miles of treacherous rivers by boat and hiked through mountains and took "cautious strolls" in forests that were uninhabited because of marauding tigers. In Africa few of the pioneering French and Dutch botanists who hacked their way through the jungles escaped dysentery and malaria; that most-botanized region of the early days is also known for the number of expeditions in which plant hunters perished.

Today's plant hunters aren't preoccupied as much with finding undiscovered flora. Their ventures are usually guided by commercial demands on already discovered plants; perhaps that's why most of them are called plant "collectors" and not "hunters." But are the pioneering days of plant hunting a thing of the past? There are an estimated twenty thousand edible plants in the world. But only three thousand have been used throughout history by mankind, and of that only twenty species account for most of the world's food crops. Before coming to Bolivia with Eshbaugh I discussed plant hunting with Enrique Forero, the director of research at Missouri Botanical Gardens. "Our concern is collecting them before they disappear," he said. "We have been inventorying the forest species in the last five years. But the world doesn't have all the botanists we need to get the job done. We don't have enough people with training and interest who are willing to go to the tropics and work there. It takes a lot of effort to move around in the forests. You have to risk dangers—the snakes, the guerrillas, and the natives that become hostile when you walk into their sacred area. In fact, the number of trained botanists here and in Europe has been on the decline."

When Eshbaugh first set foot in Bolivia, back in 1970, he didn't know where to start. "I made deals with taxi drivers. I showed them a map and told them I was a botanico. The taxi driver would then simply go door to door in a village, and get back in the car and drive a little further and repeat the process." In later years, when Eshbaugh figured out the elevations and climatic conditions preferred by various wild peppers, he began to employ novel approaches. In 1976, for instance, he transposed a map of Bolivia that had elevation measurements onto a vegetational map of the country that had just been published. Elevation measurements and vegetational descriptions suggested that the areas around Aiquile and Mizque would be ideal habitats for ulupica. He wrote to the principal priests of those towns, requesting that they ask their parishioners if they knew of the pepper. Eshbaugh enclosed a check for fifteen dollars and promised to send the same amount for each collection he received from the natives. "I figured that the priest would be an educated person," he says. "I ended up with a hundred and fifty different collections from little towns in the middle of nowhere in Bolivia. I didn't have to even leave my office."

In 1971 Eshbaugh was collecting in Peru, but couldn't get into the region eight miles from Ayacucho, an area of intense guerrilla activity. He was interested in a tiny hot pepper that Oscar Tovar, a research scientist at the University of Lima, had collected there. Few outside the region had seen it in its natural habitat. When Eshbaugh was flying from Ayacucho to Lima, en route to Bolivia, he noticed an American missionary on the plane. "This guy said, 'I have been a missionary in that area for seventeen years, and I can tell you there are no wild peppers in that area.' And I said, 'I would like you to ask some people there when you go back.' We exchanged cards. Then in April 1971 I received a letter from this Harry Marshall. It said: 'Dear Hardy, much to my surprise when I asked my parishioners about the pepper, they told me it is all over the region. My daughter, who will be returning to the United States in a month, will bring you a package of the fruits.'"

That Peruvian collection is now the subject of major research. A peculiar thing about the pepper, locally known as mukúru, is that it doesn't self-pollinate early in the season, but if it isn't pollinated by another plant by the end of the season it finally self-pollinates, producing a few fruits, avoiding extinction. "That fail-safe mechanism is a matter of much curiosity," Eshbaugh says. The mukúru, moreover, has turned out to be genetically related to Bolivian peppers rather than to the peppers found in Peru. "That will be more information that will perhaps argue, as I have argued, that Bolivia is really the center of the genus."

For plant geneticists it's important to pin down the origin of a genus because that's where the population is likely to have the useful primitive genes. In the 1960s plant geneticists collected wild ancestors of corn in South America thinking that that's where it originated. Later a number of geneticists demonstrated that the birthplace instead was southern Mexico and northern Guatemala. South America was where selection by humans had given rise to the greatest diversity in that crop. Eshbaugh says he doesn't want to see that mistake repeated in peppers. Sure, Peru and Brazil have a lot of peppers, and many of them appear to be primitive, but these regions may simply have become secondary centers in evolution. He says increasing evidence that points to Bolivia's being the birthplace underscores the importance of collecting the wild relatives of Capsicum in that country.

• • •

Local markets are another source for samples, usually for cultivated peppers, and on some days Eshbaugh forgoes botanizing in the fields. As he walks through the weekly market in Punata, thirty-one miles from Cochabamba, this afternoon he sees disturbing signs. "The varieties are far fewer than I saw twenty years ago. No doubt," he says. "I used to find a lot of small orange and red fruit types that usually come from un-domesticated plants, but this time I see only four such types."

The regular markets, nevertheless, offer a good selection of different types of peppers that are still close to their wild ancestors. The Punata market, which occupies an area the size of a football field, was a collage of ramshackle stalls. Vendors were selling goats, sheep, cows, chickens, and pigs, and such agricultural implements as hoes, machetes, shovels, and spades. They were hawking soap, plastic bags, toothpaste, and clothes; there were beans, corns, yucca, radish, onions, apricots, and grapes. But if there was one item that overwhelmed the market in sheer volume, it was peppers: long row after long row of locoto peppers, piled on blankets—in huge mounds, or in tiny heaps of ten or so fruits. Sometimes these small mounds of

locotos, each representing a unit of sale, were topped off with a green herb called quillquiaña, which adds a very agreeable flavor to a salsa made of the pepper and tomato. Behind the peppers sat the vendors, Quechua and Aymara women, in their traditional baggy skirts and bowler hats and brilliantly colored rectangular shawls. "How can they make money when everybody is selling the same thing, the same pepper," Eshbaugh remarks as he walks along the pepper rows. Even though shoppers, with their plastic and straw bags, were reaching for these mounds of locotos more than for any other produce, I wasn't sure if they would so much as make a dent in the supply by the end of the day.

Locoto—or rocoto, as it's called in Peru—is by far the best pepper I have eaten raw. It's a bulbous, fleshy pepper with black seeds. The pepper looks like a tiny papaya. Its color ranges from forest green to yellow to pink to bright red. A deep red locoto with its glistening black seeds exposed is a beautiful object to behold. When green and yellowish, it's as crispy and cool to the bite as cucumber, and yet it has a pleasant pungency that oozes out of its firm walls to satisfy the most discriminating of pepper aficionados. Bolivians crush the pepper with tomato, onion, and the herb quillquiaña. They call the sauce Llajw'a; and a chopped salady version, salsa cruda. The cold-tolerant locoto plant grows at altitudes between forty-nine hundred and ninety-five hundred feet and produces fruit for ten years. The other widely used pepper here is the ají, a long and thick pepper cultivated in lowlands below the elevation of thirty-six hundred feet. This pungent red and yellow pepper is generally used in sauces.

But locoto clearly is the Bolivian's favorite. And I would pine for its crisp and pleasant bite in fresh salads upon my return to the United States. It's the only hot pepper I have come across that can be eaten raw without sniffling and gasping for air. It's a perfect garnish, tossed or sprinkled raw into anything that requires a slight edge. Unfortunately, efforts to grow locoto in New Mexico and Texas, the two pepper-growing regions in the United States, haven't been successful. Locoto requires cool temperatures without frost; the plant takes 150 days to bear fruit, but in most cool regions in North America a killing frost usually arrives within 110 days. The alternative is to ship the fruits from the Andes, but their fleshiness makes them un-economical to transport long distances.

Walking through the market, Eshbaugh takes pictures of locotos and buys a handful selected from the mound he has just captured in his camera. He puts the peppers in a plastic bag along with a piece of paper on which he has scribbled the information he gathers from the vendor.

"*Y de dónde viene?*" He asks another vendor where the pepper has come from.

"Chapari," says the woman. Eshbaugh selects half a dozen of the pods, pays for them, and moves on.

"I have not seen this before," Eshbaugh says, staring at a pile of peppers at another vendor. "The shape of their necks is strange," he says of the bulbuous red pods that look like Christmas tree lights.

When he comes across a mound of long, fleshy peppers that look like ají, he isn't sure if they are ají or some other species of pepper. He buys a handful. "They could be Capsicum baccatum var. pendulum, or they could be Capsicum annuum. I wouldn't know until I grow them out," he says. He moves on to another vendor, an old woman who just sits there motionless and expres-sionless and declines to respond to Eshbaugh's curiosity. Eshbaugh makes all the polite gestures and smiles, which he intuitively flashes from his years of collecting to smooth his entry. "Maybe she doesn't understand my Spanish. Or maybe she just doesn't want to talk to me," he says. Eshbaugh knows when to move on quickly. And he does. He has learned from his previous forays into local markets that native Indian vendors are superstitious about such outside intrusions, especially if their produce is photographed. The locals believe the camera also captures their souls. Once in the U.S. Virgin Islands he was taking pictures of peppers in a market when all of a sudden he saw something pass in front of his camera. He looked up and saw it was a broom. He realized this woman was coming after him. "She chased me right out of the market," Eshbaugh says. But Eshbaugh takes risks for the sake of botany whenever he thinks he can get away with his intrusions in the Punata market. Several vendors get up and leave their stalls when he trains his camera on their produce, allowing him to photograph the peppers only.

Before we leave the market, we witness a bizarre scene at a spice stall, its vendor the only one selling dried spices in the market. She has dried peppers (two different kinds of ají), cinnamon bark, cumin, bay leaves, and in open sacks turmeric roots, allspice, and powdered red pepper. A bee has descended into the sack of red pepper and is packing its legs with the red powder while its fluttering wings keep its body hovering like a helicopter. It then flies out. Minutes later, while we are still speculating what the bee was up to, another bee (or perhaps the same one) ignores all the other sacks of spices and descends into the sack of red powder, thrashing its legs in the red heap. Slowly its tiny hairy legs are packed red. It flies out again. It seems quite clear what even the bees prefer in Bolivia, the supposed birthplace of the pepper.

At the end of each collecting day, the romance of botanizing in the fields ends and Eshbaugh gets down to what he calls "the real work." In his hotel room he lays out on his bed the peppers he has collected. He spreads an old newspaper on the desk and lines up the tools of his trade: a Hoffritz tweezer, a pair of scissors, a scalpel and four blades, a straight single-edge blade, a caliper, a ruler, and a stack of No. 3 coin envelopes. "You can't find these tweezers anymore," he says. "I have had them for fifteen years. They don't slip and rotate in the hand like the new ones do," he says, rubbing the points of the tweezer on his pants.

He then takes each batch of peppers, one pepper at a time,

and gets down to cataloguing. He measures the pepper's dimensions, notes the color and shape, and writes them down on the front of the coin envelope. He then runs the scalpel across the belly of the pepper and carefully pulls apart the sections. With the tweezer he gently shakes lose the seeds from the placenta and slides them into the envelope. "These envelopes absorb the moisture and air-dry the seeds nicely," he says. He doesn't count the seeds, which he says he will do when he is back in Ohio. But he expresses surprise when the number of seeds he extracts looks unusual, too low or too high. "This one has only ten seeds, almost one-third the others in the same batch," he says, examining an orange pod. He checks the size again and finds that it's about the same as the others in that batch, about seventeen inches long and thirteen inches wide. He coughs and sniffles.

Now he cuts open the pods whose elongated necks had puzzled him in the market. "I don't know what I am dealing with here," he says, staring at the seeds. "They have very few seeds, and a number of them are aborted seeds. The seeds should be black, but they are very white." He shakes his head and declares that they were not locotos as he had initially predicted. "I am really interested in seeing what happens when I grow the seeds in the greenhouse." He puts the seeds in envelopes—one envelope for each pepper—and draws the shape of the fruits, accenting their elongated necks, on the front of the envelopes to remind himself of the pods' unusual shapes.

The dimensions and the number of seeds give important clues about how removed the fruits may be from their wild ancestors; the smaller the fruits, for instance, the closer they are to their ancestral species. Eshbaugh already has compared the physical characteristics of locotos collected from different valleys. "I wanted to see the variations in locoto throughout its range and measured fruit size in every location I had collected, from Peru to Bolivia. What became obvious was that the smallest fruit types were all from Bolivia. In other words, if you started from Bolivia and went north, you began getting larger and larger fruit types in that species. I maintain that the fruit difficult to put a dollar value on the crop improvements that are brought about by these genetic materials collected from poor nations. Some indications exist, however. In 1962 Hugh Iltis of the University of Wisconsin in Madison collected a "ratty-looking" wild tomato in the Peruvian Andes. That single collection turned out to be a "germplasm" jackpot: it crossed with a commercial variety and produced large red tomatoes with a vastly higher sugar content, which added $5 million annually to the coffers of the tomato industry, according to Iltis.

The development of sophisticated gene-transfer techniques has only increased the West's appetite for collecting ancestral genes. These biotechnological methods are more ef-

fective than the breeding techniques that can take as long as ten years to incorporate desired traits into a crop. Now a useful gene can be precisely inserted into a commercial crop to produce improved varieties in a couple of years.

But a number of Western countries are opposed to paying any royalty or fee for the genetic material they collect. Neither do they want to give developing countries any free access to the high-yielding and disease-resistant seeds that are bred from those countries' primitive plants. The United Nations' Food and Agriculture Organization has established a Commission on Plant Genetic Resources to resolve the issue. But the United States and a number of Western countries have refused to join the 125-nation commission. These countries, with their highly developed seed companies, object to the commission's 1983

declaration that "plant genetic resources are a heritage of mankind and consequently should be available without restriction."
To agree to that motto would mean that these Western countries would have to give others free access to their improved
seeds. "Right now there's a tremendous amount of resentment
building in Ecuador and Brazil among scientists and agricultural officials who are saying, and rightly so, you got the material
from us to begin with," Eshbaugh says.

It seems Western botanists and plant geneticists who freely
rummage through the Andean countries don't bother to share
even their research with the botanists of their host countries.
When one afternoon Eshbaugh and I visited the Bolivian Agriculture Research Center in Pairumani, it was clear that the
botanists there had no idea of the kind of research U.S. and
European botanists are doing with South American peppers.

"Do you know the parents of locoto?" asked Gonzola Evilla,
a top researcher at the center.

"Ulupica," Eshbaugh replied, and pointed out that his research showed that "resistance genes" for locoto could be found
in these wild species.

"I see. So we need to collect and save ulupicas in a seed
bank," the Bolivian botanist said. Evilla explained that his
agriculture center had been busy with corn and quinoa and
other local staples. "Pepper has been put on the back burner,"
he said.

Eshbaugh promised to send him copies of his latest research on the peppers. He told Evilla that he would also put in
the mail a copy of the "Lost crops of the Incas," a recently
published report by the National Research Council in Washington, D.C. I found it startling that as important a publication
as this on Andean crops wasn't distributed to the country whose
crops had formed the basis of this study. Eshbaugh told me
later: "These people cannot afford to subscribe to even the most
essential of botanical journals."

• • •

It is midnight and Eshbaugh is still measuring and slicing away peppers. The wastebasket has filled up with dissected pepper pods. He wonders what the hotel maid must think every morning when she sees the basket. A large number of peppers and stems in plastic bags are still scattered on his bed, waiting to be catalogued. Eshbaugh says he will get up early to finish up the rest, before heading out for another round of collecting.

Next morning, when I pass his room at about seven his door is ajar. He is at it again, cutting pepper pods and pressing ulupica branches between newspapers and frowning over some puzzling thing he has encountered in a batch of pepper. "The calyxes of these pods are coming off so easily," he tells me, pointing at a group of seven small pods. "This indicates to me that they are a hybrid between locoto and some wild species. I wonder which wild fruit is crossing so easily with this cultivated type in the open environment," he wonders aloud. The answer would unravel an important link in pepper genealogy. He says he will extract the seeds of all seven. "Normally, I would cut open only two or three from the same batch. But they are so intriguing."

As I stand at the door of Eshbaugh's room, my eye is snagged by the stupendous Tunari mountain range in the distance, and I momentarily consider the overwhelming odds this man faces in tracing cultivated pepper species back to their ancestors and the ancestors to the "mother pepper." The dense vegetation on the formidable mountain range and the parched foothills taunt him with so few clues it all seems a futile exercise. Peppers won't, of course, disappear from the face of the earth if Eshbaugh never solves the puzzle. And he doesn't even eat peppers. But here he is obsessed with going back to the beginning of time and solving a riddle of evolution just for the sake of seeing it through. When I turn back to look at him, Eshbaugh is still hunched over his tweezers, prying seeds from a pod.

5

Pimentologos

When plants from the New World arrived in Europe they were scrutinized for medicinal value before they were considered food. In his "Joyfull Newes Out of the Newe Founde Worlde," the sixteenth-century Seville physician Nicolai Monardes speculated about "the rare and singular vertues of diverse and sundrie hearbes, trees, oyles, plantes and stones" brought by the early explorers. "Of the peper of the Indias," he wrote: "Not onely it serveth for medicine, but it is moste excellente, the whiche is knowen in all Spaine ... It dooeth comforte muche, it dooeth dissolve mindes, it is good for the breaste, and for theim that bee colde of complexion: it dooeth heale and comforte, strengthenyng the principall members. It is hotte and drie, well neere in the fourth degree."

Not surprisingly, some of the early medical applications of hot pepper in Europe occurred in Spain. Spanish sailors took chiles to sea for the same reason English sailors took limes: to prevent scurvy. Ripe red pepper's rich vitamin A content was believed to make eyesight keen; in the seventeenth century some Spaniards ate "two roasted chili peppers after each meal" to improve vision, according to one account.

But as medicine, peppers made a stronger impression in other parts of the world, where they continue to be put to far-reaching applications. In the Malay peninsula, peppers are used to treat digestive problems, and folk healers prescribe them for jaundice, scarlet fever, cholera, malaria, and even gonorrhea, though there is no proof that the fruit cures any of these diseases. Juice from the leaves of pepper plants is used in Indonesian villages to stimulate childbirth. In the Philippines, leaves of the pepper plants belonging to frutescens species are pounded and mixed with lime and applied to reduce swelling; the same leaves combined with spices become poultices for ulcers. According to the Indian *Materia Medica,* three species of peppers—annuum, fastigiatum, and minimum—made into a paste and combined with mustard is a counterirritant; pills made of equal parts of capsicum, rhubarb, and ginger are a carminative; chiles and hot water make a "particularly benefi-cial" gargle for sore throat and hoarseness; the whole plant steeped in milk is "successfully applied to reduce swellings and hardened tumors"; and capsicum with cinnamon and sugar "is a valuable drink for patients suffering from delirium tremens, as it satisfies the craving [for alcohol] in dipsomaniacs." In Ayur-vedic applications pepper sometimes is used as a "fire" to open up the body's system to accept other medicines. In homeopathic medicine a tincture of capsicum made from ripe and dried pods is suggested as a cure for diarrhea, and regular use of ten to fifteen drops in a hot liquid diet is said to suppress the desire for alcohol.

Long before peppers reached Europe and Asia, they were already in wide use in the New World as medicine. The Maya Indians of northern Guatemala made a potion they called *ic,* which they took orally to cure cramps and diarrhea and which they rubbed on the gum to relieve toothache. The Aztecs applied mashed hot peppers to aching bones and muscles, and it worked the same way as some of today's topical medicines whose active ingredient is the pepper's pungent chemical. To this day, West Indians prepare a stomachic called mandram, with cucumbers, shallots, lime juice, Madeira wine, and mashed pods of the highly pungent bird peppers. Brazilian folk healers who prescribe medicines made from chiles are known as pimentologos.

Dr. Irwin Ziment is an unlikely pimentologo. He's the chief of medicine at the prestigious Olive View Medical Center in Los Angeles and a professor of medicine at the University of California–Los Angeles School of Medicine. He is a leading expert on respiratory medicine and has written several textbooks and a vast number of papers on respiratory pharmacology. Bush doctor he is not, but his rising reputation has something to do with his faith in hot pepper. He recommends it to patients, or anyone who will listen, as a treatment for cold, flu, and bronchitis. He has spent months in India investigating pepper's pharmacological uses, has put together an extensive collection of slides on peppers from around the world that he frequently presents at medical conferences, and he seizes opportunities to slip into scholarly papers serious references to peppers.

One Sunday afternoon he invited me to join him at the Ritz-Carlton Hotel in Laguna Beach, California, where he was attending a conference on an old drug called theophylline, which once was used for treating asthma. The German pharmaceutical company Boehringer Ingelheim, sponsoring the meeting, had gathered about two dozen pulmonary experts and other specialists from around the United States to discuss whether the drug should be revived or whether it should be completely written off because its toxicity might be unacceptable to regulatory agencies. Drugs are like women's clothing—they go in and out of fashion—and theophylline, a drug that goes back to 1888, had fallen out of favor, Dr. Ziment told me.

When I arrived at the hotel, brunch was being served on a

terrace overlooking the vast blue expanse of the Pacific Ocean. The modern medicine men and women, clad in greens and pinks and yellows, colors suggesting a respite from their demanding scientific schedule, were settling down in the shade of bright yellow umbrellas with glasses of wine and platefuls of food. The number of colleagues who approached Dr. Ziment to exchange pleasantries or to eavesdrop suggested he was a celebrity.

"People think I am an eccentric," Dr. Ziment said. "There're a lot of over-the-counter drugs for colds and coughs and bronchitis on the market, but they don't have any proven clinical remedies and it's difficult to authenticate the value of these drugs. They act more like placebos, and the doctors say, well, they have to prescribe something to the patient. So they prescribe to please patients. I am more honest. These drugs do exactly what peppers do, but I believe more in peppers. Peppers don't cause any side effects." During the course of our conversation, Dr. Ziment would often pause to recount an anecdote or to delight in a diversion that wasn't too far from the subject. "By the way, Christopher Columbus might have had a respiratory problem himself, which might explain his passionate search for pepper. People usually get interested in their own diseases." He let out a short laugh.

It soon became clear to me that Dr. Ziment liked to talk pepper. It was the longest uninterrupted discourse on pepper I had heard, during which the venue shifted from the hotel terrace to the hotel library to the balcony of his hotel room (where he held out nearly three dozen slides to the sun for me to see) to the beach and to a private yacht that had been hired to entertain the bronchial experts. His wife, Yda, sat listening to him in rapt attention, as if hearing all this for the first time.

Dr. Ziment was born and educated in Britain. With his salt-and-pepper hair and goatee, and his sonorous voice, he could have played the model for a venerable college dean. He often finished his thoughts with a short giggle, the sort of little outburst that might erupt from a grown-up recalling childhood mischief. I asked him how he'd become interested in peppers. He said that while he was conducting research for one of his textbooks, *Respiratory Pharmacology*, published in 1978, he had learned that hot pepper was used widely in ancient times as a remedy for the cold.

Yda, who was now sitting on the bed in the hotel room, jumped into the conversation. "Let me tell you something," she said. "I met him twenty years ago, and the love letters he used to write started out, 'My dear pepper,' and so he was into it probably long before he met me." Dr. Ziment blushed. Yda continued: "If he called another woman pepper then I would be really jealous, because then I would know for sure he was in love with her."

Dr. Ziment laughed, and looked guilty for not telling me the whole truth, that he liked pepper for its own sake too, and not solely for its medicinal properties.

"You see, my area of expertise is mucus. Ha! I was very impressed that a drug called Robitussin, which is the major drug used as a so-called expectorant to loosen mucus, has a chemical called guaifenesin, which is derived from guaiacol, which has the same chemical structure as capsaicin, the chemical in pepper. In other words, capsaicin is structurally related to the principal chemical in Robitussin. Guaifenesin is a compound in many other cough medicines, tablets, and prescription syrups, such as Vicks Formula 44D and Sudafed. All this struck me as being very interesting. So the scientific interest I gained in pepper was the outcome of my orthodox interest in drugs used to clean up sputum."

The idea of using hot spices to cure respiratory diseases is an old one. Traditional Ayurvedic remedies listed as expectorants hot peppers—including black, long, and cubeb—and in addition ginger, turmeric, radish, and onion. Cardamom, cinnamon, asafetida, ajowan, cumin, aniseed, eucalyptus, and caraway were said to have antibacterial properties for the management of bronchitis. The basis for using pepper as a remedy for the cold was the belief that conditions making one feel cold should be treated with hot substances. The Chinese believed in the same principle: their yin-yang theory called for treating cold (yin) physical conditions with pungent hot (yang) spices. This was also practiced in Greco-Roman medicine. Hippocrates prescribed vinegar and pepper to relieve respiratory infections. Claudius Galenus, one of the greatest physicians of the second century and royal physician to the emperor Marcus Aurelius, prescribed Sabine wine with a dash of black pepper for stomachache. He also recommended black pepper for the treatment of malaria.

The berrylike pepper called cubeb, which is native to Malaysia and is used mainly as a spice, was incorporated into cigarettes for the treatment of asthma and other respiratory diseases. Jewish philosopher-physician Moses Maimonides (A.D. 1135–1204) was one of the earliest enthusiasts of chicken soup for the treatment of respiratory illness. His recipes for asthmatic conditions included rue, mint, lemon juice, and vinegar—and hot spices: coriander, ginger, and cloves. In 1802 the distinguished English physician Herberden also recommended spicy chicken soup for bronchial afflictions.

However, Dr. Ziment said the ancient chicken soup recipes, which are effective in soothing the body and mind, lack the appropriate pungency to be medicinally effective. He thinks the soup should be as nose-tingling as the one concocted by the cook in Wonderland while the Duchess was nursing a baby in the kitchen. Rising steam from the caldron of soup sent the baby into a howling and sneezing fit, and this annoyed the Duchess, who shook the baby severely as she sang the lullaby:

> Speak roughly to your little boy,
> And beat him when he sneezes:
> He only does it to annoy,
> Because he knows it teases.

The Duchess was, of course, unreasonable; even the adventurous Alice, who had just walked in, sneezed and said to herself, "There's certainly too much pepper in that soup!" Sneezing and sniffling are what pepper makes you do, and that's precisely what Dr. Ziment wants chicken soup to do to someone who's nursing a cold. The Duchess's cook, of course, used black pepper, presumably the only kind that was available at the time in Lewis Carroll's Wonderland. Dr. Ziment recommends the hotter green or red varieties of the Capsicum species and has modified the chicken soup recipe, which appears as a footnote—giving his wife credit for helping develop it—as "Yda's chicken soup recipe" in his book, *Practical Pulmonary Disease*. It may be the only modern-day medical book that includes a recipe:

> Twenty-eight ounces of chicken broth
> One bulb of garlic
> Six sprigs parsley
> Six sprigs of cilantro, minced
> One teaspoonful of lemon-pepper
> One teaspoonful minced mint leaves
> One teaspoonful minced sweet basil leaves
> One teaspoonful curry powder (and red pepper
>   to level of tolerance)

With a serious tone that befits such a weighty medical book, the recipe instructs: "The fumes of the boiling soup can be inhaled during its preparation. The soup and its constituents can be divided into 4–8 equal portions, each of which should be taken at the beginning of a meal, one to three times each day. Patients are encouraged to add additional ingredients (e.g., carrots, bay leaves, chili pepper flakes) to taste. A more diluted preparation may be deemed preferable, both personally and socially, until adaptation to this therapy occurs." Dr. Ziment said the soup was arrived at after "experimenting with different levels of pungency till it was pungent enough to clear his stuffed nostrils." He said he wanted it to be a "gourmet concoction" as well as a medicine. "We wanted it hot enough that when people eat it they would sweat and cough and the nose would run and clear the sinuses. You should be able to sweat out the cold."

The purpose of employing hot pepper, or any number of modern medicines, is to dislodge mucus when the body is afflicted with a cold and fever. When the body is healthy, mucus moves through the sinus system so inconspicuously and effortlessly that the body is hardly aware of the presence of this sticky liquid. It is moved by cilia, tiny cells with hairlike projections in the mucous membrane. These cells rhythmically propel themselves, like an army of rowers, a thousand times a minute. Acting against gravity, they move mucus in waves from the lower part of the lungs up through the breathing passages and then out of the bronchiole tree. Then the mucus, in droplets, rises to the throat in a continuous flow, a total of 100 milliliters a day. This gravity-defying plumbing system works effortlessly when the mucus is thin; respiratory diseases make mucus thick and sticky. Then the tiny cells can't row the heavy mucus, and the resulting accumulation causes coughing and inflames airways, and the body develops all sorts of respiratory problems. The idea of an expectorant drug is to provoke the body into secreting more water to thin the sticky mucus so that it can be easily transported out of the lungs by the hairy cilia or through coughing.

Pepper, garlic, and modern cough medicines all work the same way: they first stimulate the receptor cells in the stomach, which in turn trigger a reflexive action that travels through the vagus nerve up to the "mucokinetic center" in the back of the brain. That center then sends the vagal reflex to bronchial glands, which are commanded to secrete water into the mucus. (Next to the mucokinetic center is the "vomiting center," which is charged with the operation the name suggests. The two centers are peculiarly linked: a chemical that stimulates the mucokinetic center in a larger dose activates the vomiting center. The same capsaicin that helps move mucus thus is the basis for a modern drug for inducing vomiting.)

Capsaicin is believed to have another duplicitous characteristic: while it dilutes mucus in the chest, in the stomach it stimulates mucus production with a benevolent effect. "It coats ulcers," Dr. Ziment said. "It's a remedy in Indian folk medicine. We did meet doctors in India who said they prescribed pepper for the treatment of peptic ulcers, and certainly some Ayurvedic literature mentions that treatment. The question is, what does pepper stimulate, acid production or mucus production? My theory is that in the mouth it stimulates saliva production, and in the stomach it stimulates mucus production. The mucus protects the stomach lining from irritation.

"I must admit that this concept has not been analyzed as well as it should be, perhaps because it can't be analyzed," Dr. Ziment said, adding that medical opinion on ulcers has been transformed in recent years by the revelation that they tend to come and go spontaneously. For lack of a better treatment, doctors often prescribe bland milk-and-potato diets for ulcer patients, and give the diet credit for spontaneous recovery. "It has became evident that bland diets were irrelevant," said Dr. Ziment. "On the other hand, if a patient knows that jalapeño sauce or General Tso's chicken gives him trouble, he will probably be happier without them."

I asked whether pepper can also cause an ulcer. I told him I had come across a report that suggested that Asians were prone to peptic ulcers. "There's very little evidence of greater incidence of peptic ulcer in Indians who eat peppers than a group of people in Iowa who don't. There is no connection between high amounts of pepper in your diet and ulcer in your stomach." (One of very few studies in this area has been done by J. Szolcsanyi and L. Bartho at the University Medical School of Pecs in Hungary. In 1980 they presented a study showing that the pepper's chemical in low concentration prevented the formation of ulcers in rats. But a high concentration desensitized the rats' stomachs, which promoted ulcer formation.)

• • •

Dr. Ziment feels that there's strong enough evidence about hot pepper's beneficial medicinal properties to warrant not only its free use as food but development of modern respiratory drugs that are based on it. "We have all these people here so wrapped up with the modern chemistry and synthesis and so on, but they never pause to study the roots of the drug," Dr. Ziment said, referring to the pulmonary experts gathered at the hotel that afternoon. "Take, for instance, the drug theophylline we are discussing today. The Greek word means divine tea, and as the very name suggests, the synthetic drug has its roots in tea leaves. The tea leaf contains a number of important drugs basic to the management of asthma and bronchitis in China."

Dr. Ziment cited other examples of modern drugs that have been derived from nature, although they are now synthetically made. The drug atropine came from datura stramonium, or jimsonweed, which belongs to the same botanical family, the Solanaceae, as the pepper. Datura's antiasthma benefits were noted in Ayurvedic medicine two thousand years ago. Cigarettes containing datura were introduced in Britain and America in the early nineteenth century. Marcel Proust used to retire to his cork-lined smoking room and smoke atropine cigarettes. And to this day the ground-up herb is sold by the British firm of Potters as "Potters' powder," which is burned in a saucer and inhaled by patients with bronchitis, the "English disease." (It's said that British doctors can find a bronchitis patient's house just by following their noses.) Atropine is used in many cough and cold medicines, most notably in Atrovent, which is inhaled to treat bronchitis. Ephedrine, now taken by mouth in the West for the treatment of asthma, is derived from the Chinese drug *ma huang,* which comes from the bush Ephedra sinensis. In China it's a popular modern medicine for the treatment of fever, nasal blockage, chest congestion, and coughs. In the West ephedrine is found in such medicines as Bronitin and Primatene, and Tedral tablets. "Why, then, is hot pepper being overlooked?" Dr. Ziment asked aloud, and then proceeded to respond to his own question.

"In the organized pharmaceutical industry, the modern medicine men are very worried about using food as medicine, because it is old-fashioned," he said. He recalled the humiliation of the man who insisted that the lowly bran was an effective medicine for the bowel. "Before he was proven right, he had to deal with a lot of ridicule."

Peppers, of course, will not replace Anacin, or nasal sprays, or trips to the doctor. Pepper supporters seem only to want recognition by doctors and the pharmaceutical community that they are on to a good thing. One person who is battling the organized drug industry is Dounne Alexander-Moore, who makes herbal pepper concoctions in London with the fussiness of an apothecary and has launched a commercial venture. While Dr. Ziment's battle against the Establishment is more on the philosophical level, Alexander-Moore's is in the streets, where she is seeking endorsement of her products by the practicing medicine men. After venting her frustration to Dr. Ziment, she called me one day. "I have knocked on so many doors. But every physician I have approached says he would lose his job. The interesting thing is that they agree with me about the beneficial properties of pepper. But they are promoting all these pills and syrups and they say they will lose support of the manufacturers. The whole system of medicine is based on synthetic drugs, and it is a closed shop."

Alexander-Moore moved to London from the West Indies in 1963 at the age of sixteen, and she is one of a growing number of African immigrants who have taken to London the practice of using herbs and spices as medicine and health foods. She was born in Trinidad, where she grew up eating the scotch bonnet and the tiny "bird pepper," two of the hottest peppers in the Caribbean. In London she makes her sauce based on her grandmother's "secret" recipe. She said her grandmother regularly dispensed the pepper potion to villagers as a medicine. "I am marketing my sauce with the same claim that it promotes general health," she said. She operates out of her home, where, she said, the West Indies scotch bonnet peppers are delivered within twenty-four hours of being picked. The peppers are pureed, combined with "twenty different healing herbs and spices," and the mixture is cooked down to a thick concentrate.

If newspaper clippings and television appearances are any measure, Alexander-Moore, who describes herself as an herbalist, has become quite an advocate in Britain for hot pepper. She has been on British TV, pitching the Caribbean "hot toddy"—hot water, lemon juice, honey, and a pinch of hot pepper—as "the most effective remedy for asthma." In December 1989, "which was a particularly bad winter month for cold and flu," she was on TV urging the English to put hot peppers in their foods and to gargle with hot water and hot pepper. "My youngest daughter doesn't like hot pepper, but when she catches a cold she puts it in hot water and says that pepper is the only flavor she can taste when she gets a cold," Alexander-Moore said on TV. As a preventative measure she has also recommended that a bit of hot pepper be put in baby food. "I have made twenty-one TV appearances, fourteen radio appearances, and more than one hundred interviews in newspapers," she told me.

She said that Britain is a good market for her pepper campaign. "Have you noticed the way the English breathe? The Englishmen breathe heavily. Why? Most of them are constantly suffering from cold or bronchitis. It is a big problem with them. Peppers are also very effective in keeping the body warm, and in this country hundreds of old people die of hypothermia in the winter. Just imagine the amount of money peppers can save the British Social Services," she said without stopping to catch a breath, and then added with a hint of agitation, "And I cannot get a British physician to endorse my product. The English do need pepper in their diet."

She has managed, however, to get one-and-a-half-ounce jars of concentrated pastes in different degrees of pungency on the shelves at Harrods, Fortnum and Mason, and other upper-crust London stores. Alexander-Moore said her tenacity in trying to get products on the shelf paid off at elite establishments but not at the run-of-the-mill middle-class places like the corner supermarkets because of what she senses as a peculiarity of British racism.

"As a woman and black you have to first deal with the prejudices in this country," she said. "But the upper-class English, especially if he's educated, actually likes the black woman. If the woman is attractive and well built, that is. In fact, the upper-class English accepts other races at an intellectual level that the middle-class English can't. The middle-class English have a unique way of smiling when he exercises his prejudice, and only later you find out that you have been dealt with discriminatingly. I have been given that unique smile far too many times. At least the educated upper-class Englishman is receptive when he sees something good."

That the folk-medicine people were on to something valuable in peppers was scientifically established in 1932 by Albert Szent-Györgyi, the Hungarian scientist who won a Nobel Prize for discovering ascorbic acid. The professor at the Szeged University of Medicine inadvertently found a rich treasure trove for it in peppers.

It all started with Szent-Györgyi's interest in the activity of the adrenal gland, located above the kidney. The impairment of this vital organ causes Addison's disease, whose symptoms are a bronzelike skin pigmentation and anemia. Plants also display such symptoms when their respiratory system is harmed. Szent-Györgyi decided he would investigate the breathing mechanism of plants, and in the process he isolated from the plants a substance he thought might have something to do with the condition. He called the compound hexuronic acid. He later found the same chemical in the adrenal glands of animals. To study the substance, he needed a lot of it. But only a minuscule amount of it could be collected from plants and animals, and isolating it from plants was more difficult. So Szent-Györgyi traveled to the United States and spent a year in Minnesota slaughterhouses, collecting adrenal glands of slaughtered cattle and extracting the substance. At the end of his stay he was able to isolate only twenty grams of pure hexuronic acid from the several hundred kilograms of adrenal glands he had collected. The quantity was too little for any extensive experiment, but the Hungarian scientist, with an American collaborator, was able to establish its structure—it turned out to be vitamin C itself. He called it "a-scorbic" acid, since it cured scorbutic disease.

This discovery added all the more importance to isolating vitamin C, which scientists around the world had been trying in vain to do. They had isolated the compound from citrus fruits but the minuscule amounts they managed to extract would easily oxidize and perish during chemical analysis. Scientists, almost blindly, pursued citrus fruits because the fruits were then widely known to have the compound that cured that horrible disease of the time: scurvy. Szent-Györgyi himself, unable to extract any appreciable amount from citrus fruits and vegetables, decided to give up trying to isolate this compound. His involvement with this chemical was a sideline anyway; his main research was in intracellular metabolism.

Then one evening his wife prepared a dish of paprika pods. Paprika was daily fare in many homes in Hungary, which was then already established as the paprika capital of Europe, and Szeged, where Szent-Györgyi lived and researched, was a center of paprika cultivation. Whole sweet and mildly pungent paprika dominated main dishes and side dishes, and on restaurant tables salt and hot paprika (not black pepper) shakers were common. Szent-Györgyi didn't care for paprika as food, but not wanting to disappoint his wife, he took the food to his laboratory adjoining the house. When he stared at the pepper dish he realized that he had never tested it for its compounds. The results surprised him. He set aside all other projects that had been under way in the laboratory and for the next few weeks turned the place into a paprika-mashing center. His assistants bought up all the fresh pods, much to the surprise of vendors in the local markets and on street corners. Szent-Györgyi's wife and daughter lent a hand too, as the entire laboratory staff was mobilized to turn cartloads of peppers into juice, filling up fifty-liter flask after fifty-liter flask. In one week alone the Hungarian professor extracted half a kilogram of pure vitamin C, a quantity unthinkable for research chemists at that time.

The scientist found that a Hungarian paprika contained five to six times more vitamin C than an orange or lemon, both of which until then had been considered the richest source for the substance. It was the first time that such quantities of vitamin C had been produced and at so little cost, and the breakthrough turned Szent-Györgyi into a national hero. He dispatched portions of his product to other scientists around the world who were investigating its properties and to the World Health Organization for distribution to countries plagued by scurvy. He saw other immediate reasons for using vitamin C: "A partial lack of this vitamin manifests itself in a decreased resistance of the body. The many colds in this [winter] time of the year may be due, in part at least, to this decreased resistance." He patented a canned paprika preserve for use on crackers, sandwiches, and meat dishes; he initially called the product Vita-Prik, but after learning that English-speaking countries shunned it because of the name he changed it to Pritamin.

Peppers are a storehouse for other important vitamins too. Carotene, an orange-yellow or red hydrocarbon, is a pigment in many plants and is converted by the liver into vitamin A. Carrots were believed to have the highest concentration of this compound, but they contain only a fraction of what peppers contain. Vitamin A is important for normal cell growth in the body, and its deficiency causes night blindness. Because a deficiency also degenerates skin and mucous membranes, the vitamin is recommended to protect the body against germs that can penetrate the body weakened by the common cold. Peppers also contain in great quantities vitamin P, also known as the bioflavonoids, which function in the maintenance of the walls of small blood vessels. "We have succeeded in curing certain diseases accompanied by hemophilia," Szent-Györgyi wrote about this new vitamin he later discovered with another scientist.

Peppers are now coming under increasing scientific scrutiny for other reasons. At the inaugural meeting of the Japan Spice Study Society in Kyoto in 1986, several researchers presented papers on the potential uses of peppers' chemicals. Professor Yoshinori Tsuda of Toyama University's pharmaceutical department reported that a chemical element in hot pepper called koshoamide can kill roundworm, or nematode, in dogs and other pets, and proposed developing a nematocide as a medicine against it. A group from Kyoto University, citing experiments with rats, reported that a heat element in hot pepper could prevent obesity because it promoted metabolism of fat.

Researchers in Thailand have reported that capsaicin, the pepper's chemical, reduces blood-clot formation by increasing fibrinolytic activity, or FA. The group compared the anticlotting characteristics of the blood of native Thai with those of fifty-five Americans at the U.S. Army Hospital in Bangkok. It found that the Americans were considerably more prone to clotting than the Thais, who are renowned for pepper eating. The researchers then fed peppery meals to the Americans and observed an almost immediate drop in the "clot-ability" of their blood. "The daily stimulation of FA is perhaps sufficient to prevent thromboembolism," the group concluded.

While capsaicin astonishingly has no harmful effect on the tongue and the lining of the stomach when digested, it has a startling effect when a highly concentrated solution of it is rubbed on the skin: it acts as an anesthetic. It first stimulates pain and warmth and then changes into an inhibitor of pain. It does so by suppressing, eventually destroying, the pain messengers, called Substance P, which carry the message from the point of contact to the brain. This pain-relieving property of hot peppers has been exploited in ancient medicine in Asia and Latin America in the treatment of toothache and chilblain. In 1850 the Dublin Medical Press recommended that a drop or two of hot-pepper extract be applied to a sore tooth to bring instant relief. But the remedy wasn't taken seriously by the medical community, because there existed little understanding of how this worked.

The first major investigation of this phenomenon was begun in the late 1940s by Hungarian pharmacologist Nicholas Jancso at the Szeged University of Medicine, the site of much of Szent-Györgyi's research. Jancso was apparently intrigued by the physiological changes he saw in children who ate peppery food. The study of capsaicin's pharmacological effects on mammals' sensory systems has continued at a brisk pace in Szeged since Jancso's death in 1966. Capsaicin studies were widely presented at a 1983 Dublin symposium, which was held to honor Ulf S. von Euler, the father of Substance P. In taking note of the Dublin gathering, the British journal *Lancet* said the tremendous scientific interest in hot pepper's chemical vindicated "the empirical approach of our ancestors to toothache."

The increasing understanding of how capsaicin acts on Substance P—the P stands for pain—has created a surge of interest in hot peppers among neuroscientists. For the first time there's a magic chemical that can eliminate pain and potentially obviate incapacitating surgery. Extensive experiments with rats and a number of other animals show that capsaicin relieves pain by first selectively attracting and then destroying the messengers responsible for taking pain messages to the brain. This messenger-chemical is one of a number of chemicals—others being chemicals that carry such senses as touch, temperature— that reside in neurons, which are message centers. These message centers are interspersed throughout the brain, the spinal cord, and the body's peripheral nerves. The job of the specialized chemicals is to relay their specific impulses or information from one message station, or neuron, to another, and ultimately to the thalamus, a sensory center in the brain. Only when the pain message sent by Substance P reaches here does the body become aware of its cause. The brain then figures out the location of the pain and its intensity and releases endorphins to diminish the pain.

The pepper's chemical acts against pain this way: When capsaicin is applied to the body, it first attracts Substance P from the nerve endings at the contact point. Substance P starts to signal a burning sensation to the brain, but soon capsaicin begins to destroy the attracted messengers. As more Substance P is sent, it too is destroyed. Capsaicin, which is 8-methyl-N-vanillyl-6-nonenamide, thus bleeds the neurons of Substance P until they no longer manufacture it. As a result, there are no more pain messengers left at the point where capsaicin has been applied, and the sensory nerve endings become insensitive to chemically induced pain. What's extraordinary, according to scientists, is that capsaicin destroys only the pain messengers and leaves intact, in the neurons, the others charged with relaying tactile sensations, physical pain, heat, cold, taste, and other sensory messages. That's not the case when anesthetics are administered or when a nerve is severed, as is often done in severe cases, to relieve chronic pain.

Pharmaceutical companies are now starting to exploit this

$$CH_2NH-\overset{\overset{\displaystyle O}{\|}}{C}-(CH_2)_4CH=CH-CH(CH_3)_2$$

Capsaicin

unique attribute of capsaicin, which has long been an active ingredient in muscle relaxants, to treat people who suffer chronic pain from rheumatoid arthritis, cancer, and herpes zoster, commonly known as shingles. The U.S. Food and Drug Administration has approved a capsaicin-based topical cream for the treatment of herpes zoster, a viral infection along a nerve path that manifests itself as an extremely painful rash, particularly among those sixty years of age and older. In many cases, even after the skin lesions have healed, the pain persists and becomes intractable. What causes this chronic pain is still very much a mystery, and it can be so unbearable that it drives some patients to suicide. Treatments, generally ineffective, have included morphine, potent analgesics, tranquilizers, acupuncture—and, as a final resort, surgery to cut either the nerves causing the local pain or the nerve tracts in the spinal cord and brain. The surgery has as debilitating an effect on the patient as the symptom it aims to remedy. It isn't surprising, then, that hot pepper is attracting tremendous attention in medicine. The treatment for the disabling pain of shingles has been "revolutionized by the introduction of topically applied capsaicin cream," wrote Joel E. Bernstein, clinical associate professor of dermatology at Northwestern University Medical School in Chicago, in the October 1988 issue of the journal *Resident & Staff Physician.* Evaluating the results of a preclinical trial, he reported that "about 75% of all patients [with chronic pain] obtained complete or substantial relief from their pain" with this cream. Separately, researchers at Tulane University School of Medicine in New Orleans have reported that a capsaicin-based topical oral drug substantially relieved a patient's previously intractable pain of the gum and tongue, and they suggested that capsaicin be used to treat chronic oral pain. At the John B. Pierce Foundation Laboratory in New Haven, Connecticut, researchers are developing a drug from capsaicin to treat the "burning mouth syndrome," an intense pain in the mouth that was treated as a psychiatric disorder in the past and now is believed to be caused by abnormalities in pain fibers.

"The reason we are excited about this drug is that it acts only on the pain sensation and not others. The sensory feelings, for instance, are not affected. That's most unusual," said a researcher.

These and other applications have led Northwestern University's Dr. Bernstein to pronounce: "Topical capsaicin may someday take a place next to aspirin as one of the most significant products for pain ever introduced."

Scientists unraveling the mysteries of hot pepper often compare it to the sun when discussing its menacing sides. Treated with respect, the pepper is soothing and life-enhancing; abused, it's scorching. It is thus urged that precaution in handling pepper should start in the kitchen itself. As much as pepper is craved by the tongue, it can deliver an uncomfortable burning sensation to the hand and worse to the eye and other sensitive parts of the body that the hand touches. Exposing sensitive tissue to pepper can land a person in the hospital. I came across an extreme case of this in a letter to the *New England Journal of Medicine* from a physician at the University of Chicago. "I feel compelled to report a case of a very painful but entirely preventable disorder: Hunan Hand," he wrote. A thirty-two-year-old male student had showed up at the university clinic, moaning with pain and waving his hands rapidly in the air. The man was dizzy and in acute distress and his pulse had dropped to 120. The student had been sanding furniture and afterward prepared a Chinese lunch of chicken with peanuts and red pepper. His fingertips had become abraded from the sanding; when he washed the red chiles, the pungent chemical got directly into the skin's pain fibers, which are most abundant in the fingertips. The pain "appeared to radiate up his arms in throbbing waves," the physician said. When the patient immersed his fingers in ice water it only aggravated the pain. He was successfully treated with lidocaine gel on his fingertips. This letter prompted another physician, in Bethesda, Maryland, to respond with "some kitchen lore" of residents along the Texas-Mexico border who are familiar with "Hunan Hand." He mentioned one remedy that he himself had tested: "Bathing or immersing the irritated area in vinegar . . . offers almost total relief even if initiated thirty minutes or more after exposure."

Peppers have been blamed for internal disorders. Not withstanding Doctor Nicolai Monardes's endorsement of pepper in his "Joyfull Newes Out of the Newe Founde Worlde," when the fruit was introduced in Europe some people automatically reasoned that owing to its bite it could only be harmful. Matthiolus, a sixteenth-century Sienna physician, declared that pepper caused liver and kidney diseases. In the seventeenth century Dodonaeus also looked at hot pepper suspiciously. More recently, two physicians at the University of Texas studied participants in a jalapeño-eating contest and asserted in a letter to the *New England Journal of Medicine* that hot pepper, contrary to its reputation as an expectorant, didn't increase sputum production in the contestants. Instead, the physicians warned, jalapeños may cause "jaloproctitus," a term they coined to describe the syndrome of burning defecation. But the symptom resulted from excessive ingestion of the pepper, three to thirteen by each contestant.

Some researchers—in the minority, as far as I could tell from surveying the medical literature on Capsicum—have claimed that peppers may cause cancer, particularly colon cancer. Peter Gannett is among a group of researchers who are studying whether capsaicin can cause human cells to undergo a change through mutation, promoting or initiating cancer. Gannett and co-researchers work at the Eppley Institute for Research in Cancer and Allied Sciences at the University of Nebraska Medical Center in Omaha. When I called Gannett he said, "When I joined the institute in 1985 it was to prove that hot pepper caused cancer, but now our studies are leading us in the other direction. We are now researching its anti-carcinogenicity."

Gannett said the assumption that capsaicin may cause cancer was a reasonable one—even though epidemiological studies don't indicate that people in Mexico or India are prone to cancer more than, say, the people in Idaho—because large doses of the pungent chemical have been shown to destroy or mutate mammalian cells. "People think that something that can alter cells is also carcinogenic. But that isn't true. We looked at mammalian cells subjected to heavy dosage of capsaicin and found that mutation didn't result in cancer," Gannett said.

He now believes that the chemical in hot pepper may actually counter conditions that promote cancer. He and his associates have discovered, for instance, that capsaicin has the ability to immobilize a select group of enzymes or "free radicals" in the body that react with a whole slew of chemicals that routinely enter the human body to form potentially cancer-causing compounds. These chemicals may be nitrosamines, which are in overcooked bacon and in cigarette smoke, or the aromatic hydrocarbons in the exhaust gases of automobiles. Normally certain enzymes in the body convert these chemicals into water-soluble compounds so that the intruders can pass through the body without causing any harm. But some enzymes in the body, such as the group designated as cytochrome P-450j, aren't that nice, and they react with the intruding chemical and form cancer-causing compounds that go off to vandalize tissues and cells. Gannett found that these unfriendly enzymes have a tendency to rush and "grab" the capsaicin ingested into the body, only to be deactivated by the pepper's chemical. As a result this P-450j class of enzyme is unable to react with a vast number of intruders, such as nitrosamines. Although singing the virtues of hot pepper, Gannett cautioned that he wasn't recommending that people should start consuming "tons of hot pepper" to reduce cancer risk. "Too much can cause acute toxicity and can irritate, and even destroy, the stomach lining and other parts of gastrointestinal tracts," Gannett said.

"To assemble the entire capsaicin story," as he put it, Gannett and other researchers at the institute are isolating capsaicin's individual compounds, or capsaicinoids. They have identified seven of the dozen or so capsaicinoids that make up the pungent chemical in hot pepper. These compounds vary slightly in chemical structure. Essentially, each structure is a hexagon that is attached to an open zigzag chain of carbon atoms. The hotness diminishes as the chain lengthens or shortens, suggesting that there's a midpoint at which hotness peaks. (These peculiarities of capsaicinoids may explain why some hot peppers offer a rapid bite, some in the front of the mouth rather than in the back, why some moderately pungent peppers linger on in the mouth and cause discomfort, and why some seem intolerable at first bite but leave behind a pleasant feeling.)

"The perception of heat is felt when the chain gets to be three or four carbons long. It disappears when the chain gets longer than eleven. The hottest range seems to be eight or nine carbon lengths." Gannett conjectured that perhaps the tongue's receptor cells "can't fit chains that are too short or too long," and, as a result, the burning sensation isn't felt. "It's quite possible that if the chain doesn't fall within the narrow region of the mouth's receptor cell, hot sensation isn't perceived," he said, and noted that the same loss of perception occurs if the chemical structure of capsaicin is modified slightly. Gannett hopes that the study of these individual capsaicinoids will help develop drugs that will have anticancer properties. "The capsaicin story is fascinating, but we don't know a whole lot yet."

6

Tabasco

O n Avery Island, a bayou-rimmed twenty-five-hundred-acre plantation at the southern tip of Louisiana, McIlhenny Company manufactures Tabasco Pepper Sauce with the air of vintners and vestigial Southern aristocracy.

In a storybook setting, rows of pines stand as a windbreak against the sea and shelter fenced-in pepper farms, green-houses, barns, and processing plants that are scattered amid live oaks and gardens of Chinese timber bamboos, azaleas, and irises. The island is a self-contained village, with its own roads and general stores for the workers. A century-old antebellum mansion blending into a new red-brick structure to accommodate expanding business serves as the administration building. It houses computers, secretaries, marketing specialists, salesmen, accountants, and executives of the company. The entrance opens to a wide spiraling stairway that rises to a floor of glassed offices and wood-paneled meeting rooms resembling the hushed inner sanctum of a luxuriant art gallery. From these offices, fourth-generation descendants of the founder, Edmund

McIlhenny, run the business in the tradition established by the company in 1868.

When I drove toward Avery Island I had half expected to encounter a region like Burgundy or Beaune or Dijon, where sloping vineyards run into each other under the languorous glances of stately mansions. But that wasn't what I saw. Avery Island sits alone in its magisterial superstructure, isolated. Not far from its perimeters are highways and gas stations and malls and other urban tangles of ordinary American landscape. As if having failed to hold back these unwanted intrusions, Avery Island has gone deep into seclusion. It is reached by a private road that shoots off the main highway, jumps over a canal and comes to a screeching halt at the guarded entrance.

Southern Louisiana once was lush with tabasco peppers, I would learn later. The pepper was brought to the region about 130 years ago. But a couple of decades ago the pepper farms began to die out. Many succumbed to local plant diseases. Growers also lost any incentive there was to plant the pepper, because rising labor costs made it too costly to harvest, a labor-intensive task. Now Avery Island is tabasco's last holdout in the United States. It has to hold out—after all, it is home to Tabasco Pepper Sauce. But the two hundred forty thousand plants that grow on eighty acres here represent less than 10 percent of McIlhenny's annual requirement. For the rest the company contracts with farmers in Mexico, Venezuela, Honduras, and Colombia, where growing conditions and economics of growing are more favorable.

Before tabasco, Avery Island did a booming business in rock salt—the marshy land sits on a salt dome thirty thousand feet deep and one and a half miles in circumference—and sugarcane under John Craig Marsh of Rahway, New Jersey, who

settled the place in 1818. His daughter married a Yale-educated Louisiana Circuit Court judge, Daniel Dudley Avery. And in 1859 a daughter of that union married Edmund McIlhenny, a bearded New Orleans banker and gourmand of Scottish-Irish descent.

The story has it that a Confederate soldier, returning from the Tabasco region of Mexico, gave McIlhenny some peppers. McIlhenny, who moved to Avery Island with his family after New Orleans was captured by Union troops in 1862, planted the seeds. But before he could harvest the fruits the federal forces attacked the island, which had been supplying salt to the Confederate Army. The McIlhenny and Avery families fled to Texas. When they returned to the island in 1865 it lay in ruins, but Edmund McIlhenny apparently found a single tabasco plant that had stood its ground against the marauding federal forces. Supposedly tooling around in the kitchen, he crushed the peppers and combined their juice with vinegar and salt, and distributed the sauce to friends. He saw the commercial potential and three years later, in 1868, sold a concoction in 350 used perfume bottles—whose outlines are retained in today's Tabasco sauce bottles—through wholesalers. In 1870 he patented his method of preparing the sauce:

> The ripe fruit is mashed to pulp and mixed with fine vinegar and rock salt, in the proportions of one pint of vinegar and one handful of salt to every gallon of pulp.
>
> The receptacle containing this mixture is closely covered, and the latter macerated for about six weeks, when the pulp is worked through a sieve that is just fine enough to not permit the seeds to pass. About one drop of bisulphate of lime is then added to every ounce of mixture, for preventing fermentation.
>
> The skins and suds not passed through the sieve are potted for about twenty four hours, with an ounce of alcohol to each pound of the residue.

This mixture is thoroughly agitated and then placed under a press, by which the remaining pulp and juice are forced out.

A drop of bisulphate of lime is added to every ounce received from the press. The two mixtures thus prepared are now put together, and the whole compound worked through a fine flour sieve. The sauce is thus completely prepared and ready for use.

The reputation of the sauce spread so quickly that by 1870 McIlhenny had opened a London office. In 1898, according to one story, his wife, Mary Eliza Avery, received letters on the same day from her three sons—Edward in Moscow, Paul in Pretoria, and John in Beijing—who wrote to say that the family's Tabasco sauce had preceded them in restaurants and hotels at their respective ports.

Even in Britain, the nation of unadventurous palates, the sauce was noticed. It came to light during the 1932 "Buy British" campaign. Several members of the House of Commons wanted the sauce excluded from an import ban because, they confessed, they couldn't do without it on the House of Commons oysters. When the proposal stirred a tempest in Parliament, even the chairman of the Kitchen Committee stepped in and offered support for Tabasco with the alibi that only "eight or nine bottles" a year were used anyway. But the opposition prevailed, and the honorable chairman of the Kitchen Committee promised to discontinue the American item. (That resolution prompted William Randolph Hearst in the United States to wage a "Buy American" campaign through his chain of newspapers. "The English will probably find that the banishment of Tabasco from the Commons restaurant is a two-edged sword," warned one editorial.)

McIlhenny's Tabasco Pepper Sauce remains a fixture in oyster bars today; even those who avoid hot pepper at meals routinely shake a drop or two of this sauce on oysters. The Bloody Mary wouldn't have its character without the dash of this fiery liquid. Tabasco sauce traveled with American GIs' C rations in Vietnam. It accompanied astronauts on the Skylab. Even earthbound travelers tuck along a bottle of it as a weapon against the bland or the unpredictable. The sauce accompanied Kitchener on his African campaign, and a correspondent who followed him around in Khartoum complained that "a correspondent cannot live on soda water and Tabasco alone." Tabasco labels are currently printed in English, Chinese, French, Greek, Italian, Japanese, Spanish, German, and Swedish. (The Japanese are McIlhenny's biggest customers.) So ubiquitous is the sauce that its name has found its way into the dictionary. The company ships 50 million two-ounce bottles annually to more than 100 countries.

Tabasco's worldwide preeminence in a crowded field of hundreds of hot sauces makes it an envied target. McIlhenny Co. gets frequent offers of purchase, but the heirs promptly turn them down. The company's stock is held by the family clan, a brood of sixty or so descendants. In the jealously guarded family enterprise, the business mantle has passed from one McIlhenny to another—from Edmund to his sons John and Edward ("Mr. Ned") and then to John's son Walter; Walter's second cousin, Edward (Ned) McIlhenny Simmons currently heads the company.

When I paid a visit to the firm, Paul McIlhenny, who is Walter's cousin and is in charge of manufacturing and sales operations, was preparing for his daily trip to the processing plant, a mile from the administrative building. I went along. On the way he told me that the most important part of his job is approving the pepper mash, which is aged for three years in oak barrels. Until he offers his subjective nod, the mash can't be processed. From the inception of the business this inspection has always been done by a McIlhenny. There are other longtime traditions at the company, he said. At harvest, for instance, a McIlhenny always does the weighing when pickers bring their baskets of harvest. Paul takes turn at that duty too. He said that when picking finishes at three o'clock, he climbs up a special tractor and sits behind a scale. The tractor edges past the line of waiting pickers. The boxes of peppers are lifted onto the scale and he calls out the weights and at the same time looks over the pods to be sure they are the right color. An employee riding on the tractor punches out a card and gives it to the picker; he in turn presents the card to a field man who carries a box of money to pay the picker cash on the spot. There is also tradition in the way plants are selected for the next year's seeds. That ritual always falls on the head of a member of the McIlhenny family, who ceremoniously twirls a twine around the plants of his choice. The seeds from these plants are stored in a local bank vault. "By the way, we always have a tie and jacket on when we weigh peppers," Paul said.

A definite air of formality, perhaps to create a mystique and aura for the sauce, was introduced by John Avery McIlhenny, the founder's son. He usually wore black tie in the evening; when important guests were expected for dinner, he switched to white tie. His son Walter, a brigadier general in the Marine Corps Reserve and a lifelong bachelor, continued the tradition of formality, down to the way he ran the day-to-day business. He would start his workday in his cluttered office precisely at 6:30 a.m. After sessions with foremen and supervisors he would walk to his stately Georgian home for breakfast promptly at 7:30, and by 8:00 he would be out in the fields or back in the office. At 11:00 sharp he would head to the factory to inspect pepper mash and return home at 12:00 for lunch. (To this day the entire company, including the switchboard, shuts down between 12:00 and 1:00 p.m. for lunch, as it has since the beginning.) Meals were always served by white-gloved attendants. On the dining table, in front of each place setting, would be a bottle of Tabasco in a silver holder that matched the Bradford antebellum silverware and goblets that once belonged to his great-great-grandfather (on his mother's side), Zachary Taylor, the twelfth president of the United States.

• • •

Paul McIlhenny took me on a circuitous drive to the factory,
stopping briefly to show me the nursery and the sheds that
house barrel upon barrel of aging pepper mash. When we
arrived at the processing plant, a long red-brick building, a
dozen oak barrels full of red slurry had been laid open. Two
workers in khaki uniforms were standing alongside, one with an
incandescent lamp and the other with a scooper, and the plant
supervisor was there too, with his clipboard. At the back, uni-
formed workers were washing burlap bags or moving barrels
around on forklifts. Paul said he inspects 90 percent of the mash
before it's processed. The responsibility for the remainder falls
on the nostrils of the plant supervisor.

The barrels of mash brought here had been sitting un-
disturbed for three years in storage barns scattered in the
compound. The barrels are color-coded, each color identifying
the pepper's country of origin. In the processing plant 200
barrels, each containing 400 pounds of mash, are opened every
week. When the lids are opened, they give off a blast of acrid air
that causes throats to choke and eyes to tear. The top layer of the
mash is usually dark from oxidation and is skimmed off. The
barrels are then covered with burlap sacks and turned over on
their bellies for three days to drain out the brine. Then the
barrels are uprighted and lined up for a McIlhenny nod.

As I coughed uncontrollably moments after stepping inside,
I asked the man who was stirring a barrel if he ever used a mask.
He wasn't coughing, and neither were the other employees.
"We are now used to it," he said. The human body, strangely,
does get accustomed to the pepper's aggravating personality.
But for a long time the fixtures in the plant didn't; before the
invention of stainless steel and plastic, Paul said, the concrete
floor and steel pipes and valves and filters and other hardware in
the factory had to be replaced periodically because the air
would eat through them. "For the longest time it was hell on the
equipment," he remarked. I wondered if the workers were truly

spared this wrath and whether a long exposure wasn't insidiously affecting the pipes and valves inside their bodies.

The man with the incandescent lamp lowered it into the first barrel. The red slurry took on a slightly purplish hue. Paul leaned into the barrel, ran his eyes up and down, and after straightening himself approved the color with a nod. Then the man with the scooper gave the mash a swirl and held a glob chest-high. Paul brought his nose to a respectable distance and gave another nod. The supervisor ticked off something on his clipboard. Paul and the employees exchanged few words during the ritual. "Smell this," Paul said, turning to me. "It's acrid but has a sweet smell. I look for this smell. It's not putrid, which would be rejected. It has to have the right color. Bright as this. The right juiciness, just as this has." The crew then shuffled to the next barrel, and so on. Thus was the inspection completed, and the batch pronounced fit for processing.

Not all barrels contain mash of uniform color and juiciness, however. To avoid unevenness, the mashes from different points of origin are blended; one-third from Honduras, one-third from Colombia, and one-third from somewhere else. "We end up rejecting about one barrel out of a hundred, but a few years ago we were rejecting more," Paul said. One of the problems in the past was that the wooden barrels would develop leaks on the way from Honduras or Colombia. "If you have a leak, moisture and flies get in. Flies lay eggs around the openings, and maggots and worms crawl into the mash and survive very well. The pungency doesn't seem to bother them, but the mash turns black and putrid. Barrels are handled much more carefully now."

The processing part of the plant consists of vats and holding tanks and looping pipes, and the setup looks like one of those petroleum storage facilities in Newark alongside the New Jersey Turnpike. The inspected barrels are rolled to the nearest pumps located at several points on the floor, and the mash is sucked through pipes into forty-four stirring vats, which sit on raised platforms. Hundred-grain vinegar, twice as strong as the vinegar used in salad dressing, flows into these 2,000-gallon vats, one gallon of vinegar for two gallons of mash. A mechanical stirrer in each of the forty-four vats stirs the blend for fifteen minutes, every hour and fifteen minutes, Monday through Friday, between 8:00 a.m. and 5:00 p.m. After four weeks the blend is pumped into three "brush finishers," or filtering machines, where the seeds and pulp are removed. The filtered juice, which is now almost clear, is periodically tested by lab technicians to ensure that it matches a formula established by McIlhenny statisticians for pepper solids, salt, and vinegar before it's bottled on automated assembly lines in an adjoining building.

McIlhenny Co. notes proudly in its publicity brochures that neither the process nor the standard for the sauce has changed since its creation, except that the stirring and the final bottling are done mechanically. "But we still stir the sauce in the vats exactly the way the ladies used to in the old days," Paul told me. "They would stir one drum and then move on to the next, and then the next and by the time they came back to the first one to repeat the process it would be an hour and fifteen minutes. So today each barrel gets an hour and fifteen minutes of rest before it's stirred again. In the old days we didn't have people around to stir the blend at nights and weekends, so we don't stir at nights and weekends, even though we have an automatic system now."

The by-products of the sauce don't go to waste. The seeds and pulp are dehydrated and sold to companies that extract oil from them. Known as oleoresin, the concentrated capsaicin easily measures 1,000,000 Scoville units, compared to 40,000 Scoville units for the pepper sauce. The oleoresin is so hot that its handling requires special safety measures, including gloves and goggles. This resin goes into making topical muscle relaxants and, in much diluted forms, candies and chewing gum. Just one drop of oleoresin is sufficient to spice a whole caldron of boiling shrimps. When I was at the plant I heard the story of a caterer who used to buy cases of Tabasco sauce to spice crab and other shellfish. He was a big-time caterer who specialized in cookouts for big crowds. One day he discovered this oleoresin at the processing plant and bought a couple of bottles of it. He hasn't been seen for years.

McIlhenny doesn't have any problem finding buyers for its sauce. But it does have a problem finding enough peppers. One reason is that the tabasco, more than other peppers, has become particularly vulnerable to plant diseases. That's because the tabasco, confined to southern Louisiana and without the infusion of genes from other peppers, has a narrow genetic makeup. "If there's a virus or any other disease near a tabasco plant you can be sure that it will make its way into it," I was once told by Dr. Lowell Black, a plant pathologist at Louisiana State University who has done considerable research on tabasco pepper diseases. "The viruses easily multiply in tabasco plants. That has the effect of compounding the virus population in the weeds in and around the tabasco farm, and that makes it even more difficult for the next planting to withstand diseases."

While low labor costs make it economical to cultivate the pepper in Mexico, Venezuela, Honduras, and Colombia, there, too, it has been falling victim to disease in field after field. As a result McIlhenny constantly finds itself in a situation of living hand-to-mouth, unsure of where the next supplies are going to come from.

The person who worries about it a lot and has the responsibility of maintaining the company's lifeline is Gene Jefferies. He is one of only three nonfamily members who hold high positions in the company and is the director of McIlhenny's agricultural operations. When I saw him one morning in early July it was pouring buckets.

"We need thirty inches of rain between April and November to get the best pepper crop. But we have had twenty inches just in June alone. It looks like we are getting the rest today," he said. The rain didn't bode well for the island's crop. Jefferies said the pods, which should start to turn red by July, hadn't even become yellow yet. "There're some yellowish pods at the bottom, but you have to look very hard." Tabasco pods ripen from the bottom of the plant up. As a result, at midseason, a tabasco plant looks like a yellow-green shrub with its bottom on fire. That sight always brings relief to Jefferies, but now he was worried about a "waterlogging effect," in which water saturates the soil, slowing down the supply of nutrients to the roots and stunting the plant's growth. "It can kill the plants."

Because of the constant attack on the tabasco by one enemy or another, Jefferies's spartan office looks like a general's war room. He sits in it facing a huge map of North America on the wall, his back to a map of South America. Red thumbtacks cluster on the maps, mostly on the isthmus. The position of the tacks indicate where his pepper supplies come from: Mazatlán and Tampico, Ciudad Valles and Ciudad Victoria and Mérida, in Mexico; San Juan, Lean, La Entrada, El Progreso, and La Flecha, all in Honduras; coastal plains near Cartagena and Cauca Valley, in Colombia; and near Lake Maracaibo and El Pinal in Venezuela. Jefferies finds himself frequently in those places, climbing mountains or wading through waist-deep weeds in jungles to check on his farmers.

McIlhenny Co. initially turned to these places more to cut labor costs than to run away from plant diseases, which weren't that rampant at the time. The company had made an unsuccessful effort to mechanize pepper harvesting on Avery Island. In 1978 company engineers rigged up a picking shroud beneath a Hagie spray tractor. On each side of the shroud they mounted nozzles capable of thrusting jets of water with considerable force. The whole contraption rode on oversize tires so that its underbelly cleared the tops of the plants. When the tractor traveled, straddling a row of pepper plants, jets of swirling water shook the plants. It was supposed to pry loose only the ripe pods onto the conveyor belts on each side of the shroud. But the engineers found unripe yellow pods, leaves, and twigs all mixed in with the ripe red pods. So they had to develop a mechanized sorting process. Using this assembly the engineers made trial runs and tallied up the costs: It cost thirty-eight cents a pound to pick tabasco with the mechanized harvester. In contrast, hand picking cost twenty-five cents on Avery Island, and ten cents less in Honduras and Colombia.

"We played around with this mechanized thing for several years, and then we gave up. Fortunately, we have been quite successful in getting farmers to grow pepper for us in Latin America," Jefferies said.

Jefferies, in fact, had just returned from his first trip to the Dominican Republic, where he was exploring the possibility of getting farmers to grow tabasco. But he wasn't sure how good an idea it was. "You are pulled over every few miles by cops and you have to give them a few pesos. If you don't bribe you don't go anywhere. If things don't work out there I would have to go to Jamaica, and God knows where." Actually, Jefferies doesn't balk at giving any place a try.

In December 1977 Jefferies received a call from Nicaraguan Minister of Defense General Heberto Sanches, who said he had an underemployed son and a lot of land. Jefferies sent him a packet of seeds and planting guidelines, as he does routinely to people who enthusiastically offer to grow tabasco for McIlhenny. "Ninety-nine times out of a hundred they never come back after they find out how hard it is to grow tabasco pepper," he said. So he was quite surprised when, on July 12, 1978, the general's son, Ricardo, called him to say he had 6,000 beautiful tabasco plants and asked what was he to do with them.

"I was immediately on the plane and looked the plants over. He got great germination in that rich soil. We shipped him empty oak barrels and a grinder. He mashed the peppers and filled eight barrels. I also sent more seeds," Jefferies said. Before the barrels could be shipped to Avery Island, the politics of Nicaragua during the Somoza regime abruptly turned for the worse. The Sandinistas, supported by embittered local peasants, deposed the Somoza family. General Sanches's family was close to the Somozas. "The general's son walked away from the pepper mash and the new crop he had planted," said Jefferies. "When the shooting stopped, we sent our man in Honduras to retrieve the pepper mash from Nicaragua. But he couldn't find anybody who would take him to the farm."

With his tall, wiry body, steel-blue eyes, and soft drawl, Jefferies cuts the figure of a Texan cowboy who has abandoned the rough ranch life for a quiet farm. He told me he was born in Los Angeles and grew up in Arizona, where he worked summers at his uncle's cattle ranch. He studied economics at the University of Arizona, spent twelve years in Brazil as an agricultural supervisor, and then moved to Venezuela. When he heard McIlhenny was looking for someone with farm experience in South America, he applied. "It looked like they were looking for someone like me to hire, but I knew nothing about growing pepper. I remember when I came up to see Walter McIlhenny, the president, whom everyone addressed as Mr. Walter, and I said I didn't know anything about pepper. Mr. Walter greased his long handlebar mustache and said, 'Gene, you don't have to worry about that. We have been growing pepper for one hundred twenty years. We can teach that part.'"

Jefferies runs a far-flung network of tabasco farmers through point men. In Colombia and Venezuela there is George Baker, who once looked after Nelson Rockefeller's agricultural enterprises in South America. Jefferies told me that Baker leads a nomadic life, moving from pepper farm to pepper farm and putting up a hammock wherever he happens to be at sunset. But Jefferies's man in Honduras, a former combat soldier named Roberto Mealer, has a much tougher job. He has to run his cooperative of some six hundred farmers in the face not only of political turmoil but of an invisible army of pepper diseases. Every time pepper fields come under siege, Mealer would shepherd his farmers to another location, sometimes to unclaimed lands. I envisioned a whole colony of farmer-settlers, moving from one valley to another, like the Bedouin tribes of the North African deserts.

When I arrived in San Pedro Sula, Honduras, Mealer looked harried. "I have been working round-the-clock building a new mashing station," he told me. The mashing station was being constructed in a valley where a large number of farmers on the run had relocated from other areas devastated by pepper diseases. "The peppers have to be mashed within twenty-four hours of picking. That's the rule. So the mashing station has to be close to farms," he said.

Honduras was in a turmoil when I was there. Mountains and jungles were sheltering Contra guerrillas from Nicaragua who were trying to depose their communist government. In pursuit of the guerrillas, Nicaraguan soldiers would venture into Honduras. And Honduran soldiers, backed by U.S. military men, were hunting for the infiltrating Nicaraguan soldiers. The border skirmishes had created a tension that was palpable in the streets, which were fortified with roadblocks and military checkpoints. Through this obstacle course Mealer was keeping up with the daily routine of visiting pepper farms, supervising mashing operations, and overseeing weekly shipments to Avery Island.

Mealer looks cut out for the job. Tall and muscular, he gives the impression of being tough, especially when he puts on sunglasses and an American accent. He told me he was born in Honduras, where his father, an American citizen, worked for United Brands. Mealer studied in Louisiana, joined the U.S. Air Force, and was posted in Iceland, but quit after he found himself "covered up to my ass in ice." He returned to Honduras and joined United Brands and, to earn some extra money, planted a small patch with tabasco peppers for McIlhenny. The Louisiana sauce maker eventually hired him full-time to supervise its entire cooperative of pepper farmers in the country.

One morning Mealer picked me up early at my hotel, and we drove for three hours—past dozens of checkpoints and the gazes of military vehicles—to the San Juan Valley. The fields there had produced the best harvest of the season, and this was the site of his new mashing station.

We drove into the valley through a maze of villages and found ourselves surrounded by stupendous San Juan mountains, veiled in heavy clouds. Trees, packed dense, streaked down the foothills and abruptly gave way to low shrubs and bushes—and then clearings. In that partly tamed but mostly wild expanse, fields of red peppers stretched as far as the eye could see. At first glance the valley looked as if it were smoldering. As I neared the fields, their bold strokes of red sprang into sprays of tiny dots; the inch-and-a-half-long red pods, growing upright, had overpowered the green leaves with sheer brilliance. Not many poets have been inspired by sights of pepper farms, but I later came across a haiku, "The Pepper-pod," perhaps inspired by a sight like this.

It was composed by Kikaku, one of the ten disciples of the Japanese poet Basho, as he strolled through an autumn field.

> Take a pair of wings
> From a dragonfly, you would
> Make a pepper-pod.

Basho told Kikaku, "That's not a haiku. You kill the dragonfly." The sixteenth-century master, who had journeyed through Japan in search of the meaning of life, recomposed the lines.

> Add a pair of wings
> To a pepper-pod, you would
> Make a dragonfly.

The association of pepper with the dragonfly intrigued me. The archetypical flying insect recurs in Japanese poetry as a symbol of summer, a time when open fields come alive with frolicking children stalking *tombo* from shrub to shrub. Dragonfly is the harbinger of summer—as is pepper, the wingless dragonfly.

The only country in the world where pepper fields today vibrate with exuberance is Hungary. Pepper harvesting doesn't attract much fanfare in India or China or South America, but it's entwined with the Hungarian psyche. Paprika, as it is called in Hungary, not only lends character to the country's national dish, a fish soup, it comprises a significant agricultural commodity. In the fields of Szeged, the paprika capital and the biggest center in the world for scientific research on pepper, harvesting starts on the Feast of the Holy Virgin's Nativity, the eighth of September. Women in colorful costumes stream into the fields, bringing the plains alive with their constant bustle and murmur. At lunch break pickers crowd around caldrons of goulash-stew prepared at the edge of the fields, and settle down with the hot food, loaves of bread, and flasks of wine.

Harvested peppers are piled in mounds. Women sit next to them and string the pods into garlands with steel needles. These pepper garlands, eight to ten feet long, are then hung from special wooden stands or on the walls of farmhouses, many of which face south or east to catch the maximum amount of sun. At the turn of the century Hungarian novelist Zsigmond Moricz wrote: "Under the eaves, over the fences, on the trees and on dovecotes—garlands of paprika, everywhere. So exotic is this decoration that for its sake tourists will want to come from Calcutta, London and other places, because this is a wondrous specialty. Beautiful! Inconceivably beautiful is the village court-yard at such times. . . ."

In Honduran pepper fields, in contrast, harvesting is cheerless. In the fields I was visiting, fifty or so people were picking tabasco, a vast number of them young boys and girls. With oversize hats on their heads these little pickers were going about their jobs silently. The only cheerful moment, so it seemed to my own mischievous side, was when a commotion broke out among the pickers. Apparently in the distraction caused by our unannounced visit, one little boy got caught emptying someone else's bag into his and was being pursued by the victim, also a young boy, through the pepper fields. Pepper harvesting, picking one pod at a time, is back-breaking drudgery. Lacking an organized custom of eating peppers, the pickers here aren't interested in the harvest as the Hungarian or Mexican pickers might be in theirs. The farmers grow peppers under contract, and as soon as they harvest them they dump their loads quickly and collect their money to buy bread and kerosene. A picker shook his head in disinterest when I asked him if he didn't care to take a handful home with him to spice up his food.

But McIlhenny doesn't take pepper farming casually. The Honduran farmers have to comply with strict standards laid down by the Louisiana company. Each pepper has to have a minimum of seven drops of juice; otherwise the pepper is rejected. The pepper has to have the right red color; farmers are issued a red stick that has the appropriate shade, to hold against the pepper if they are in doubt. Mealer hangs a cardboard sign in every mashing station to remind the farmers:

> *Aviso: sales recuerda*
> *que según contrato*
> *solamente chile*
> *rojo se recibirá*
> *sin excepción*
> *—Roberto Mealer*

"The right color is crucial, since we don't use any coloring agents," Mealer told me.

Tension builds up when farmers can't meet the requirements through no fault of their own. A drought can shrivel peppers dry. Viruses and microbes can turn the pods prematurely yellow. And this is occurring more often. How do farmers react when their harvest is rejected? When I asked that question, I had in the back of my mind the security measures at

Mealer's home—the fenced compound, guards, the two Dober-
man pinschers he lets loose at night, and the two guns he keeps
at home. He attributed those precautions to the general "delin-
quency" in the country.

Mealer said he had had a serious problem only once. In
1983 a drought caused peppers in another valley, on the river
Lean, to ripen prematurely, and the pods turned yellow instead
of red. When the pods showed up at the mashing station,
Mealer's men rejected them. The farmers blamed the situation
on God and wanted to be paid. Mealer pointed out what the
contracts called for. The farmers wouldn't accept that. So some
of them decided to kidnap him. They worked out a plan to
ambush him from behind a bridge near the Lean mashing
station when Mealer arrived the next day. Word leaked out, and
one of Mealer's assistants bicycled eighteen miles in the night to
his home to alert him.

"Instead of calling the police, I invited the farmers to my
office. We talked and talked, and I showed them the contract.
Finally they calmed down, and I gave them fresh seeds and
fertilizer and said let's give it another try. It's very important to
make the farmers feel that they are not being exploited. I treat
them with respect."

While the farmer doesn't get paid if his crop is inferior, he is
guaranteed a price if it meets McIlhenny's standards. Under the
contract McIlhenny is also obligated to buy, no matter how
much the farmer produces at that price. The contracted price at
the time of my visit was thirty-six cents a pound. "It's not a bad
price," Mealer said. "Tomatoes, for instance, sell for ten to
twelve cents in the local market, and their price can go down to
as low as four to five cents. They don't have any price guarantee." Mealer calculated that an acre of tabasco brings the
farmer a profit of $700, after paying for fertilizer, pesticide, and
labor. An acre of corn or beans, on the other hand, generates
only $200 to $300 profit per acre.

If farmers have problems growing tabasco, that has less to
do with bad weather and more to do with plain carelessness

during planting, Mealer said. To preempt explosive situations at harvest, Mealer and his assistants supervise farmers closely early in the planting season, which begins in March. His men help them with selecting land, transplanting seedlings, and planning offensive actions with pesticide and fungicide.

Pepper plants, which can't withstand environmental stress as easily as most common crops do, require extraordinary care. A critical stage in pepper cultivation is the time when seeds are being germinated. The little plants are most vulnerable at this point to various microorganisms, especially rampant in the tropics. As a protection, some farmers in the United States and Mexico first plant the seeds in greenhouses; this practice, however, is on the decline because of the costs involved. An increasingly common method is to plant the seeds in small, well-tended patches called seedbeds. The seedbed's soil is sterilized by heating it to 60°F for thirty to sixty minutes or by fumigating it with methyl bromide.

The ideal temperature for seed germination is between 80°F and 90°F, and to maintain the temperatures farmers sometimes cover the seedbeds with mulch or plastic sheeting. When the seedlings appear in a week or two, the farmer has to scout the seedbed each day for signs of insects and other organisms and apply the appropriate fungicide and insecticide sprays without causing chemical burns. The liquid arsenal varies, but Mealer's planting guideline recommends Zineb, Maneb, and copper sprays as fungicides, and such insecticides as thiodan, malathion, Lannate, Cygon and Diazinon.

The cultivation guidelines also urge farmers to disinfect hands in isopropyl alcohol every time they handle the seedbeds. Spades and trowels and clippers must be washed in a water-formaldehyde mixture before and after use. Pepper planting requires meticulous attention, more so than, say, cotton. Mealer said a cotton farmer may be able to grow a pepper crop if he is given ready seedlings, but more than likely he will fail if he has to start from scratch with seeds.

The seedlings are transplanted into the fields when they are six to twelve inches high. They are clipped periodically in seedbeds to induce them to grow more branches. The more stocky the seedlings, the less shock they will feel when transferred to the field. The seedlings are so sensitive at this stage that they can be infected with the tobacco mosaic virus by a handler who smokes. A California pepper breeder once told me, "You can tell a row planted by a smoker from a row planted by a nonsmoker." One precaution usually taken against such infection is dipping the seedlings in milk—milk contains a protein that apparently deactivates the tobacco mosaic virus—before planting them in the field. But this has had limited success; the virus is very stable and can persist on greenhouse benches and tools for weeks, even through the entire winter, and then is easily transmitted mechanically.

Growing healthy seedlings is only half the battle. In the fields about half a dozen viruses lurk in weeds and brush, and they attack all types of peppers. They are carried into the plants by aphids or plant lice. Tobacco etch virus—unlike the mosaic type, in which the disease is confined to spots on the branches—is lethal: the entire plant wilts, as if its roots had been severed, and it dies in seven to ten days. Potato virus—so called because the virus was first detected in potato plants—destroys the roots' ability to take in water and thus reduces yield. Cucumber mosaic virus doesn't engulf the entire plant but stunts pepper growth on the branch it infects. Tomato spotted wilt virus causes "dead spots," and leaves drop off and eventually the plant stops producing fruit altogether. Pepper mottle causes dark spots on leaves and stems and distorts plants' growth.

Then there are the fungus diseases: phytophthora, a soil-borne fungus that loves humidity, rots roots, and is devastating bell pepper and jalapeños from the tropics to as far north as Texas and New Mexico; verticillium wilt, which seems to have made particular targets of peppers grown in California and Europe, also attacks from below ground, causing plants to wilt and die. Many of these diseases aren't unique to pepper, of course. But other crops are economically bigger and thus have attracted more attention from researchers who are developing disease-resistant strains, using such modern techniques as genetic engineering.

Mealer instructs farmers to avoid growing peppers near tobacco, tomatoes, eggplant, or potatoes. For many years Honduran farmers bordered their fields of tabasco with ten-foot- to fifteen-foot-wide strips of corn, sorghum, or sugarcane to hold back migrating microorganisms. That doesn't do much good now. The viruses jump those barriers so easily that farmers have given up on bordering their fields, Mealer said.

With pesticides becoming less and less effective against the enemy, Honduran farmers increasingly are abandoning besieged fields and moving on to new land. Mealer worries that eventually his farmers may run out of places to run to. Overwhelming viruses have made it almost impossible for McIlhenny to grow tabasco in many parts of Mexico; the company abandoned Guatemala for that reason in 1984. As Mealer and I walked through the fields in the San Juan Valley, he would frequently stop and break a pod from a wilting plant and show me a wiggling larva, or he would squeeze a pod to show how little juice it gave out. Mealer said he hadn't visited these fields in weeks, because he had been so busy with the new mashing station. I saw him darting from plant to plant. He had a glum look. He waved at a man, who I learned later was one of the owners, and told him that he would have to find another field for the next planting. It was bad news for Francisco, the owner, who was in the midst of only the first week of harvesting. He had hoped to coax a second harvest from the same crop with the help of pesticides and nutrients. As perennials in the tropics the same pepper plants can produce again in the next season. Francisco, covered with sweat, looked with disappointment at the deformed yellow pods in Mealer's hand.

Mealer told me later that the farmer would either swap land somewhere else for the next planting or just clear unclaimed lands. Farmers also take over unused lands that the wealthy have appropriated through fictitious deeds but have never bothered to put to use. The government hasn't done much to help farmers under its much-touted land-distribution program, so it usually looks the other way when angry farmers squat on lands that have questionable proprietorship. Sometimes Mealer's farmers end up moving half a mile away, sometimes ten. When farmers relocate quite a distance, as they have by moving ten to twelve miles into the San Juan Valley, Mealer has to worry about a mashing station that is accessible to them.

The day I was visiting the farms in the valley happened to be the day Mealer's newest mashing station, his fifth such facility in the country, was gearing up for a trial run. When we drove the short distance from the farms to the station in the late afternoon, we found that farmers had already begun to trickle in with their harvests, even though they weren't supposed to: the mashing station wasn't yet officially opened. Word of a trial run had leaked out and brought in farmers anxious to unload their harvest at the nearest possible station. Otherwise they would have to lug it twenty miles or more to an old station.

Standing inside the mashing station, which was actually a large shed with a cement floor and grinding machinery in its center, Mealer looked out to the entrance of the barbed compound. He wasn't sure what to tell the farmers. A donkey was pulling a cartload of sacks through the gate. Right behind was a blue pickup so overladen with sacks of tabasco that it scraped against the uneven ground, swaying precariously from side to side. The truck had barely pulled up when two horses staggered in through the gate with piles of sacks, followed by three farmers in blue jeans and cowboy hats. Mealer shook his head and ordered his men to get the machinery cranking full blast.

The machinery didn't look like much. It consisted of a set of parallel steel rollers, flush against each other, which rotated in opposite directions. The whole contraption sat on a platform. Adjacent to it, a raised platform held peppers, which came down through a funnel into the rollers. The rollers were driven by a diesel engine, which received its fuel through a blue plastic pipe from a rusty drum hanging from the ceiling. The worn but still visible advertisement on the drum read, "The superior quality of this Texaco product is your assurance of dependable performance." Calling into question the Texaco advertising, the engine kept sputtering and failing. The workers finally located the problem in the choke. To me the most striking thing about it all was how primitive the contraption was—the blackened motor; the scooper, chunks of which had been lost to rust; the old dented fuel drum—as if the whole thing had been put together with parts from a salvage yard. After fits and starts, the diesel motor finally cranked up, and the pace in the shed began to pick up. Workers started scrubbing old empty oak barrels with water, and two men pumped a Coleman kerosene lamp to get it going. Mealer sat and watched the flurry of activity.

Over at one corner the peppers that passed inspection were scraped into crates, each holding roughly 100 pounds, for weighing. As soon as the scale registered 100, a young boy scooped up salt from a sack and dumped it into the crate till the scale read 108. The crate was then emptied on the raised deck. Using a rectangular piece of wood Mealer's men pushed the contents into the funnel, which channeled them into the whirring rollers. Down came a deluge of red mash, which Mealer allowed to fall on the floor for several minutes in order to inspect consistency and color. Then two men rolled up oak barrels to catch the red slurry. The burst of flowing mash sent a spray of pungent mist up into the air, overpowering the fumes of the diesel engine. Children who were watching the spectacle sped away, coughing and laughing. The farmer whose crispy harvest had been turned into a mush grinned, baring his gold teeth.

Since Mealer is required to mash the peppers within twenty-four hours after they arrive, to extract the maximum possible juice from the pod, he predicted an all-night operation of machinery that was intended to have had only a trial run that afternoon. "We are often open twenty-four hours in the season, and there have been times when the mashers have worked nonstop for days," Mealer said. At harvesttime there is no telling when farmers will show up with their sacks. Some finish harvesting in the evening but may not get to a mashing station till midnight. When rivers flood, some arrive at two in the morning. They line up with their harvests in the order of their arrival. Mealer said that in years past some mashing stations had such long caravans of mules, horses, motorcycles, and pickup trucks that his men issued tickets so that the farmers didn't have to stay in line to maintain their turn. "One time we had sixty-five farmers all at once at one station," Mealer said. Fortunately, village women showed up with their stoves to prepare tortillas and meats, and professional vendors peddled their own menu alongside.

The constant drone and sputter of the engine in the mashing station now echoed in the valley and bounced back from the mountains, bringing farmers along with it. Children left their play and gathered to watch the mashing. Machete-carrying farmers returning after a day's work streamed into the compound out of curiosity. Some even eagerly lent their hands to unload sacks of pepper.

Next day Mealer and I were back at the mashing station. The shed was silent, except for gurgling sounds from barrels of mash scattered around. The oak barrels are shut tight with a lid secured by steel hoops, and the top has several holes to allow the air from the ripening mash to exit. The lids are covered with a thick layer of salt so that insects and other organisms don't find their way into the barrels. Several workers were fast asleep when we arrived at eleven in the morning. One of them woke up as he heard Mealer's truck and told him that the last of the previous evening's harvest was mashed at about five in the morning. Much of the mashing was done under the dim light of candles and flashlights because the Coleman lamp, their main source of light until electricity arrives in a few weeks, went out of action late in the night.

After inspecting the mashing machinery and the mash-filled barrels, Mealer said he would show me fields that had recently been devastated by viruses. We drove west, near Honduras's border with Guatemala, to Copán. On the way, at La Entrada, six or so miles from the border, Mealer stopped briefly at another of his mashing stations, checked the barrels that were ready for shipment to Avery Island, and collected some papers. Then he pulled up near a supermarket that sat incongruously on the main highway, next to clusters of thatched huts selling food and soft drinks. The supermarket sold contraband goods— from brand-name soaps and toilet papers to cereals. Mealer went straight to the canned goods section. A few minutes later he returned with a can. "Finally, some Salvador jalapeños," he said, paying at the register. "This is more flavorful than the stuff from Mexico."

For the next few hours he drove past vacant fields, eating jalapeño strips on saltine crackers. He pointed at the valleys and foothills where farmers once had grown peppers for him. Occasionally he would stop and describe excitedly how far the lush fields stretched. Sometimes he would drive off the main road and edge close up to a field. The fields were covered with tall weeds and shrubs, the outlines of once-cultivated plots barely discernible. After some hours of driving around, Mealer pulled up to the edge of a shrubby ravine, off the highway. He said he wanted to show me "a famous hammock bridge." A track, now overgrown with grass, still showed signs of having once been heavily traveled. I followed Mealer and one of his men through a clearing, toward the sound of a rushing stream. Tiptoeing on the muddy bank, we stepped onto the hammock bridge. Underneath, the water cascaded over rocks before picking up speed and moving on in swells and rushes. On the other side of the bridge were vast fields that, Mealer said, once had been thriving pepper farms. The land was overgrown with weeds. Only the relatively low height of the weeds compared to the surrounding wild vegetation suggested that the area once had been cultivated.

Mealer said the site, which once bustled with the comings and goings of the locals, held a special meaning for him. He leaned on the hammock bridge, looking a little meditative, and pointed to the huge rocks in the stream. "The village women came in the afternoon and washed their laundry in this stream. There was this girl, actually a beautiful young woman. Maybe nineteen or twenty. She would come with a group of her friends, and they would all sit right there and carry on for hours. It was a sort of social hour for the young women," Mealer said. "I used to stand here and admire her long hair that fell all the way to her waist. She was a beauty. With the pepper fields, she disappeared, too. But I still stop by."

7

The Tabasco War

Although McIlhenny Company is by far the dominant hot-sauce maker in the United States, restaurants in its hometown had been compelled to place a rival product on their tables, too: Trappey's Pepper Sauce. That's because right across from McIlhenny's Avery Island sat the headquarters of B. F. Trappey's Sons in New Iberia Parish.

While the eateries judiciously avoided taking sides with either of the region's big employers, their customers sometimes had little choice. The cap on McIlhenny's Tabasco sauce bottles wouldn't open—which wasn't an accident. It was the work of Jack Blenderman, the president of B. F. Trappey's. Whenever he went into the local eateries, he would habitually reach for his rival's sauce and twist the cap way past the bottle's grooves. Diners, frustrated, would reach for the only other sauce on the table—Trappey's.

"It's a modest revenge," Blenderman, a big man with strong wrists and an earnest face, told me when I called on him.

Blenderman's ire goes back to the very roots of the companies' rivalry over who had the rights to the tabasco pepper.

The dispute started at the turn of the century. McIlhenny Co. claimed that its founder, Edmund McIlhenny, developed the pepper from a handful of nondescript pods brought from the Tabasco region of Mexico and that he gave it the name it bears today. Trappey's founder, Bernard F. Trappey, said that was nonsense, arguing that the pepper predated McIlhenny and was already known as tabasco in New Orleans. After five decades of acrimonious court battles in Galveston, Philadelphia, New York, Washington, and New Orleans, McIlhenny Co. mysteriously emerged in 1948 as the winner in the Louisiana courts after a string of defeats in other parts of the country. The tabasco pepper then disappeared from the public domain and became, in effect, a proprietary item: only McIlhenny had the right to call a sauce made from tabasco peppers a tabasco sauce. Trappey's couldn't even say "Made from tabasco peppers" to describe its sauce; it was allowed only to include the tabasco name, in fine print, with the other sauce ingredients.

In fact, soon after Blenderman took over the helm of Trappey's ten years ago—he's the first non–family member to run the company—a member of the McIlhenny clan called to remind him of the 1948 restraining order from a Louisiana federal court that set the labeling restrictions.

Trappey's was the last holdout in the battle over the name tabasco; nearly a dozen other companies, under the heft of McIlhenny's legal machinery, simply quit.

A year after my visit to the two companies, Trappey's too would disappear as an independent concern. Crushed and financially strapped, it had been limping along for some years in the shadow of its big rival. McIlhenny took the company over in May 1991, stamping out its last rival.

"What McIlhenny got away with is mind-boggling. No court would allow that today," Jack Blenderman had told me, at the time unaware of his company's impending fate. When he surveyed the battle-scarred history of the rivalry, he saw only foul play aimed at driving his company out of the tabasco business.

"If you knew anything about Louisiana politics, you would

understand why we lost at the end. The McIlhennys were powerful and well connected," Blenderman said, in an obvious reference to the state's reputation for outlandish politics. "If we had deep pockets today, we would give them a run for their money."

The way Blenderman saw it, not being able to call a tabasco a tabasco is like being forced to sell Darjeeling tea simply as tea. Or having to leave out the name Idaho from a bag of Idaho potatoes. Or not being able to identify an Indian River orange as an Indian River orange.

I would have considered the controversy nothing more than an interesting story, except that I came across other people in Louisiana—which is to pepper sauce what Florida is to orange juice and Idaho is to potatoes—who get easily riled up over how the tabasco pepper has been usurped by McIlhenny.

"If there's anyone whose name should be associated with tabasco pepper it should be my great-grandfather, Maunsel White," declared John Tobin White, age eighty-three, who bottles a "private label" pepper sauce in New Orleans, which he prepares in accordance with a pre–Civil War recipe of his ancestor. It's made of what's known as Louisiana hot peppers. He labels it Maunsel White 1812. "Maunsel White was the first to cultivate the tabasco pepper. He was the first to make a sauce of it, but he never cared to make a business enterprise of it," White told me. He said that after his great-grandfather and grandfather died, "Edmund McIlhenny tried to get my grandmother to testify that it was he and not Maunsel White who invented the name tabasco." John White's grandmother was Betty Bradford, a niece of Jefferson Davis, president of the Confederate States between 1861 and 1865. "She said she had no interest."

I dug up the suits, testimony, correspondence, exhibits, and other evidence in federal archives and the Library of Congress. What emerges is that there wasn't much basis for anyone to claim an exclusive right to the name; the McIlhenny claims were based on stories that, like the pepper sauce, were a blend of esoteric ingredients—fact and hearsay. Ultimately, how the tabasco pepper became, for all practical purposes, private property is a story of how business sometimes is done.

The McIlhenny clan has maintained that Friend Gleason gave Edmund McIlhenny a handful of tabasco peppers. He was the young Confederate soldier who, returning from Mexico, it is said, brought the peppers from the Tabasco region. And they contend that it's those peppers that Edmund McIlhenny planted on Avery Island in 1862 that launched his pepper-sauce business in 1868. The McIlhennys also have argued that over the years, through the protective family custody that has prevented infusion of outside genes into the fruit, their tabasco peppers have taken on unique physical and sensory qualities that make them distinct from those found in their original habitat. More important, they have maintained that it was they who gave the pepper its current name. Prior to that, they assert, the pepper wasn't known as the tabasco but as the "bird pepper" or by some generic name. This story is now a McIlhenny legend.

The recorded history of tabasco sauce, however, starts with Maunsel White in Louisiana and predates Edmund McIlhenny's venture.

First, a bit about White, who seems to have had just the right dash to bottle the elixir. He had landed in Louisville, Kentucky, as an orphan from Tipperary, Ireland, and in 1800, when he was nineteen, he moved to New Orleans to make his fortune. The small city was rapidly growing then into a busy commercial center; ships and steamboats plied the waters with goods and slaves. Ambitious and cunning, White wasn't going to lurk in the bottom layers of the predominantly French society. Soon after finding a job as an accounting clerk, he set out to learn French and spent half his monthly salary of sixteen dollars on his lessons. Before too long, with his dashing looks and a cultivated fondness for silk vests, scarves, and fine wines, he slipped into society life. It was natural that he should one day meet General Pierre Denise de la Ronde and marry his daughter. White settled down into the secure life of a banker and plantation owner, befriending the likes of Andrew Jackson.

Eating was then, as ever, a favorite pastime of the city's wealthy merchants and the landed gentry. "Good eating held the place in people's lives that TV and the World Series hold today," Bernard F. Trappey, Jr., would write in a newspaper column in 1956. It was Trappey's father who had founded the pepper sauce company of that name. Trappey wrote that it was the discovery of herbs and spices that lent a dimension of gaiety to New Orleans cooking and eating. The tradition started, he wrote, with the arrival of Acadians in 1755 to Louisiana's bayou country. The settlers from Nova Scotia, who had been rejected by other American colonies, took to the native herbs and roots used by the Attakapas Indians and combined them with the piquant spices brought by the Spaniards. Then the French added refinements. At wealthy plantations, hospitality was expressed with bubbling Acadian or Creole secrets in iron caldrons. In 1885 the Ancient Order of Creole Gourmets was formed in New Iberia, the heart of Creole and Acadian country.

"A high-liver and epicure" is how a contemporary described Maunsel White. At his Deer Range plantation on the Mississippi River south of New Orleans, White loved showing off as a consummate gourmet before invited guests. He even sent two of his kitchen slaves to Paris to learn French cooking. He was especially adept at making sauces, having been influenced by the French predilection for coating, basting, and bathing foods in buttery sauces. He experimented with herbs and spices. When he discovered tabasco, he found his talisman.

White's attention must have been drawn by the tabasco because, unlike any other hot peppers, it is juicy: a squeeze easily yields six to eight fiery drops. There were other peppers available at that time, brought by slaves from Africa and by the Spaniards from Mexico, but they were good for garnishing a dish or for using in cooking. Now here was a pepper that didn't need to be chopped or puréed to extract its pungency, just squeezed like a lemon. It was ideal for making a refined pepper sauce.

White combined tabasco juice with orange wine and spices in several different proportions until he hit upon the one that met with his approval. The sauce became a fixture on his dining table; he would habitually reach for it to douse his eggs, oysters, fish, peas, beans—even corn muffins. When he traveled, the sauce went along with him, in his vest pocket. At the Gem Restaurant in New Orleans, he was often found sitting behind mounds of oysters with a bottle of his concoction in one hand.

Now the question: Where did White find tabasco peppers in the 1850s? That was years before Edmund McIlhenny reportedly planted his first tabasco seeds. The peppers, more than likely, were arriving from the Tabasco region of Mexico with American soldiers returning from the Mexican War. New Orleans was a major port. Bags of tabasco pepper were being sold in local markets. Some vendors, perhaps taken by the novelty of this pepper, even advertised in local newspapers. By 1851 the pepper had become a popular and regular import from Tabasco. That year *Schooner Manuelito* arrived in New Orleans with "200 qtts. logwood, and 33 bags of pepper," among other items. In December 1854 *Schooner Rayo* brought "33 hides, 11 bales of pepper, 118 pcs of mahogany, 8000 oranges." It must have been a popular item, for in his 1872 history of the Mexican province, "History of Tabasco," Manuel Gil y Saenz documented the region's attributes thus: "We have, besides Tabasco pepper. . . ."

Maunsel White was the man who popularized tabasco sauce. The story has it that the sauce made its formal debut at a dinner White gave for Andrew Jackson. Visitors to his plantation usually left with a bottle of the potion, and even acquaintances demanded one. To keep up with the private demand, he had his slaves plant fields of tabasco pepper. And before he knew it he had launched a pepper-sauce business, supplying private clubs, restaurants, and apothecaries. The enterprise was driven not so much by commerce but as a diversion. Highly esteemed as a successful merchant and banker and as overseer of the construction of the state capital in Baton Rouge, White delighted in the eccentricity of his tabasco connection.

The sauce was sold under the name Maunsel White; although White and his plantation slaves called the pepper tabasco, his name had a greater cachet. His son once said about him, "First he made a name, then the name made money."

So closely linked was White's name to tabasco that it gave the impression that the maverick businessman had built his entire reputation on the pepper. "Col. White has introduced the celebrated Tabasco red pepper, the very strongest of all peppers, of which he has cultivated a large quantity with a view of supplying his neighbors, and diffusing it through the state . . ." said a story in the *Daily True Delta* of New Orleans on January 26, 1850. It also extolled the sauce's virtues:

> A single drop of [his] sauce will flavor a whole plate of soup or other food. The use of a decoction like this, particularly in preparing the food for laboring persons, would be found exceedingly beneficial in a relaxing climate like this. Col. White has not had a single case of cholera among his large gang of Negroes since that disease appeared in the South. He attributes this to the free use of this valuable agent.

White's slaves would deliver the sauce to grocers in big "porter" bottles, which sold for five dollars each. The grocers then transferred it into vase-shaped four-and-a-half-inch-tall glass bottles and labeled them Maunsel White. Some added the description: "Tabasco Pepper Sauce." The seasonal arrival of his sauce created the same sort of fuss among the high livers as Beaujolais Nouveau does today soon after leaving the French wineries each autumn. An announcement in the *Daily True Delta* of New Orleans trumpeted on March 9, 1853:

Amateurs, Connoisseurs, and Bon Vivants
Attention!!!
Maunsel White's Concentrated Essence of Tobasco
Peppers
The undersigned has just received a consignment of
the above celebrated Pepper Sauce which he offers to
the public at reduced prices.
—E. Monteuse, Wholesale Druggist, Corner
Chartres and Bienville Streets

Maunsel White died in 1862. While his descendants didn't
make a serious go of the sauce business, a number of other
tabasco sauces soon entered the market. But no one among them
would make an entry as forcefully as did Edmund McIlhenny.
Edmund's tack was to patent his recipe. White never had; in fact,
he gave his recipe out freely to anyone who wanted it, and a lot of
sauces on the market were slight variations of his. Edmund
McIlhenny wanted his sauce to be unique in the market. Thus he
patented in 1870 not the name "Tabasco," which was already
used generically in Louisiana to describe pepper sauces, but his
method of preparing the sauce. "This invention relates to a new
process of preparing an aromatic and strong sauce from the
pepper known in the market as Tabasco Pepper. This pepper is as
strong as Cayenne pepper but of finer flavor," McIlhenny declared in his patent application.

One thing peculiar to pepper sauce and not to tomato or
Worcestershire sauce: no single formula appeases equally a
majority of the populace. Even though Tabasco is the most
widely used sauce in the world—much of it to spice drinks and
oysters—pepper eaters generally have developed loyalties to
other hot sauces to spike their soups and stews. Proof is the
huge number of pepper sauces currently on the market.
Louisiana alone puts out an estimated 100 different varieties
of pepper sauces. One collector in Louisiana told me he had in
his possession 402 bottles of different sauces—collected from
Mombasa and Mozambique, from Cochabamba and Calcutta,

from Yucatán and Jamaica, from Cambodia, Malaysia, and Thailand. The main reason so many sauces exist is that the pepper works on people's imagination as no other fruit or vegetable does. Secret recipes are handed down, and even auspicious moments and rituals are observed in their preparations. At the turn of the century, medical claims—the pepper's ability to improve digestion and cure cholera and yellow fever—also sparked the proliferation of these fiery sauces. In Louisiana, tabasco sauce was once the hottest-selling item on the shelves of the apothecary.

McIlhenny came up against some tough competition. Bernard Trappey, the feistiest of McIlhenny's rivals, launched his tabasco sauce in 1896. In 1901 C. P. Moss of New Iberia was bottling tabasco sauce, as was Christian Shertz of New Orleans; Hirsch Brothers Tobasco Co. of Louisville was making Hirsch Tobasco Sauce the same year. In 1898 J. O. Grevenburg at Morgan City, Louisiana, was bottling Grevenburg's Tobasco Pepper Sauce; Sunset Tobasco Sauce was being made by Louisiana Tobasco Pepper Sauce Co. in Lake Charles, Louisiana; Francis H. Leggett & Co. was making tabasco sauce in New York, as were McMechen Preserving Co. in Wheeling, West Virginia; Reed, Murdock & Co. in Chicago; A. E. Mass in Atlanta; Gust Feist & Co. in Galveston, Texas; H. J. Heinz Co. in Pittsburgh; and Campbell Soup in Philadelphia.

Edmund McIlhenny, who died in 1890, had spent considerable sums to popularize his tabasco sauce, and his heirs felt that the name tabasco had become closely associated with McIlhenny Co. So they claimed the pepper's name exclusively for themselves.

Enter: Confederate soldier Friend Gleason, the man who supposedly gave Edmund his first peppers. When the McIlhenny heirs sued competitors, they presented General Dudley Avery, Edmund's brother-in-law, to corroborate the story for the court. The sixty-eight-year-old general was ques-

tioned on November 14, 1910, at his home in Iberia Parish, where he had been living since coming out of the army in 1865.

Q: "Were you present at the time that this pepper was given to your brother-in-law by the . . . Confederate soldier?"

A: "No, sir, but I remember his speaking to me about it when he came home, and showing me the peppers, which were dried, and he had them in his vest pocket, wrapped in a piece of paper, a half dozen of them or so."

Who was this mysterious chap, the Confederate soldier? It's puzzling that he wasn't put on the witness stand. Perhaps he was never found. I asked Paul McIlhenny, the head of McIlhenny's manufacturing and marketing, about that. "All that is known is that his name was Friend Gleason," he said, and added that he had been trying to trace this man's history. He showed me a letter he had recently received. "Take it with a grain of salt, although the name and the dates sort of make sense," he told me.

The letter, dated April 28, 1988, was from one Harvey G. Gleason, supposedly Friend Gleason's grandson. It read:

> I asked the family historian, my aunt Helen Kingsley of Alexandria, [who] doubted that anyone named Friend Gleason would have passed through Avery Island in the 1840s . . .
>
> She said the most likely Gleason would have been Cyrus King Gleason, [who] was taken prisoner by the Mexicans; suffered by their cruelty, but finally escaped by digging under the prison walls; got aboard a vessel and arrived in New York in June 1844; . . . After leaving Mexico, he probably never wanted to see another pepper for the rest of his life, and he dumped all he had at Avery Island.

Neither the dates nor the place make any sense, for Edmund planted his seeds some twenty years after this Cyrus Gleason's ship touched New Orleans, if it did, en route to New York. In any case, after this mysterious Gleason "dumped" his peppers on Avery Island, the peppers apparently took on an altogether different profile from that of their ancestors in Mexico. They became bigger, redder, and juicier, the McIlhenny heirs asserted. Lest the courts didn't believe it, John McIlhenny, the founder's son, was ready as a witness. He told the courts that when he traveled to Mexico in 1890 to procure tabasco peppers because much of his father's crop had failed the previous year, he found none that resembled the peppers of Avery Island:

> I went to the City of Mexico and made a careful search in the markets and failed to find any pepper

which resembled Tabasco pepper. . . . I rode from the City of Mexico down to Oaxaca and not finding any pepper there I rode down to the City of Chiapas. . . . I then went into the state of Tabasco, going as far east as the capital, San Juan Batista, but I didn't find any Tabasco pepper and I returned to the United States without a pod that at all resembled Tabasco, a sample of which I had taken with me. I can state that in the year 1890 there was no pepper in the State of Tabasco known as tabasco pepper.

The McIlhenny heirs also marshaled the help of prominent botanists, who obliged, ignoring the fact that the founder had already acknowledged in the 1870 patent that the sauce was made from "the pepper known in the market as Tabasco Pepper." (His descendants later would go to lengths to explain that the patent application was in error; what Edmund McIlhenny meant was not "Tabasco" but rather the pepper commonly known as "bird pepper.") Nor did the botanists acknowledge the existence of periodicals in the Library of Congress in which Maunsel White was credited with cultivating tabasco peppers as far back as 1850, twenty years before Edmund McIlhenny obtained a patent for his sauce.

The variety "now recognized as Tabasco pepper undoubtedly had its origin in the pepper grown by Mr. McIlhenny at New Iberia," declared Lyster H. Dewey, assistant botanist of the U.S. Department of Agriculture, on February 7, 1901. Support also came from one of the most prominent botanists of the time, H. C. Irish of the Missouri Botanical Garden. In 1898 Irish had published *A Revision of the Genus Capsicum,* the first comprehensive classification of peppers. He testified that he had credited in the book Dr. E. L. Sturtevant of the New York Botanical Garden for naming the pepper Tabasco, and that Dr. Sturtevant had named the pepper after McIlhenny's sauce by that name. Irish also told the court that he hadn't come across any prior reference to the tabasco pepper in his garden's extensive library, which he described as "one of the best in the country."

It's possible that the elusive Friend Gleason did give some tabasco peppers to Edmund McIlhenny. It is also, of course, entirely possible that Edmund obtained the pods from local markets that were getting shipments from Tabasco and then, seeking a commercial advantage, used the story of the soldier to establish his pods' uniqueness.

It's also possible that his source was none other than the easygoing Maunsel White himself. Edmund's brother-in-law, General Avery, knew White well and was a frequent dinner guest at his Deer Range plantation. Sallie Huling, who was about twenty-five years old when Edmund is supposed to have concocted his sauce, often stopped by at Deer Range to see the Whites and their four children. She would later testify that she had heard on her visits that "a Mr. McIlhenny had come down to Deer Range" and that Maunsel White gave him "a number of pods of pepper, and also gave him the secret process" for making the sauce.

In 1905 or 1906—Sallie Huling wasn't sure—Edmund's widow, Mary McIlhenny, traveled from New Iberia to visit Maunsel White's widow in New Orleans. Mrs. McIlhenny, who all these years had been in the midst of the tabasco tempest and probably had no reason to doubt the company legend, wanted to hear firsthand who actually had invented the name tabasco for the pepper. "When Mrs. White told her the truth," Huling said in her testimony, "she cried."

The tabasco controversy reached the courts when Mc-Ilhenny tried to register the name tabasco under a newly instituted trademark law. Congress's Trademark Act of 1905 allowed registration of a product that had been manufactured exclusively for ten years prior to 1905. Soon after McIlhenny obtained the registration, Bernard Trappey, the founder of Trappey's, petitioned the U.S. Patent Office in Washington, D.C., to cancel it. The patent office agreed in 1909 with Trappey, as would the court of appeals in Washington later, that tabasco was not only the name of a place but also the name of a recognized pepper and thus couldn't be claimed as an exclusive property by anyone.

The McIlhennys would later find themselves in more trouble in connection with their registration application. They had claimed—as they had to in order to qualify under the new law—that McIlhenny was the sole manufacturer of tabasco sauce in the ten years prior to 1905. That wasn't, of course, true because during that period there were nearly a dozen manufacturers that had been competing with their company. The misrepresentation became an issue later when Trappey sued McIlhenny in the Louisiana Supreme Court for informing grocers, restaurants, and other customers that it had obtained a patent that gave it the exclusive right to the name tabasco. In imposing a $5,000 fine on McIlhenny Company in 1912, the court chastised it for deceiving the U.S. Patent Office. The court was particularly miffed because the false registration application had been signed by John McIlhenny, the founder's son, who was now a U.S. Civil Service Commissioner in Washington. (John, who signed on with Teddy Roosevelt's group of Rough Riders, left the company to his brothers in 1906. He was the first member of the family of Confederate supporters to swear allegiance to the United States after the Civil War.) The infraction was brought to the attention of President Roosevelt, who, in turn, directed an aide to look into the matter.

To "relieve himself of the moral fraud implied," John McIlhenny admitted "his grave error"—and blamed it on his lawyers. He said he had sworn to the false statement "upon the advice of counsel and against his own convictions."

Such setbacks, however, didn't deter the McIlhenny heirs from going after competitors. And they did, one at a time. Gust Feist of Texas was one of their first targets.

Feist was from New Orleans and was familiar with Louisiana hot sauces. After moving to Texas, he devoted a few years to formulating a tabasco sauce that would keep in a bottle for a long time without the mashed tabasco separating from the liquid. (It was a difficult feat; the sauces that separated into a clear liquid in the top half of the bottle and red sediment in the bottom failed in the market.) Feist succeeded in preparing his "perfect blend" in the fall of 1895, and by the next year his sauce was showing up on tables in Texas restaurants and hotels. That same year Mary McIlhenny happened to vacation at one of those hotels. Feist recalled that he was visited at his factory by a mysterious "lady" who identified herself as a customer charmed by his sauce. Feist would later recall that this charming lady was none other than Mary McIlhenny. Soon he was charged by McIlhenny lawyers with illegally using the name tabasco. And not resting there, McIlhenny also cut its prices to take business away from Feist's in Texas. An incensed Feist fired off an angry response:

> . . . After all my years of work to perfect my Tabasco
> Pepper Sauce, I do not propose to stay out of the
> market nor be cut out of its sale, for, if compelled, I
> shall cut my price half in two before I stay out. . . . I, as
> well as anybody else, can manufacture Tabasco Sauce
> and call it such and sell it . . .

McIlhenny sued Feist. But the U.S. District Court in Galveston refused to give the McIlhenny heirs "exclusive use or ownership of the name Tabasco" on the ground that it was the name of a Mexican territory as well as a pepper.

The case, however, ended with a peculiar turn. McIlhenny paid Feist $2,500 for whatever "rights" to the word tabasco he had won as a result of the favorable court decision. In return, Feist agreed to drop the tabasco sauce from his product line. That arrangement wasn't all that bad for Feist, for he wasn't dependent on this product. Moreover, competition was heating up. For McIlhenny, on the other hand, pepper sauce was the entire business.

McIlhenny targeted restaurants as well, including Whyte's Restaurant at 145 Fulton Street in New York City. When Edward McIlhenny went there for lunch on February 26, 1914, and asked for tabasco, he was served a Louisiana sauce made not by his father but by Lowell Gaidry. McIlhenny sued the restaurant owner for carrying an "illegal product." Gaidry, the manufacturer, promised to join in the fight on behalf of the restaurateur but withdrew at the last minute for tactical reasons: he wanted to fight McIlhenny on their home turf, New Orleans. Without Gaidry's support, Whyte's had little choice but to sign a decree that prohibited it from serving a tabasco pepper sauce that wasn't made by McIlhenny.

Whyte's capitulation in New York and Feist's agreement in Texas to quit the tabasco sauce business gave the impression that McIlhenny was winning his claim to the tabasco name. Indeed, McIlhenny sent out circulars to its distributors and customers informing them that two courts had acknowledged its right to the name tabasco. That sent Gaidry's customers into a panic. "Do not ship us any more Tabasco Sauce. See letter," telegrammed Sprague, Warner & Co. of Chicago, on May 26, 1915. Corbett & Schmitt, a manufacturers' representative in New York, wrote that another wholesaler had "four or five cases of Gaidry's Tabasco Pepper Sauce upstairs now and would not dare to sell it."

But Lowell Gaidry was not a pushover. He had built a considerable reputation for his sauce and was known outside of Louisiana. In 1914 directors of a new industrial park in Atascadero, California, had taken on the challenge of selling 100,000 bottles of his tabasco sauce in order to get him to move his factory to the industrial park. Even the *Woman's National Weekly* had taken up the cause, urging under banner headlines that every reader of the paper "not only send in an order for at least one bottle of the delicious condiment, but also insist upon his or her grocer placing an order for a dozen or more under the assurance that you will help him dispose of them."

With much at stake, Gaidry sued McIlhenny, and won in the U.S. District Court in New Orleans. Judge Rufus E. Foster agreed that Gaidry had been financially damaged by McIlhenny's false claims, which had scared customers into shunning Gaidry's sauce. The judge awarded Gaidry $1,000 plus interest.

One would have thought that after all these debilitating setbacks, the McIlhenny clan would have pulled in their horns and competed on marketing prowess and sauce quality. But the McIlhenny heirs relentlessly pursued their fight from one court to another, primarily in Louisiana, where Edmund's father-in-law once had been a Circuit Court judge. And for reasons that puzzle many, McIlhenny's luck suddenly began to change in the early 1920s.

McIlhenny now was claiming that even though it didn't have a registered trademark for tabasco it had earned one through its long use of the name. Its biggest break came in a surprising ruling by the federal appeals court in New Orleans, the Fifth U.S. Circuit Court of Appeals, which agreed that tabasco sauce now meant a McIlhenny sauce and reversed Judge Foster's $1,000 award against the company. The court, just one step below the U.S. Supreme Court, ruled that McIlhenny's claim of "a common-law trade-mark" for the word tabasco was in "good faith" and its warnings to dealers against invasion of its supposed rights didn't make it liable for damages. This opinion meant that Trappey and others who described their product as Tabasco Pepper Sauce weren't trading fairly.

The decision astonished Trappey's lawyers, who now held out little hope that they could get the court to reverse itself. "It is most improbable that a serious court like the Circuit Court of Appeals of the Fifth Circuit will admit any error upon a plain question of unfair competition," they advised their client. They suggested compromise.

All was not lost, the lawyers consoled Bernard Trappey. The court hadn't, after all, enjoined McIlhenny's competitors from using the word altogether. The court had merely held that only McIlhenny could use the form Tabasco Pepper Sauce. The lawyers suggested four alternative labels for Trappey's sauce:

> Decoction of Tabasco Pepper
> Essence of Tabasco Pepper
> Extract of Tabasco Pepper
> Sauce of Tabasco Pepper

But Bernard Trappey wasn't going to be intimidated. After all, he hadn't made it to where he was by being a wimp. He had started his career as a blacksmith for Edmund McIlhenny; and then one day he had walked off Avery Island with a pocketful of tabasco peppers to launch his own sauce. He didn't have the McIlhenny lineage, but in the bayou country he was now commanding no less respect. He was prepared to take the issue all the way to the U.S. Supreme Court. Trappey decided to defy the federal appeals court, as did other McIlhenny competitors— ultimately such contempt of court would contribute to their downfall.

Other courts in which McIlhenny had sued one or the other competitor were irritated that Trappey, who was leading the fight, continued to market his sauce as Tabasco Pepper Sauce and even advertised it thus on a big billboard near his factory in Jeanerette. In a strange reversal of position, Judge Foster himself ruled that Trappey was trading on McIlhenny's "goodwill" and fined him $5,073. To send a strong message to other sauce makers, another Louisiana court slapped Edward Bulliard with a $5,000 fine. Bulliard had described his sauce as Made from Tabasco Peppers, all right, as he was supposed to under a 1926 decree he had signed, but he had refused to add the rest of the long and ludicrous qualifying message: "But this is not the old, established tabasco sauce, which is the pepper sauce manufactured for many years by McIlhenny Co. and its predecessors."

Trappey was counting on the U.S. Supreme Court for help, but the nation's highest court didn't come through. It declined to hear his petition on the ground that the matter didn't affect a sufficient number of people. Facing contempt of court in Louisiana and no chance of an appeal, Trappey found himself cornered.

McIlhenny, now seen increasingly as the victim by the Louisiana courts, became reluctant to give any ground to Trappey, as it might have before; in fact, it went for the kill. Its lawyers wrote Trappey that they would try to prevent him from using the name tabasco altogether on the ground that "as a practical matter" his sauce would be bought and sold and served whenever "tabasco is asked for." The lawyers taunted him that they wouldn't have any trouble getting affidavits to that effect from restaurant owners. "If Trappey wants to prevent the entry of such a judgment, or to put it mildly, the danger of having such a judgment entered against him, which we believe is an imminent danger, the way is open to him," McIlhenny's lawyers asserted.

The nearly five decades of battle against McIlhenny had worn Bernard Trappey down. A good part of the company's resources had been drained in the fight against his rival. In May 1926 Citizens Bank of Jeanerette, in which Trappey had accounts, filed for liquidation. "From indications, it appears that the business of this bank was carried on very loosely; money was loaned without sufficient security and that in many instances the banking laws were violated," Trappey wrote to his lawyer in New Orleans. "If such should be the facts, would this have any bearing in our particular case?" He was desperately trying to get the court damages against his company waived.

The Trappey heirs also were getting nervous about spending more money to continue the fight. Trappey considered banding together with other McIlhenny competitors to raise money and support to prove to the U.S. Supreme Court that the tabasco issue affected quite a large number of people. He apparently ran into opposition from within his own family. Says Jack Blenderman, the former head of the company, "Trappey's descendants were totally dependent on this company for their livelihoods. They didn't want money wasted anymore on hot sauce. The company was canning dozens of other products. The pepper sauce was just one."

Broken by the long battle, B. F. Trappey's Sons would sign a series of restrictive agreements to meet McIlhenny's demands—some under court order and some under the threat of more suits—and relinquish, among other things, the name tabasco. Its sauce would become simply Trappey's Pepper Sauce.

McIlhenny's victories, however, haven't altogether stopped others from calling their sauce tabasco. Most of them are blatant violators; they even copy McIlhenny's familiar bottle to the last detail. In his office, Edmund McIlhenny Jr., the great-grandson of the founder, points to imitation tabasco sauces from all over the world. Nine such bottles are neatly lined up on his desk. An antique china closet in the office contains six dozen more. Most look identical to McIlhenny's brand—the diamond-shaped label, the concentric circles, the familiar octagonal red cap, the green neck band. "All imitations," Edmund told me. The counterfeits were from India, Zaire, Japan, Colombia, Turkey, Mexico, Louisiana, and Tennessee. "At least we are being noticed, but I have three children to educate."

The proliferation of counterfeits keeps him busy fighting trademark infringements. He's the company's in-house legal counsel, but he relies heavily on two law firms that specialize in trademark cases, one nationally and the other internationally. Like his ancestors, he said, he pops into local supermarkets and grocery stores when he travels. If a bottle resembles Mc-Ilhenny's even slightly, he buys it and launches an investigation. "We welcome competition, but we say please do not trade on our goodwill. There is no secret ingredient in our sauce; it is pepper, vinegar, and salt. It is not difficult to duplicate. But the sauce without the Tabasco name will be hard to sell."

Infringement invites McIlhenny's wrath with full force. And you don't have to be a sauce maker to get onto McIlhenny's bad side. Consider the case of Ms. Evangeline Tabasco, a New York City artist.

Ms. Tabasco received a letter in 1979 from McIlhenny's head of marketing and manufacturing, Paul McIlhenny:

> Can you shed some light on the origin and background of your name? Could you or your forebears have come from St. Martinville, Louisiana?
>
> As I'm sure you are aware, the word TABASCO when applied to a food product is the registered and active trademark of our company. We do know that a state, a river, and several towns go by the name Tabasco in Mexico, but we've never seen it used as a person's name. Any information you can provide us with would be appreciated.

Ms. Tabasco, it turned out, was the professional name of Sam Wiener, who specializes in collages and assemblages intended as visual puns on art itself. Why did Sam Wiener adopt the name Evangeline Tabasco? He had come from Louisiana, and "so the name came naturally from Evangeline hot sauce and Tabasco sauce, both native products . . ."

When that information reached Paul McIlhenny, the next letter naturally came not from him but from his lawyer, Julius R. Lunsford, Jr., who is based in Atlanta and whose firm represents major American corporations in trademark issues. "This use of our client's registered trademark is both improper and illegal . . . ," Lunsford wrote.

The exchanges continued for a while (with no resolution to the dispute):

> Your letter reminded me of a friend I haven't seen for many years. I think it was right after the war that Kraft, or was it Borden Co., got real mad at my friend Willie Philadelphia, and tried to get him to change his name. Willie, as you may recall, achieved some notoriety back then as a flagpole sitter. The case never reached court, as I recollect it, because the company backed off when the city of Philadelphia offered to send in a bunch of Philadelphia lawyers as friends of the court or something.
>
> —Tabasco

> . . . We would like to remind you that this situation occurred prior to the enactment of the present Federal Trademark Statute commonly referred to as the Lanham Act. . . . It is sincerely hoped that you will appreciate and respect our client's position by adopting a name that will not falsely suggest a connection with McIlhenny Company. . . .
>
> —Lunsford, Jr.

> . . . I can only say that if you saw my art work, rather than focusing solely upon my name, I feel certain you would understand that it is the work that's important. For as Will Shakespeare put it: "What's in a name? That which we call a rose / By another name would smell as sweet" . . .
>
> —Tabasco

> Dear Mr. Wiener or Ms. Tabasco . . . Your quotation from Romeo and Juliet is interesting but the quotation from Othello is much more important. You may recall that Shakespeare said therein: "He who steals my purse will not enrich him, but will make me very poor indeed." . . .
>
> —Lunsford, Jr.

• • •

When Walter Greenleaf, professor of horticulture at Auburn University in Auburn, Alabama, got in trouble with McIlhenny, the exchanges weren't all that witty. They were vitriolic.

At issue was a new variety of tabasco pepper the professor developed in 1970; he called it Greenleaf Tabasco. The company wanted this pepper banned or given an altogether different name.

Actually, McIlhenny initially was ecstatic that this pepper was being developed by Dr. Greenleaf, because it was, unlike all other tabasco peppers, resistant to the debilitating tobacco etch virus. Dr. Greenleaf stumbled onto it rather unintentionally; he had been trying to develop a pimiento pepper that would be resistant to the virus. This virus originates in tobacco plants and devastates a number of different varieties of peppers, most ruthlessly the tabasco. So even though the pimiento, the sweet bell-type pepper, was his target he decided to first study the behavior of the virus in tabasco.

Dr. Greenleaf had learned from a plant pathologist at Campbell Soup that there was a Peruvian pepper, a chinense species, that had a gene resistant to tobacco etch virus. He procured the pepper and found that the tabasco accepted the Peruvian gene more readily than the pimiento did. Considering how difficult it is to transfer a desirable gene into a plant, his accidental feat created a sensation in the pepper industry. When McIlhenny heard about it, Dr. Greenleaf said that top executives of the company came to see him and gave him financial support to complete the development work. It took ten years of crossbreeding to come up with a tabasco that was proven to be permanently resistant to tobacco etch virus. That should have been a cause for celebration for McIlhenny— except that Dr. Greenleaf called his pepper Greenleaf Tabasco, as required by the protocol of research. He and his colleagues reported their work in a glossy ten-page pamphlet published by Auburn's Agricultural Experiment Station in December 1970.

That sent the McIlhenny people into a rage, said Dr. Greenleaf, because the work of an agricultural station funded by taxpayers becomes public property. "Since McIlhenny couldn't have an exclusive right to this pepper, they wanted me to call it just Greenleaf Pepper." A high-level McIlhenny executive had suggested other names as well: Louisianne, or Acadian, or Auburn, or Greenleaf wilt-resistant pepper. "To our way of looking at it, however, by attaching your name to the development, you would achieve the maximum benefits you are trying to accomplish," the executive urged Dr. Greenleaf in a letter.

McIlhenny's concern was obvious. Now there was a pepper that was out of the hands of the company but still a tabasco. What claim could it lay to this pepper that was genetically different from the tabasco Edmund McIlhenny, the founder, had asserted was unique and proprietary? Even the name tabascan, which Dr. Greenleaf had suggested at one point as a compromise, wouldn't meet with McIlhenny's approval. "As you can appreciate, a manufacturer of hot sauce emphasizing a word such as tabascan would tend to dilute the McIlhenny Company trademark TABASCO and force us to take costly legal action. We appeal to your sense of justice," the McIlhenny official implored.

I asked Dr. Greenleaf, who's now retired, why he hadn't just called his new variety Greenleaf Pepper.

"Why should I have?" he said. "It was a tabasco pepper."

When he refused to change the pepper's name, McIlhenny threatened to sue him and the university. "I received all kinds of nasty letters from the company lawyers," he said. "The university people—the administrator and the director of agricultural station—instead of supporting me told me I was embarrassing the university. The atmosphere was inimical, but I had tenure and they couldn't fire me." Auburn University's attorneys declined to comment on the incident.

"The matter was finally put to rest when it was turned over to the U.S. Attorney General's office," Dr. Greenleaf said. Meanwhile, Dr. Charles B. Heiser, professor of botany at

Indiana University in Bloomington, had been enlisted by McIlhenny to investigate whether Dr. Greenleaf's christening of the pepper could be voided under some loophole in the International Code of Nomenclature of Cultivated Plants. "Since the name Greenleaf Tabasco has been validly published I'm afraid that we shall have to live with it," Dr. Heiser informed McIlhenny.

Dr. Greenleaf now sells the seeds of Greenleaf Tabasco to seed companies and prepares a sauce from the pepper for himself and his friends. "I want to keep this Greenleaf Tabasco alive," he told me.

Dr. Greenleaf had an epilogue to tell. Some years after his skirmishes with McIlhenny, he was visited by "a McIlhenny field man." It wasn't to pick another fight; the visitor wanted some seeds of Greenleaf Tabasco, and Dr. Greenleaf obliged.

"The field man said McIlhenny needed them, because the virus was devastating its tabasco plants in Louisiana," Dr. Greenleaf said. "There won't be any tabasco sauce if there isn't any tabasco pepper left."

The Habanero

Mexico produces more varieties of pepper than any other country, and the varied uses to which it puts them frame its cuisine. In this crowded pepper field everyone has developed loyalty to one variety or another. With certain types of peppers this allegiance catapults culinary preferences into downright battles drawn along geographical and genealogical lines.

Take the habanero. About the size and shape of a walnut, it is the hottest pepper known to exist. It's also fragrant. In Mexico the Mayas claim it as their own. The pepper grows almost exclusively in Yucatán, the region in southern Mexico that is home to the Mayas. These natives eschew almost all other types of peppers with the same disdain that they have for the country's dominant European race, the legacy of Spain's "discovery" of the New World. These "outsiders," on the other hand, much prefer the milder-mannered jalapeño and serrano.

"I consider it to be a very 'off' pepper within the Mexican

context," said José Antonio Laborde, when I asked him what he thought of the habanero. He is a noted pepper expert at the Instituto Nacional de Investigaciones Agrícolas, or INIA, in Mexico. In case I'd missed the point, the urbane and scholarly man of European stock grimaced and made faces in mock convulsion. He pointed to the wide popularity of the jalapeño, which to non-Mexicans has come to symbolize the country. The dark green pepper, about two inches long, is plump and conical and imparts a sharp bite to a meal. Laborde also noted the "beautiful and crisp" serrano, a slender pepper that dons a bright green skin on its well-tapered inch-and-a-half body, and is luscious and amiably pungent. But the habanero? "Habanero is not preferred by many Mexicans because it smells like a perfume," he said.

When I repeated this to Evaristo Ordoñez Pool, a Maya, it provoked a snide smile. He is a government agricultural official in Uxmal, near Mérida, the capital of Yucatán. During my travels in Mexico one summer my curiosity about the habanero had led me to him. He said he was aware that the Europeans looked down on the habanero. "That may be because it's a Maya pepper," declared the deer-eyed, serene Maya. But then, he countered, the Mayas wouldn't be caught dead biting into a jalapeño. He described this most popular pepper as tasteless and flavorless and asserted that it causes an "intense" pain and indigestion in the Maya stomach. Some Mayas resort to the jalapeño, not grown much in Yucatán, when habanero isn't available or is too expensive. "Before I touch jalapeños, I'll eat max, or I'll eat xcatic, if I can't have habanero," Ordoñez Pool said resolutely, referring to two peppers that grow wild in Yucatán (today xcatic is also cultivated) and that the Mayas once offered to their gods. "Actually, if you ask me," he said, "if I don't have an habanero I may not eat."

I quickly sensed that the habanero in a way symbolized for the Maya their fierce independence within Mexico and that the jalapeño symbolized the European Mexican, the invader.

• • •

Before the habanero-jalapeño rivalry unfolded before me, I was strolling down the main avenue in Cancún, a tourist mecca whose every inch has been fashioned to serve the visitor. Even in the tangle of hotels, shops, and restaurants that line the boulevard facing the ocean, it was hard to miss the green-canopied restaurant bearing the name Jalapeño's. What attracted me to it was the name: it suggested specialization and, of course, a passion close to mine.

True to its name, the restaurant's menu is peppered with jalapeños: jalapeños stuffed with shrimp and Chihuahua cheese, jalapeño burgers, the day's catch with jalapeños, and strips of beef with sautéed jalapeños are but a few of the dishes. Lest the customer consider the jalapeño motif overdone, the menu takes pains to describe *Ensalada de la casa* as "House salad, without jalapeños." The menu tries to keep within boundaries tolerable to the tourist's palate, but for the asking one can get jalapeños—fresh, sautéed, puréed, or jellied—on practically every dish. There are other peppers in the kitchen refrigerator too, and some get into the customer's meal without having been advertised on the menu.

Then there also are peppers in the inventory of the kitchen but, out of respect for the uninitiated customer, absent from the menu; they are for the cooks and kitchen help and, of course, for the man who is responsible for the restaurant's peppery creations. He is a young Peruvian, Lalo Garland, who grew up with a strong affinity for hot peppers and a yearning for an unhurried life by the ocean. Those two needs were met in Cancún.

When my inquiries about peppers turned a little too complex for the man waiting on my table, he beckoned to Garland, who was in the dining room, in a white apron, chatting up patrons. Pulling up a chair, Garland declared himself "a pepper fanatic." Even something as basic as the salad he prepares for himself is generously garnished with slivers of serrano. With an impish smile spreading over his handsome face, he said he liked to "play around" with peppers in his dishes. Looking around at the packed dining room, it was clear his customers approved.

Garland is the chief chef and part owner. Summoned to the kitchen, he invited me to follow. Delighted, I jumped from my chair. On the way he suggested I start with his favorite item on the menu: jalapeño rellenos, stuffed jalapeños. He would prepare it before my very eyes, he said.

I asked him how he happened to take up cooking. Garland said he'd gone to a technical college in Houston but all along harbored the idea of becoming a chef. But not just any chef—he wanted to specialize in hot peppers. He had grown up eating the hottest of the peppers of Peru. And as a college student in Houston—a period he described as "Miller time" because of all the partying he did—he impressed young women with his improvisations in the kitchen and enjoyed watching them squirm and sweat. When he graduated, his father enlisted him to work for his oil-trading business in Houston. The oil business, fast-paced and tense, involved buying oil contracts and selling the secured supplies at higher prices, betting on demand and supply and currency-exchange rates and political events. Any one of these variables threatened to send bets asunder and turn millions of dollars of anticipated profits into sudden losses. "One mistake and you paid for it," Garland said. "One day I decided I wanted to worry about just medium-rare and well-done. The worst you could do is overcook."

He didn't go to a culinary school; instead, he took jobs in the kitchens of local restaurants. He washed dishes and worked his way up to the cutting board, to the fryer, and then to the sautéing pan. "I just wanted to learn the basics and not waste my time learning cuisines. I wanted to reserve my own imagination for that."

Garland got together with three others, formed a business partnership, and moved to Cancún in 1987, opening Jalapeño's. He became the head chef and recruited Bruce Bignold for the kitchen. Bignold, who had worked in a restaurant kitchen when he was a student, left his job as a financial analyst in Seattle to become an investor in the restaurant.

When I entered the kitchen, I thought for a moment that I was in the back of a restaurant in Chinatown. A dozen men with very Oriental features were busy at the sink, at cutting boards, and at the stoves. They were Mayas, I learned, and almost all were from Mérida. I had heard of the gentle-looking Mayas and their attachment to the ferocious habanero, but I had never seen them before. Now surrounded by all these Mayas I thought they must be an asset in a kitchen that specializes in the preparation of peppery dishes. But Garland, who hired them precisely for that reason, now finds it can be a liability. Bignold, who has the job of keeping an eye on them, told me the Maya cooks forget that not all customers have their iron stomachs. "I have to keep reminding them that they are cooking for tourists," he said.

Once in a while they ignore him, as they did one evening when one of them spotted a group of diners and was elated at the rare sight of fellow Mayas in such an upscale eatery. After the dinners were served, a minor commotion broke out among those patrons. Bignold investigated and returned to the kitchen, flustered. "No, no. They are not Mayas. They are Japanese tourists," he screamed at the cooks. Bignold said the Mayas were upset not because they had overdone it with the pepper but because the patrons turned out not to be Mayas. Not many Mayas have "made it" economically in Mexico. The sight of what looked like a prosperous group of them at Jalapeño's had given the cooks a surge of pride. "They were quite disappointed," Bignold laughed.

None of the Mayas in the kitchen spoke Spanish, so Bignold was teaching himself their language, Yucatecatl. It's a tough language, he said. At least he had succeeded at the other challenge in his job, he said: that of stomaching hot peppers. Before he joined the restaurant, he had never eaten hot food, let alone seen a fresh hot pepper. "Now I eat peppers with breakfast, with lunch, with dinner. I stop when I feel my tail is going to fall off."

Garland opened the giant refrigerator—not a walk-in, but giant nonetheless—and pulled out a straw basket of jalapeños. "I bought these this morning. Very fresh." He grinned. (Pepper, it has been my observation, often brings out a mischievous grin in the person offering it.) The inside of the refrigerator looked like a greengrocer's display: red and green tomatoes, eggplants, cucumbers, green onions, white onions, potatoes, avocados, squash, zucchini, lemons, limes, sprigs of parsley, cilantro, celery, piles of romaine lettuce, and mushrooms. Among this stock were neatly placed baskets of jalapeños and poblano, habanero, and serrano peppers. "I try not to stock too much," Garland said. "All this will be gone by tomorrow."

He selected six jalapeños, large and dumpy, and walked over to a deep fryer heating over a hot gas burner. He dropped the pods in. "I like to start with firm and crispy pods; otherwise they turn soggy by the time they're cooked." Half a minute later he retrieved the sizzling pods and wrapped them in a small towel, to induce sweating. A few minutes later he rubbed the pods between his thumb and index finger and peeled off the loosened cellophanelike skin. The once shiny pods now were an olive green with a surface porous enough to hold the breading and other ingredients that would eventually coat the pod. With a sharp knife he cut the pods from the stem down to the tip and removed the seeds and veins. Into each he rammed a thin slice of Chihuahua cheese and a large shrimp, and then he rolled the pod in a mixture of flour, crushed walnut, salt, ground peppercorn, and parsley, dipped it into an egg batter, and then gently released the whole assembly into the deep fryer. He retrieved the peppers when they had turned golden and arranged them on a plate of shredded lettuce.

I followed Garland back to my dining table. The jalapeño rellenos were hot and nutty. The dish easily beat out every other jalapeño dish—jalapeño stuffed with herring or cold tuna or cheese—I had ever eaten. Garland offered an entrée of red snapper sautéed in wine, garlic, shredded onion, tomato, and slivers of serrano pepper. "Serrano is a spicy pepper. It's hot and sweet at the same time," he said. Although it doesn't at Jalapeño's, at some restaurants this pepper also substitutes for the customary olive in a chilled martini.

Garland is at the vegetable market practically every day, early in the morning, even when he doesn't need to stock up. Even a hard night of imbibing and dancing in the local discos doesn't prevent him from observing that ritual. He will show up groggy and stroll through the market, and the ambience and the aroma of fresh produce, he said, seem to cure him immediately of the night's trauma. Actually, Garland simply loves the sight of the bounty of farms, in bursting colors and shapes, all piled high haphazardly. "I touch them, squeeze them. I bite into them. I am very happy when I am surrounded by fresh produce. I can smell the earth. I can taste the sunshine. That makes it all meaningful when I put on the apron and go to work in the kitchen," he said.

When we arrived early one morning at La Flor de Puebla, his wholesale market, he told me that he detests spices that are bottled or powdered. He fusses over the freshness of oregano and parsley. That morning, it was clear, he was going to fuss over peppers, perhaps because he had me as an audience. It was his chance to show off his infatuation with this fruit.

The market, nestled among crowded downtown shops but out of the path of the tourists, belongs to that breed of wholesale markets that are congested and noisy and slippery-floored. Empty wooden boxes are precariously piled on top of one another; air-conditioned trucks are backed to the edge of the store entrances, being emptied by carriers who are scurrying with sacks, crates, and bundles on their heads. Inside, the stores are bustling with retailers, restaurateurs, and a few housewives and maids. The scent of fresh vegetables and fruits is as strong as the musty, stale odor of the damp floors that are strewn with rotted leaves and packing straw. The combined odor is neither repulsive nor pleasant. But the balance is tipped in favor of pleasant when one draws a fresh fruit close to the nose. In selecting a pepper Garland said that one must frequently rely on the nose: sometimes the most vicious-looking pod may turn out to be as wimpy as a cucumber. "I break them open when no one

is looking," Garland said, as he made his way through alleys flanked by crates, sacks, baskets, and shelves.

Garland compared the vibrancy of the produce at the market in Cancún with that of the monotonous and faded colors in American supermarkets and greenmarkets. The green of spinach is brilliant, not muddied; the bulb of the scallion is milky white and not the yellowish hue of spoiled milk; the eggplant doesn't look bleached; the red of the tomato is so brilliant that it appears unreal. On his way to the pepper section Garland stopped to squeeze this or that vegetable. Ruby onions. White onions. Onions the size of melons, and onions the size of cherries. Yellow squash and squiggly little green squash. White eggplant, round eggplant, and eggplant the shape of cucumber. Piles of leeks and Swiss chard. Piles of cilantro, spinach, Bibb lettuce. Melons the size of onions, and melons the size of soccer balls. Tomatoes so thick with meat that the fragile skin barely contains it. The piles looked like the crumbling pyramids at Maya ruins. Shoppers said *"Perdón"* and squeezed past each other in the aisles, making sure they didn't turn the store into a giant bowl of tossed salad.

A man scratched a jalapeño with his right thumb and smelled the pepper. "How much are the jalapeños?" he shouted across to the register.

Garland bit a chunk out of a jalapeño, then threw the rest back into the bin. "If you want to stuff a jalapeño, you have to be sure it is not so hot that you need beer as a chaser. If it's too mild, you might as well stuff a cucumber. I look for the right balance. This balance . . . is in your mind, and you try to find a batch of peppers that matches the taste in your brain. Sometimes you

find it, sometimes you don't." Garland seemed to enjoy the exercise.

The pepper section of the market consisted of twenty-two crates—actually plastic laundry baskets—blue and red, eleven in a row, two deep, on slanted shelves. Signs identified their contents: Chile morrón. Chile poblano. Large chile habanero, and small chile habanero. Chile serrano. Chile xcatic. Chile dulce. Jalapeños. Chile pimiento.

There were as many varieties of dried and smoked chiles as there were fresh. Many of them weren't identified; perhaps they were too common. There was one that was dark red, the size of a small eggplant, and wrinkly. A crate full of flattened peppers that were black and the size of large cookies. Pea-size bright red peppers. Long salmon-red peppers the size and shape of string beans. Some were labeled: Chile piquín. Chile de arbol. Chile mulato. Chile seco. Chile ancho. Chile guajillo. Chile pasilla.

"How much the poblanos?" a customer called out.

"One thousand one hundred," one of the men behind the counter shouted back from across the room. The customer squeezed a few of the poblanos and moved on.

"Four kilos jala-pe-ños," shouted a man near the bin of fresh jalapeños.

Garland whispered to me the poblanos were not that fresh that day. A bit wrinkly, he said. "Poblanos have to be like a baby's bottom. No wrinkles, no brown spots." It was quickly apparent that the best ones were in cold storage in the back, for customers like Garland who get extra attention from the wholesaler. He walked straight into the storage room, followed by an attendant, and cracked open a poblano from the pile of grayish green oblong peppers. He ordered six dozen as he chewed the broken piece of poblano as one would a carrot. Back in the crowd, he assured me that the wrinkly poblanos in the front of the store would sell easily. "It's a staple on the menu of all restaurants."

Poblanos attracted more customers than any other chile in

the produce market. An elderly woman squeezed and smelled each poblano before she carefully dropped it in her little burlap bag. Another buyer followed, but was more finicky: he matched each pod for size and shape. The supple pepper approximates a medium-size oblong eggplant. It is Mexico's most-stuffed pepper: filled with cheese and served under a spicy tomato sauce, it is called chile relleno. Stuffed with fruit and meat, served under a sauce of sweetened farmer's cheese and walnuts and sprinkled with pomegranate seeds, it becomes an autumn classic in the red, white, and green of the Mexican flag: chile en nogada. The milder poblanos are generally light green, but Garland prefers the darker, hotter types. "The pungency of poblanos is hard to predict, however. The dark ones are generally hot, but sometimes the light green or red ones turn out to be hotter."

Garland picked up a reddish poblano, opened his jaws wide, and let his teeth dig into it. And then, as quickly, he spat the chunk out. "See what I mean? This one is very hot," he said, smacking his lips. "I would never have predicted that, looking at it." Heat levels aside, Garland uses poblano "to give an earthy" taste to dishes that already employ other peppers, such as jalapeño, which he says doesn't have any flavor. Poblano becomes part of a marinade that includes garlic, celery, onion, cilantro, and jalapeños. Chicken marinated in this and grilled becomes Pollo a la parilla on Garland's menu. At other restaurants, sautéed strips of the mildly pungent poblano are served cold inside warm, moist crepes; and in yet another variation poblano is turned into an earthy mousse.

Dried or smoked, poblano takes on new names: ancho, for the wrinkly and heart-shaped dark mahogany version; mulato, for the black and more pungent type. These dried poblanos are soaked and ground into pastes, which are used as sauces for a variety of delectable dishes. The most notable of these moles, or sauces, built on ground spices, is the mole poblano, Mexico's national dish. It's also a concoction of unlikely ingredients. To prepare the dish, ancho, mulato, and chile pasilla (another mahogany dried pepper, thinner and longer and more pungent than ancho or mulato) are first soaked and then blended together. The paste is then combined with chocolate. To it are added cinnamon, cumin, raisins, almonds, garlic, and tomato. The dark mass is then mixed with fat and stock and cooked for several hours into a thick and smooth sauce, which tastes bitter, earthy, spicy, and sweet all at once. This forms the sauce in which meats—often turkey—are stewed. It requires considerable skill to pull off this legendary dish.

The dish was created, it is said, by a nun at the Santa Rosa Convent in the city of Puebla to honor a visiting archbishop who had built the convent. To show her appreciation she blended ingredients of the New World—the chocolate and the chiles—with the others that came from the Old World. But another story has it that mole wasn't such a thoughtful and calculated culinary attempt at all. What actually happened was that a cook at the convent was preparing turkey for a visiting viceroy and had chocolate, chiles, and garlic and other spices sitting separately on a tray. A sudden gust of wind, the story goes, tossed them into a messy heap. Unable to separate the ingredients, the cook went ahead and prepared the turkey with the mingled spices.

Garland says mole isn't on his list of favorite dishes, and he doesn't even attempt to serve it in the restaurant. "I have never liked it. It's too heavy."

"Here's guajillo." Garland pointed to a pile of dried pods, about five inches long and an inch and a half wide. "These peppers are plucked when ripe, and then dried in the sun. You take the seeds out, and then boil the pods and turn them into a paste. It's my favorite for basting meats; it gives a pungent and nutty taste. Yumm!"

Garland picked up a handful of dried jalapeños called chile chipotle. They were wrinkly, twisted, and dark red, and they smelled like tar. "If you want a smoky flavor in minced or shredded meat, this is what you use."

Garland shuffled to the next bin. Chile seco, small and bright red. Chile piquín, a little round red pepper. "Very, very hot. The best pepper to fry with garlic for fish or beef. In Peru, when piquín is green we call it pipi de mono, which means monkey's little dick."

He shuffled to the next bin. "This yellowish green pepper is xcatic, a Mayan pepper. It's both sweet and hot at the same time." Garland took a bite of a yellowish pod, threw it back into the bin, picked up a reddish xcatic and did the same. "The red one is both sweet and hot. The yellow is just tangy."

He picked up five chile morróns, which look very much like the common bell pepper but are hot. "I can bet each has a different pungency." I was afraid he was going to callously bite a piece out of each to prove his prediction. "I believe you," I said quickly, and was relieved when he put the peppers—intact—back into the bin.

The truly awesome variety of chiles—in form, flavor, and pungency—attested to the fruit's unique contribution to Mexico's cuisine; no other cuisine in the world comes close to employing chiles the way Mexicans do. By one measure, 140 varieties of chiles are sold in the market. Each variety, whether fresh or dried or roasted, is used to give a specific effect. Fresh jalapeño may be used for its fire, but chipotle, the same pepper smoke-dried, imparts both a hot and a smoky flavor. The dry ancho has a hot and rich taste, but its green version, the poblano, is fleshy and is used to give a certain mouth-feel to the food it's added to. Since the peppers make their bites known differently—some burn immediately, some don't make their presence known until the food is swallowed, the impact of some is on the front of the tongue and some hit the back, while others engulf the mouth—the Mexicans select chiles and sometimes combine different types to achieve not only a certain flavor and aroma but an appropriate bite.

This alchemy has been so well developed over the centuries and fixed in the Mexican palate that it is said that gourmands can tell by tasting the food if a specific pepper has been omitted or substituted. I once discussed this with Elisabeth Rozin, who has written on food and has studied with particular interest the whole issue of food flavor. She told me: "The Mexicans manipulate peppers so as to make use of the differences in flavor and pungency to optimize the full range of their gustatory experiences. No one else does it. Other culinary cultures—the Indians, Indonesians, Chinese, and Thais—all rely mainly on one or the other type of chiles and primarily for piquancy. It isn't that Mexicans don't use chiles for hotness, but they manipulate the hotness and flavor and texture to achieve all kinds of marvelous subtleties. And this complex interaction of chiles was completely established before the Spaniards came to the New World. If you read the first Spanish explorers' descriptions of the dishes they encountered in Mexico you would find their eyes were bugging out of their heads. The dishes were so extensive in the use of chiles." Mexicans have developed a language of peppers.

Why Mexicans came to be so creative with chiles is a matter of speculation. Rozin thinks that long before the Spanish arrived the natives in Mexico had developed a sophisticated agrarian diet, and since it consisted mainly of starchy foods the natives took to different varieties of chiles to increase the foods' palatability. The Indians and Indonesians and Chinese, on the other hand, already had other pungent spices, such as turmeric and ginger and mustard and black peppercorn, all of which also imparted their own distinct flavors. So when the pepper arrived from the New World, the fruit that was hotter than anything else that existed in Asia was embraced, enthusiastically, for contributing pungency rather than subtle flavor or visual appeal. Even though Indian cuisine is closely associated with hot peppers, its distinction is the extraordinary interplay of flavors it offers with a whole range of spices.

Still, the claim that Indians aren't as creative with chiles as Mexicans are riles many Indians. Madhur Jaffrey, the Indian actress, cookbook writer, and authority on Indian cuisine, is one. "Only a person with an unsophisticated palate would say that," she told me.

I countered that Indian cuisine simply doesn't use the number of varieties common in Mexico.

"We have the most wonderful pickles made with red chiles from Banaras; the large pepper is stuffed with some fifty different spices and pickled in oil or lime juice. These Banarasi pickled chiles are famous. In New Delhi we have chiles pickled with mustard. We have all kinds of stuffed chiles, big and small. The only thing is that we have not assigned them names, as Mexicans have to theirs."

Based on what I had seen, I wasn't convinced.

In the wholesale market in Cancún, Lalo Garland was not buying much pepper; he was there largely for my benefit. But he filled a small plastic bag with habanero for his kitchen staff. Sometimes he has to worry about this pepper more than any other. "Five kilograms of this goes into the stomachs of my kitchen staff every week, all raw." Garland shook his head. The pepper isn't served to customers because its pungency is explosive. The only dish his customers get to taste it in is Taquitos de carne, sautéed meats eaten with corn flour tortillas. The habanero is in the accompanying sauce, blended with onion, parsley, olive oil, salt, and black pepper.

While strolling through the market, Garland spotted a bunch of iron skillets hanging in a shop and darted into the store. The shop also sold aspirin, soaps, toothpaste, shampoo, soft drinks, garlic, onion—and habanero. Garland picked up a skillet and haggled over the price—"If you don't bargain, you feel you have been had"—but ended up paying the full asking price after all. It was a small skillet, just big enough to hold one large fish fillet.

"This is for me," he said. "I want to make some blackened fish. Have you ever made blackened fish with piquíns?"

"I have never tried it," I said. Piquín is the tiny red pepper, the size of a small nailhead. Small "grenades," Garland calls them. But blackened fish, a Cajun dish, traditionally is made with a powder of mixed spices, mainly hot red pepper. The fish is smothered with it and charred in a scorching iron skillet. "I think that's a very unsophisticated preparation. You rub your fork on the fish and all this powder comes off," Garland said. "I want to take fresh piquín. Fresh jalapeño. Fresh oregano. Fresh poblano. Fresh onions. Mash all this up and coat the fish with the sauce. Then throw it in a real hot skillet. I can already taste it."

The next evening, Jalapeño's restaurant was swarming with American and European tourists. Women, overbaked in the sun, were sipping daiquiris and margaritas and other pastel-colored frozen drinks. Men were guzzling Corona beer. Garland sent me a plate of shrimp Corona, shrimp dipped in a batter of flour, Corona beer, thyme, coriander, oregano, salt, and serrano peppers, and deep-fried. A sauce of jalapeños, pineapple, and Dijon mustard accompanied the dish. "Isn't this sauce something," he asked, emerging from the kitchen on one of his frequent breaks.

Bignold spotted me. "Just the man I was looking for." He was quite excited. He wanted to show me a new pepper he had discovered. Actually, it was brought to the restaurant by a Maya farmer who had come to see him the previous night. The farmer was interested in supplying the restaurant with fresh produce and had left a handful of peppers as an inducement.

"I have no idea what kind they are. I tried one, and all I know is they are hot as hell and packed with seeds. I have been saving them for you."

Bignold was back ten minutes later, with an embarrassed look on his face. "They're gone. The kitchen guys ate them, raw, with tortillas, all of them. They ate them raw, can you believe it? They thought they were for them. These peppers apparently grow wild in their villages in Yucatán and when they saw them they realized how much they had missed the pepper. Maxic. I think that's what they said it's called. Sorry. I guess for them it was a special treat."

In Mexico, man developed a craving for chile when he was still foraging and hunting, some eight thousand years ago. Archaeologists found evidence of man's early attachment to this fruit when they dug up the Tehuacán Valley, in south-central Mexico, in 1960. It was a historic excavation because it shed important light on the origin and spread of prehistoric plant domestication. The oldest layers at the site, those formed before 7000 B.C., contained carbonized deposits of pepper and avocado pits. In the layers that corresponded to the period between 7000 B.C. and 5000 B.C., deposits were found of squash, avocado, cotton, amaranth seeds, corn, and pepper. Every subsequent layer unearthed—each representing a phase of civilization—contained pepper seeds, among other plant remnants.

In fact, archaeologists at the Tehuacán site unearthed a whole chile, almost intact, that dated from between 5000 B.C. and 3400 B.C. The thin, long pod is identical in shape and size to the present-day common species known as Capsicum annuum, and in Mexico it resembles the variety known as the chile pasilla.

"The consistent occurrence of chile remains, and the fact that chile didn't originate there leads me to suspect that it was planted there roughly eight thousand years ago," the excavation's director, Richard MacNeish of the Peabody Foundation for Archaeology in Andover, Massachusetts, told me when I called him upon my return to the United States. MacNeish was involved in another dig, in the state of Tamaulipas in northeastern Mexico. Chile remains there dated back to between 6544 B.C. and 6244 B.C., "plus or minus four hundred fifty years," he said. But more telling was the Tehuacán excavation, which seemed to suggest that chiles might have been cultivated before corn and squash.

Chiles were important "tributes"—the taxes paid by villagers to their chiefs and kings—very much as the black peppercorn once was a means of payment, and a measure of one's wealth, in Europe. During the rule of Mexico's militaristic Toltecs, for instance, thirteen of the thirty communities in the empire were required to pay their "tributes" only in chiles. During the reign of Nezahualcóyotl, subjects were made to pay twenty baskets of chile ancho, twenty baskets of chile menudo, and ten baskets of chile pequeños every seventy days. After the Spanish conquest, Antonio de Mendoza, the first viceroy of New Spain, demanded 400 crates of dried chiles, among other items, from the conquered cities.

In 1529, Friar Bernardino de Sahagun arrived in New Spain to chronicle the life of the Aztecs in what is now central Mexico. The friar recorded that the Aztec nobles ate stewed hen with chile, fish with chile, and frogs with chile, and prepared beverages, including a chocolate drink, with chiles. The variety they apparently preferred was a yellow pepper. "The poor Aztecs also ate chiles, except that they had less food to eat," he noted.

In the sixteenth century the town of Santa Catarina Texupa in Oaxaca threw a rousing party for a visiting bishop, and the community kept an account of the expenses: wine, hens, eggs, and two types of chiles (green and dry red).

By most accounts, the Mayan ancestors of the cooks in Lalo Garland's Jalapeño's restaurant were the most notorious consumers of peppers. In 1549 Friar Diego de Landa, a Franciscan monk known for destroying Maya idols and hieroglyphics, which he called the "falsehoods of the devil," noted:

> The Mayas toast the maize and then grind and mix
> it with water into a very refreshing drink, putting into it
> a little Indian pepper or cocoa.

In the mornings they take their hot drink with
pepper, through the day cold drinks. . . . When they
have no meat they make their sauces of pepper and [eat
them with] vegetables. . . . Their peppers have many
different pods; the seeds of some of these are used for
seasoning. Other [pods] are for eating baked or boiled,
and still others for [storing in] cups for household use.

To this day the Mayas, who occupy all of Mexico's Yucatán
peninsula and extend through Belize and Guatemala to northern Honduras and El Salvador, keep up a pepper-eating routine
more or less in that fashion. The Mayas' obsession with just one
pepper, the habanero, is unparalleled in pepper eating.

My curiosity about the Mayas' habanero habit led me to
Mérida, the capital of Yucatán. "I would say everybody in this
office grows the pepper at home," said Leticia Alvarado, a
thirtyish woman at the government's agricultural secretariat in
Mérida. She is an agricultural coordinator at the Secretaría de
Agricultura y Recursos Hidraulicos, or SARH. She looked
around the large room she shares with other agricultural officials. "I don't know of one neighbor who doesn't have at least
one habanero plant at home." (A man at a nearby desk looked up
and nodded.) "When children are three years old, they are
ready to eat habanero. In Yucatán only a small number of people
don't eat habanero, and if you ask me, they are from other
places—foreigners," she continued.

Alvarado said that in her house five potted pepper plants
hang from the ceiling. "Chickens love them. The rats love them.
The goats love them. We reach for the plants when prices are
too high in the market," she said. "Sometimes it costs two
hundred pesos for just three habaneros. A lot of poor people
can't afford habanero."

The tourist guidebook for Mérida warns that even "the
most macho might have trouble stomaching the habanero."

One of the places to test that is Los Almendros, an eatery on Plaza de Mejorada that bills itself as serving "authentic Yucatán dishes." With its plain tables and chairs and hurried waiters, the restaurant has the atmosphere of a bustling coffeehouse. When I arrived, I was immediately greeted and taken to a table. Before I settled into my chair, a tray-carrying waiter plopped down three bowls on the table and as quickly disappeared into the kitchen. One bowl held two toasted habaneros in lime juice; one had chopped habanero and slivers of red onion; and the third contained a green habanero sauce. On the picture menu, habanero is featured in most dishes: Combinado Yucateco (an assortment of broiled and baked pork), Pollo Ticuleno (boneless breaded chicken, ham, cheese, fried beans, and tomato sauce) and Escabeche de Pueblo (turkey baked with black pepper, cloves, vinegar, and onion). A whole habanero is positioned in the meal as a cherry or a strawberry is on some American desserts.

The habanero is usually toasted before it's served. In fact, the Mayas have a predilection for toasting and roasting. They toast garlic, seeds, oregano, and even tomatoes before putting them to use. To prepare one of their more celebrated dishes, cochinita pibil (pork steamed in banana leaves), the Mayas dig an oven-size hole in the ground and cover its bottom with large stones. They then light a thick wood fire inside it. When the flame has subsided, they wrap the pork with banana leaves and place the meat-and-leaf packets in a metal container inside the oven. The container is then covered with wet burlap or gunnysacks and topped with embers and hot stones taken from the bottom of the oven. The oven is filled with some of the excavated soil, and the meat is left to cook for many hours, even overnight.

The Mayas know that contact with heat brings out flavor. Roasting an habanero brings the *picante* juices to the surface of the pod, making it taste even hotter and more aromatic.

At the restaurant I cut slivers from a roasted pink habanero and sprinkled them on my entrée of Cochinita horneada con achiote (roast pork with achiote, a red seed ground to a paste and often mixed with orange juice). That first full-fledged encounter with habanero was memorable for the large amount of the local beer, Negra Leon, I consumed with the dinner and, more importantly, for the faint deafness that persisted for a few hours after the meal. About that mild deafness the waiter said, "That's so you don't hear your own screams." He laughed and then with a serious note diagnosed the symptom as "a feeling of high."

Despite the extraordinary pungency, the habanero is one of the smoothest peppers I have ever tasted. Its bite doesn't have a sharp edge, nor does its pungency linger, as the pungency of most hot peppers does. It has a silky taste, rich and velvety.

Although the Mayas disparage jalapeño, their favorite, habanero, may be a foreign item after all. The fact that habanero, unlike other peppers in Mexico, is rarely cooked or blended into the food is often cited as evidence that it is a relative newcomer to Yucatán. It's believed to have arrived from Havana, Cuba, a connection suggested by the pepper's name. The two regions once had close commercial ties. The pepper, however, doesn't exist anymore in Cuba, having vanished with the annihilation of the last Indian on that island. Mayas insist that if the pepper ever existed in Cuba it couldn't have disappeared without a trace. They use this evidence to claim Yucatán as the habanero's home. Others believe it got its name from Java, one of the points on a trade route connecting Mexico with Spain and Asia. Relatives of this pepper do exist elsewhere under different names: in Jamaica it's called scotch bonnet; in Liberia, billy-goat pepper; in Brazil, pimento de cheiro; and in Amazonian Peru, charapilla.

A relative of the habanero was recently identified growing in gardens and small plots in St. Augustine, Florida, where the locals call it datil pepper. I heard about this from Jean Andrews, the Texas artist and pepper expert, who had made a mad dash to

Florida from Austin, where she lives, to look over the plants and retrieve some pods. She told me she had sent some samples for botanical identification to Hardy Eshbaugh, the botany professor at Miami University in Ohio with whom I had trekked in central Bolivia in search of the mother pepper. "This may be the only pepper of its kind in the U.S.," Andrews told me excitedly. She would prove correct; Eshbaugh identified datil as belonging to the species Capsicum chinense, the species to which habanero belongs. The pepper, which starts out as a nearly white pod, turns lime green and then golden yellow at full maturity, and is somewhat bigger than the Yucatecan pepper. But it has the unmistakable fragrance of the habanero.

According to Andrews the pepper must have arrived from Cuba or the West Indies with Spanish settlers and traders. Local legend holds, however, that it came with the people of Menorca, a Mediterranean island off the eastern coast of Spain, who were brought in as indentured workers by the British in 1768 to work on Florida indigo plantations. Andrews said her research didn't reveal any sign that this cousin of habanero ever existed in Menorca. It's safe to assume, she said, that the pepper was already in St. Augustine and other areas on the east coast of Florida when the Menorcans arrived. The immigrants just fell in love with this very hot pepper, which remains a staple in many dishes of the Menorcan descendants. To the Mediterranean settlers the slightly wrinkled pepper looked like a date (datil in Menorcan Spanish), a fruit they were quite familiar with.

Mayas don't like to hear that their favorite pepper might have also come from abroad, that their cuisine has succumbed to foreign influence. After all, they have steadfastly resisted other intrusions.

They repeatedly fought such invaders as Hernandez de Córdoba and Francisco de Montejo. Although subdued finally in 1542, they once even hired the Texas navy to fight Mexico in an unsuccessful bid to establish their own independent nation. Maya guerrillas fought the central government as recently as four decades ago. They might have given up politically, but not on the pepper front.

When I saw Evaristo Ordoñez Pool, the Maya agricultural official at the government experimental station in Uxmal, I asked him what he found so special about habanero. He said the pepper does something agreeable to his state of mind that no other pepper does, certainly not the jalapeño. "When you eat habaneros, your head floats. You feel the head is not attached to your body. Unfortunately the feeling lasts only fifteen to twenty minutes."

Ordoñez Pool told me of a Texan who had visited him recently to explore the possibility of using habanero to make tear gas. "Why would anyone want to waste this pepper on tear gas?" he asked.

"Why would anyone want to eat something that could be turned into tear gas?" I countered.

"The pepper is hot, but it doesn't bother our stomachs. We actually sell habaneros to people outside of Yucatán, and they tell us it's the only chile that doesn't give them stomach problems. My doctor forbids jalapeños."

Actually I had heard that claim from other Mayas, even from some non-Mayas outside of Yucatán. One of them was Dr. Rubén Conde, who had a general practice in Mérida for many years before he moved to Cancún, where he now treats tourists. "Habanero is just hot in the mouth, and it is not an irritant as other chiles are," he said. "I don't know exactly why habanero is so different. Nobody has looked into it. I never found health problems in the Mayas I could blame on the habanero. From my experience I can tell you that if you eat other chiles in the quantities Mayas eat habanero they can give stomach cramps, abdominal pain, colon problems, gastritis, and hemorrhoids."

The habanero almost faced extinction in the 1970s. Ordoñez Pool was one of the principal horticulturists who saved it. All over Yucatán the pepper had turned scraggly and emaciated and was shrinking with each succeeding crop. Farmers watched helplessly, and the government agricultural experts were puzzled. Then everyone realized the cause of the problem was the farmers themselves: instead of saving fruits of the healthiest plants for the next planting, they had been selecting the sorriest-looking pods, since they wouldn't fetch a good price in the market. Ordoñez Pool and his fellow researchers collected the best available habanero pods from different parts of the state, and through interbreeding—a process that took seven years—came up with new and robust strains. The improved seeds were then distributed to farmers.

Actually, when the breeding process was completed, the researchers ended up with two distinct types of habanero. They propagated both. They named one Uxmal, for the variety that likes rich reddish soil. The other they called INIA, the acronym for the Instituto Nacional de Investigaciones Agrícolas; it prefers a rocky terrain. "We decided to develop both because Yucatán has both rocky and rich red soil," Ordoñez Pool said. The Uxmal variety bears four fruits in a bunch; the INIA, three fruits. The Uxmal pepper is two inches long and about an inch wide, slightly smaller than the INIA. Farmers prefer the INIA because the plant is compact and takes up less space, but for flavor people prefer the Uxmal. "But if you ask me, people here haven't become that picky. They are happy to have any habanero," Ordoñez Pool said.

The reason habanero is a scarce commodity in Yucatán is that the pepper, which has adapted to the region's loose and rocky soil, doesn't grow well anywhere else. A publication of the Mexican agricultural department says, "This pepper grows exclusively in Yucatán. . . . Commercial establishments in other parts of the country have been without results." Ordoñez Pool told me that after new varieties were developed the agricultural secretariat sent the seeds to the neighboring state of Veracruz, and farther north, to Guanajuato and Sinaloa. "These states grow all types of peppers but habanero. The varieties we sent just refused to grow in any of the states. We are investigating why."

The Mayas point to that botanical fact to strengthen their

claim of special kinship with the pepper, which belongs to the species chinense. Almost all other peppers in Mexico belong to the species annuum.

Some five hundred farmers grow habanero in Yucatán; together they represent about two hundred fifty hectares. Annual production totals twenty-five hundred tons, and 60 percent of this production is consumed in Yucatán itself. The rest is exported, mostly to the adjoining states of Quintana Roo and Campeche. In terms of revenue to farmers, habanero comes after corn, beans, sorghum, and melon and precedes coconut and onion and peanuts.

"But it's the most profitable of all crops," Rafael Lopez, a young agricultural coordinator at the agricultural secretariat in Mérida had told me when I visited the governmental office at the start of my journey in Yucatán. Lopez was himself an habanero farmer. "A side business to make money," he told me. He had planted a hectare, at a cost of 1 million pesos; he hoped to garner 3 million to 5 million pesos in sales but was worried that he might barely break even this season, since prices had plummeted because of robust production throughout the area.

"In cultivating habanero," he had said, "you can become very rich, or you can become very poor."

In Yucatán, retail prices of habanero fluctuate daily with the unpredictability of the stock market. The day I arrived there the pepper retailed in the supermarket for 5,000 pesos a kilogram; a month earlier it had ranged between 10,000 and 15,000 pesos. When I left a week later, the price had risen to about 8,000 pesos.

The fluctuation isn't caused by sudden changes in demand, as might be the case in stock and bond trading. Demand for habanero is by and large constant; it's the supply that's unpredictable. To start with, the peppers, which become harvest-ready at different times from farm to farm, arrive in the market in fits and starts. That causes short-term fluctuation in prices, sometimes from day to day. But the biggest reason for tight supplies is that the pepper is more difficult to grow than other peppers. The rocky soil it prefers is hard to plow and keep clear of weeds. The plant requires a lot of water, which is hard to harness in rocky soil. Farmers dig wells, or *pozos*, but in mid-season the wells can abruptly go dry.

Carmelo Chi Cauich grows one hectare, about two and a half acres, of habanero in a little clearing on a hill near Uxmal. It is one of the largest farms in the area. To get to his farm, field hands hike through rugged jungle terrain. Agricultural officials, who visit him frequently to dispense advice and to help him build a model habanero farm so that other farmers can be lured into growing this crop, use a four-wheel-drive pickup and have to dodge tree stumps and boulders to get there. One afternoon I hopped onto that pickup to reach the farm.

"A field bigger than this would be too much to take care of," the farmer told me after initiating a most unusual handshake, which involved first the usual clasping of each other's hands, followed by a cupping, and ending with interlocking each other's thumb. Wrinkles crisscrossed Chi Cauich's face, and his hazel eyes radiated happiness. "You cannot use machines to prepare the soil." He has had to dig three *pozos* in the rocky soil and the water from them is pumped by motors, a costly proposition. Chi Cauich said that in the Mérida area wells have to be dug twenty-six feet to find water. In the next largest area for habanero production, Ticul, the water level can be as far down as eighty-two feet, so pumping requires even larger motors.

"I need five or six people every two to three days just to water the plants," Chi Cauich said, pointing to the plastic pipes that snaked through his field. The day I was there, Chi Cauich had filled ten wooden crates with a total of 100 kilograms of habanero. That was the entire population of mature pods that day; pickers revisit the plants every two days or so when a new batch of peppers mature.

As I prepared to leave, Chi Cauich filled both my hands with pods he himself had selected. "In Yucatán we say food doesn't taste if it doesn't have habanero."

9

The Pepper High

A pepper eater doesn't simply like the bite of the pepper: he yearns for it. He may look forward to a meal to satisfy his hunger, but it's the prospect of the pepper accompanying his every bite that cheers him and makes eating a new indulgence every time. The pepper gives a certain sensory dimension to his dish, however elaborate and delicate the food might already be. The pepper accents his entire culinary existence.

Take the pepper away from the pepper eater and he withdraws and slips into a general malaise at the dinner table. He may even choose to starve. Or he may go to extraordinary lengths to procure his pepper. Notice the note of warmth and excitement when he talks about his favorite pepper. Listen to his "Ah!" when he bites into his choice pod. Notice, too, how amid sweating and gasping he reaches for more and more of the hot stuff and silently rocks between the crests of undulating pain and pleasure.

The pepper eater is addicted to his pepper. The craving, at the very least, rivals the more renowned addictions to caffeine and nicotine. It wouldn't be much of an exaggeration to say that it also resembles addiction to alcohol, even drugs. If Alcoholics Anonymous were to study the symptoms of the pepper eater, it would swiftly label them, I'm convinced, as signs of a progressively worsening disease. This narcoticlike behavior isn't easily apparent. After all, nobody rolls up a pepper to smoke it, or quietly slips into the bathroom to snort it. But the kinship between man and his pepper has equally bizarre and comic sides, which I have observed in the company of pepper eaters and heard in the stories of pepper habits. Here are a few.

Have Pepper, Will Eat Any Food

So dependent is Zubin Mehta on the pepper to appreciate food that he carries it with him all the time, even to the best-known haute cuisine eateries where even asking for the saltshaker would be seen as blatant disrespect for the chef's well-studied sense of balance. It wasn't at one of those restaurants but at a private dinner that a friend spotted the music conductor pulling a couple of hot peppers from his pocket.

I tracked Mehta down, over the phone, in Tel Aviv, where he had gone to conduct the Israel Philharmonic. I caught him in his hotel room, just as he was preparing to leave for a rehearsal. I introduced myself, and asked: "Is it true?"

My timing, it turned out, was perfect. The music director had just placed two dry red peppers in a matchbox, which he said he was going to carry in his pocket. "Without hot pepper I feel I am eating hospital food, even at Le Cirque," he said.

Le Cirque?

In a ritual now well established at that four-star New York restaurant he frequents, Mehta told me, waiters greet him with extended hands the moment he arrives. "My pepper box is immediately taken to the kitchen, and the chef himself puts the peppers in my food."

Even at Indian restaurants he shows up with peppers in his pocket. (Some time after our phone conversation I ran into him at an Indian restaurant in midtown New York, and he pulled out a dangerous-looking tabasco pepper from his pocket to show me.) Bringing your own pepper to a curry house is like bringing your own bread to a bakery. But Mehta must have his own brands. He grows three kinds—jalapeños, tabasco, and Hungarian cherry—in his Los Angeles garden. A full-time Mexican gardener tends to the pepper plants. But when it comes to selecting pods from his plants, "only I'm allowed to pick the peppers," Mehta said.

He usually carries peppers in a matchbox, but on formal occasions he uses a gold box, he said. At banquets he passes his peppers around the table. Call it pepper etiquette. He told me that at a recent banquet hosted by the Queen of England he passed his gold box around.

"Did the queen accept any?"

"No, she passed it on."

But his pepper habit has influenced others, he said. "Mrs. Sinatra used to carry Tabasco sauce; now she carries the real thing. Gregory Peck started growing his own chiles after he saw my garden. That's a relief, because at dinners I was always having to share my peppers with him."

Mehta said he has impressed none other than the King of Spain himself. When King Juan Carlos came for dinner at his Los Angeles home he was quite taken by the juicy red tabasco pods in Mehta's garden. "Before he left, he plucked a handful and put them in his pocket," Mehta said. "So, somewhere in his palace my tabasco peppers are growing."

I saw some irony in the King of Spain's grabbing a handful of peppers at the home of an Indian. For it was Juan Carlos's ancestors, the Catholic majesties of Spain, who had bankrolled Columbus's voyage to bring back black pepper and other spices from the Indian subcontinent. Columbus landed instead, of course, in the Caribbean and brought back an altogether different pepper from people he took—mistakenly—for Indians.

Rivera's Pepper Seed

If Lucienne Bloch Dimitroff had her way she would have Diego Rivera remembered as much for the muralist's craving for peppers as for his murals. A few years ago Dimitroff, who was Rivera's assistant, presented a seed from a Rivera pepper to the Detroit Institute of Arts to memorialize the muralist's passion for hot peppers. When I read the story in a local paper I called Dimitroff, a vivacious seventy-nine-year-old woman.

"Peppers were a big part of Rivera's life," she told me. "He worried about his peppers, like he worried about his colors and plasters." Dimitroff and her husband spent many years with Rivera as his assistants, transposing drawings from paper to walls and preparing his paints.

She found the seed in 1988 while restoring Rivera's murals at the institute. She was standing with a sponge in her hand on a scaffolding forty-five feet above the ground when she saw an oily patch on a mural—depicting the metamorphosis of iron, coal, lime, and sand into an automobile—and she gently scratched the blotch. A seed fell down. She lost it but found another one in the patch and carefully retrieved it. She put it in an empty film canister and labeled it: "A seed from Rivera's dinner." She then tied a bow around it and gave it to the institute's conservation division.

"It obviously came from his sputum," she said. "It must have been an extra-hot pepper."

Dimitroff wondered whether she might have been indirectly responsible for the lodged pepper seeds. After all, Rivera's wife Frida Kahlo had accused her of feeding the muralist hotter and hotter peppers and raising his heat threshold when the muralist's wife was hospitalized in July 1933 for a miscarriage.

In Kahlo's absence, Dimitroff had assumed the additional task of cooking for Rivera. One of the first things she learned from Rivera about cooking was how to toast dried red peppers. (Peppers were readily available in Detroit at that time, thanks to the large number of Mexican immigrants attracted by employment in the auto industry.) Apparently Frida Kahlo avoided toasting the pepper, no matter how much Rivera insisted. Toasting draws out the pepper's full brute bite. At Rivera's urging, Dimitroff would also add rather generous portions of toasted peppers to the meals she prepared to please him. Then came the day when Rivera's wife returned from her two-week hospital stay. She put in her mouth a spoonful of the previous night's leftover beef-and-cabbage dish—only to spit it out instantly.

"She said she wouldn't feed it to a dog," Dimitroff chuckled as she continued with her story. Kahlo accused her of excesses with peppers that were sure to kill her husband.

Rivera, however, came to Dimitroff's rescue. "Diego happily ate the leftovers in front of Frida and told her the story that when he was a student in Spain he would finish up a bowl of hot peppers and a bowl of cherries and couldn't tell the difference."

A Pepper Solves a Scholarly Dispute

In India, the southern part of the country is renowned for pepper eating, especially the state of Andhra Pradesh, the subcontinent's largest chile-producing region. According to government records maintained during British rule, Hyderabad, now the capital of Andhra, had the highest annual per-capita consumption of green and red chiles in the country, 6.375 kilograms, followed by Bombay's 4.713 kilograms.

Poor people accounted for most of the consumption. Hot peppers didn't figure much in the foods of the rich and the nobility, who preferred black pepper, cardamom, and saffron and other exotic spices of the time. The poor couldn't afford these aromatic spices and relied instead on hot peppers.

One summer I visited the family of a friend whose ancestors had ruled the Hyderabad state, once the seat of a powerful

Mogul empire known for its dazzling wealth—and its cuisine. I had telephoned earlier to say that I wanted to talk about chiles; I wanted to see what role the pepper played in the cuisine of the aristocracy. When I arrived at Hyder Manzil, an old baronial estate, I was greeted by Begum Husain, a woman of boundless energy, and her brother Agha Sirtaj Hasan Mirza.

"You know chile is a favorite subject of my husband. He can engage you in a lot of stories, but unfortunately he is laid up with an angina attack," the begum said as she led me into the living room, where the sprawling rugs, faded and frayed, hinted at the splendor of the bygone Mogul rule in India.

I asked if chiles were mainly a spice of the poor.

"Even aristocrats eat a lot of chiles in Hyderabad today," the begum said. "But the lower classes eat more chiles. Take my servants. I have to constantly stock up, otherwise they slow down and claim fatigue. They say, 'Oh, the head hurts,' or they say they are feeling dizzy. We have six servants, and every month they go through one and a half kilograms of red chile."

"But why blame the servants? Take your own family," Hasan Mirza, her brother, intervened.

"I am getting to that," said the begum, who likes the piquant, but only in moderation. "On my mother-in-law's side there were five people in the family. Do you know how much they consumed? Twenty kilograms per year. That's roughly two kilograms per month for five people. My grandfather and grandmother both ate two chiles each at lunch and two chiles at dinner, throughout the year. My parents put chiles in every-thing. I remember growing up praying, 'Oh, Allah mia, make chiles one rupee per kilogram! So expensive that people would stop eating chiles.' That was thirty-five years ago. At that time, five kilograms of chiles sold for one rupee. Now chiles are thirty rupees per kilogram and people are eating even more chiles."

After we finished tea, the begum wanted to show me a letter that, in her mind, said more about the pepper than any culinary application of it. Moments later I was following her into an adjoining three-story building that she and her husband were converting into a museum for Islamic scholars. It housed the family's ancestral possessions: books; letters; swords; utensils; Mogul garments; prayer beads; photographs; coats of arms; coin collections from the state of her great-great-grandfather, the Nizam of Hyderabad; and a vast collection of other memorabilia.

She paused before a glass display case and raised its lid. The case held piles of letters—from such extraordinary men of Indian history as Mahatma Gandhi, the Bengali poet Rabindranath Tagore, Maharaja Krishna Prasad, and Salar Jung—waiting to be organized. The begum rifled through the papers and, while continuing her search, read to me a portion of this or that correspondence that she thought was interesting.

"Here it is," she said finally. She had found the letter she was looking for. "This is from a famous Sufi of Delhi, Haza Hasan Nizami, to my father. There was a dispute between them over who spoke the purest form of Urdu between the two. Each claimed his was the purest. Letters went back and forth with claims and counterclaims," the begum said by way of background. "Finally, Haza Hasan Nizami wrote, 'How can my Urdu be different from yours? I have grown up eating chiles from your village.'" The begum read from the letter with great flourish.

"You see that settled the dispute."

The Arrivistes

The dependence on the pepper isn't peculiar to people of Mexican or Indian heritage. There's nothing in the genes of these people that makes them predisposed to the pepper habit. "Whenever I think of Henri Cartier-Bresson, I see him sitting at the dinner table with a tube of North African red-pepper paste in one hand and a pocketknife in the other . . ." began a profile of the famous French photographer in an October 1989 issue of the *New Yorker* magazine. Some Westerners have developed a highly discriminating palate for peppers. Sid, a Michigan businessman, for one. I had heard about him from a total stranger who surprised me in Detroit in 1986 with the tiny silver box he had pulled out of his pocket. The filigreed box seemed to have been designed with something else in mind, perhaps cocaine. But it was full of small dry red peppers, grown in Sid's backyard.

When I telephoned Sid that summer he said he had planted peppers in a forty-by-sixty-foot backyard plot. He had also planted peppers in two flowerpots that sat just outside his back door. "Sometimes I want to be able to reach one in a hurry," he said.

"You name a pepper, and I have it growing," he said, and then softened his claim. "I have planted all my favorite peppers. Of course, only those that can grow in the climate here."

He rattled off how he uses the half dozen different varieties he grows: "I put the mild chiles largos in breakfast eggs; cayenne in pasta; the very hot chipotle in meat sandwiches; the serrano in salad and as a garnish in a wide range of dishes. . . . The only thing I haven't tried peppers in is ice cream, although I have been tempted."

Once at a gathering of tweedy gentlemen at a New York club, where the members' spiciest encounter usually is with the Tabasco in their Bloody Marys, I watched with amusement the fuzzy and warm feelings hot peppers brought out in them. It all started when someone complained that the Tabasco he had just shaken into his drink wasn't hot enough. "You should try some of the hot sauces in Jamaica," he said. Another man, who had been to Peru to advise the government there on restructuring its banking system, chimed in: "I once brought these round peppers from Lima. But I haven't been able to grow the darn things." The man lived in Tuxedo Park, New York, which has hardly the climatic conditions for the Peruvian pepper. Said another: "There's this pepper in Bhutan. It's marvelous in vodka—just drop one in the bottle." Downing their drinks that Sunday afternoon, the men talked of how they had been smitten by peppers they initially had approached reluctantly during travels in Africa or South America or India. Back in the United States they were still pining with faraway looks for those faraway peppers. A week or so later, I learned, two of the men had exchanged peppers via mail.

Having been moved to an absurd action or two myself, I have come to accept such behavior as not all that odd. After my first taste of habanero at the restaurant Los Almendros in Mérida, Yucatán, I remember pondering how I could procure a supply of it back in New York. Although the pepper is the hottest known, its velvety and aromatic bite had gently set my head afloat, causing a sort of trance, a mild stupor. This was the pepper to have, and I knew it would impress quite a few friends north of the border. But I also knew it would be a problem to get around U.S. customs law, which forbids tourists from bringing fresh produce into the country. A Kansas woman once told me that her Mexican grandmother had made a special waistband in which she smuggled her fresh peppers into the United States. With customs officials now on to every trick in the books, that was out of the question for me.

I devised another strategy. On the plane back to the States I carried fresh habaneros in a brown paper bag, a big jar of water, and a small bottle of wine vinegar. Just as the Aeromexico plane landed, I quickly sprinkled a tiny amount of the vinegar into the jar of water and trundled the habaneros in after it.

"Any plants, fresh fruits, or vegetables?" I imagined the customs official inquiring of me.

"Nope!"

Technically, I was now carrying "pickled" habanero across the border. That is allowed under U.S. customs law. But customs never asked.

When I arrived at the taxi stand outside the airport I poured the liquid out of the jar to arrest any pickling action I might have started. I later parceled out much of the precious import to friends, some of whom habitually use overnight delivery ser-

vices to procure peppers—although not the habanero, which isn't easily available in the United States—from greenhouses in Texas and Louisiana. The habanero was a big hit. One recipient, Peter, a Wall Street type with an iron stomach, telephoned me a week later. He wanted to find out how he could arrange to have the pepper sent from Yucatán by Federal Express!

What's in the pepper that has taken hold of more than a quarter of the world's tongues? The craving for chocolate seems perfectly normal. A worldwide following for caviar, whose bitter and salty and slimy taste isn't for everyone, doesn't seem all that odd. Even some people's liking for anchovies is accepted. But pepper? I have looked for an explanation every time I have

sat across from a die-hard pepper eater who was happily enduring—or rhapsodizing about—a hot pepper while silently sobbing and squirming with discomfort.

I pursued the issue with some food historians, psychologists, and people who had suddenly become experts, having made their own efforts to find an explanation for their addictive habit. One theory is that the pepper eater likes the physiological change triggered by the pungent chemical. Paul Rozin, a psychologist at the University of Pennsylvania, is a proponent of this theory. It's one that I myself have come to put some credence in. According to this theory it's the brain's response to the pepper's burning sensation that the pepper eater likes.

When capsaicin, the chemical in peppers, comes in contact with the nerve endings in the tongue and mouth, the pain messengers in those nerves mimic burning sensations to the brain. The chemical, of course, doesn't actually burn the mouth

as fire or acid might. But why the pain messengers, known as the neurotransmitters, send this false signal to the brain is a mystery. It is said that the messengers can't identify the chemical and in a panic they carry the worst possible message to the brain. "Fire! Fire!" The brain—which isn't alarmed by other pungent spices, such as black pepper, Japanese wasabi, and ginger—in a reflexive action responds by turning the body's plumbing system into high gear to get rid of this substance: the heart beats faster, the mouth salivates, the nose sniffles, the gastrointestinal tract works harder, and the head and face break out in a torrential sweat.

Now here comes the best part of the physiological change: as the body tries to get rid of the pepper's chemical, Rozin told me, the brain, perceiving that the body has been injured by it, secretes its natural painkiller, endorphin. Endorphin produces the same effect as a shot of morphine or Novocain: it causes a high. The brain releases endorphin whenever the body is physically harmed. But since the pepper doesn't really do any harm—it doesn't burn a hole or peel off a layer of tissue—taking a bite of the pepper is like giving oneself a mild dose of painkiller for no reason at all. As the pepper eater takes another bite—since pepper doesn't desensitize the tongue, although the threshold for tolerance is raised—another burst of pain is perceived by the brain, and it spurs it to release more endorphin. The continued release builds into a rush. "Excessive endorphin causes pleasure," Rozin said, with a smile peering through his bushy salt-and-pepper beard.

The endorphin theory also explains why the pepper eater has a tendency to eat hotter and hotter peppers till he can't stand it anymore: it's the craving for more and more endorphin that leads him to take yet another punishing bite. "If we happened to stab our foot by mistake, the brain would release the same endorphin. But we don't get high because we don't stab the foot over and over again," Rozin said.

Rozin has fed hot peppers to humans and animals and closely studied their pepper behaviors. In association with his wife, Elisabeth (they are now divorced), a food historian, and a number of other researchers, he has published numerous papers on the subject. They have such titles as "The Nature and Acquisition of a Preference for Chili Pepper by Humans," "Some Like It Hot: A Temporal Analysis of Hedonic Responses to Chili Pepper," "Acquired Preferences for Piquant Foods by Chimpanzees," "Reversal of Innate Aversions: Attempts to Induce a Preference for Chili Peppers in Rats," and "Effects of Oral Capsaicin and Flavor Identification in Humans Who Regularly or Rarely Consume Chili Pepper."

Rozin has put forward another theory, one that he only mildly believes in. He suggests that the pepper eater derives a psychological sensation from the realization that the pepper, despite all its barking, leaves the body unharmed. Rozin compares the experience with a roller-coaster ride, a seemingly violent act that frightens the body but not the mind. The fright causes a physical discomfort in the rider, but the knowledge that all the free fall and the rolling won't result in any harm creates, at the end, a sensation of pleasure. The greater the fright, the greater the resulting pleasure from what Rozin calls the "constrained risk." "When you eat pepper you feel your mouth is going to peel off, but you know that isn't true. The pepper eater likes this benign masochism," he told me, and included among such mind-over-matter activities taking a sauna or a very cold shower. "They lead to a pleasant sensation after an initial discomfort."

Elisabeth Rozin looks at the pepper's role on a different level—as food. I met her separately in Philadelphia, at a Mexican restaurant, where the owner surprised us both with a variety of rare hot peppers that appeared in slivers and purées in our meals. When she wasn't complimenting the chef, Elisabeth was theorizing about why humans have forged a close association with this acrimonious fruit. Her conjecture is that the pepper does something to the mouth itself: it heightens the mouth's sensitivity. As a result, the mouth perceives the food to be more flavorful and tasty than it actually is. (It debunks the notion many pepper haters have that the pepper ruins the palate and thus one's ability to taste the food. In fact, the opposite seems to be the case.)

The pepper's chemical sort of bursts open the receptor cells, and the highly sensitized mouth now feels the contours of the morsel, its texture, its weight, its density, its succulency, its flavor—all the elements that make food appear delectable to the palate. Garlic, coriander, ginger, and other herbs and spices do that to some extent. Indeed, the ancient Hindus, who believed that different parts of the mouth—and the body—are stimulated by different tastes, constructed elaborate dishes with a range of different spices, a gastronomic principle that still guides the modern Indian cuisine. "But chile is very direct. In one bout, it lends plain food all the necessary dimensions," Elisabeth Rozin said. "Wham! And the food, rather the perception of it, is radically altered."

Thyme or basil or oregano or garlic enhances the food's acceptability by adding aroma and flavor to the food itself. The pepper doesn't have any of those attributes to speak of. When it's toasted or sautéed, it doesn't give off the inviting aroma coriander or garlic does; it instead stifles the throat and irritates the nostrils. Yet, when it is experienced in the mouth, it pleasantly transforms plain rice in a way that coriander or garlic or any other single spice can't.

That the pepper lends "mouth feel" to plain food is supported by the fact that it's primarily popular with people whose daily diets consist largely of such bland and starchy foods as corn, beans, and rice. All but the best tortillas are bland, but sprinkle on any of them a salsa of serrano or habanero and the paper-thin Mexican bread rises to a delicacy. That's how many of the poor in Mexico eat tortillas to nourish themselves. In India a flat wheat bread with slices of onions and some green chiles becomes an affordable and tasty meal for peasants. In *Nectar in a Sieve,* a 1954 novel about rural India, Kamala Markandaya wrote: ". . . when the tongue rebels against plain boiled rice, desiring ghee [clarified butter] and salt and spices which one cannot afford, the sharp bite of a chile renders even plain rice palatable."

"Wherever the cuisine is largely dependent on plants and vegetables, the use of spices is greater," Elisabeth Rozin told me. "That clearly indicates to me that there is something missing in vegetable food that meat offers. Meat is the most satisfactory package of nourishment, and its chewiness and bloodiness provide a psychological fulfillment not offered by plant foods. Chile gives the plant-derived foods the same sort of gustatory experience that meat offers." That may partially explain why the Irish or the German or the French haven't found it necessary to rely on the hot pepper to enjoy their meals, which consist largely of meats.

But the fact that the pepper is used liberally in meat dishes outside of Europe suggests that even an otherwise satisfying piece of beef or pork or chicken can be catapulted up the flavor scale with a dash of hot sauce or slivers of fresh hot peppers. Witness chile con carne (meat stewed with hot pepper and often beans), which the writer O. Henry described in "The Enchanted Kiss" as "a compound of singular savor and a fiery zest," or India's richly spiced chicken or lamb "vindaloo," renowned for its fire, or the Szechwan meat dishes from China.

It's the pepper's ability to enhance the "mouth feel" that sends Carol Farber, an anthropologist at the University of Western Ontario in London, Ontario, to hot peppers. "I am able to feel parts of the mouth that I can't feel when I eat Western food [without hot peppers]," she told me. She took to hot peppers, she said, while traveling with a theatrical group in Bengal. "At mealtime all the actors and actresses wanted a tiny green hot pepper on the side."

The pepper acts in another way to enhance food's acceptability: by producing saliva. The constant production of saliva helps move the food down the throat. And the gut, which is also activated by the pepper's chemical, digests faster. Thus the side effect: people who eat chiles often complain of overeating.

I have wondered if saliva is part of the arsenal of tricks the pepper plays on the brain. Usually it's the sight of "mouthwatering" foods that causes the mouth to salivate. The reverse of that cause-and-effect chain is that if the mouth waters, then the object it waters for must be something delectable. So a case can be made that the pepper-induced saliva must trick the brain into thinking that the morsel just placed on the tongue is delicious. "Go for it," says the brain. Hm! I didn't propose this theory of mine to any of the experts for comment, because who's to know!

How about the pepper itself being the repository of some rush-inducing substance that the pepper eater likes? After all, pepper belongs to the nightshade family of plants, which also includes potatoes, tomatoes, eggplants, tobacco—and the dan-

gerous plants like the hallucinogenic datura, the toxic henbane
and belladonna, all of which have alkaloids that interfere with
the human nervous system. The alkaloids in capsicum are
chemically related to caffeine, morphine, quinine, strychnine,
and nicotine. Dr. Andrew Weil, who has examined psychedelic
aspects of marijuana and certain mushrooms, says that pepper's
psychotropic effects — changes in mood and perception — are so
mild that they don't appear disruptive, as are the psychedelic or
hallucinogenic reactions caused by certain other members of
the nightshade family.

Only one pepper plant — which doesn't bear any peppers,
however — is known to have stronger psychotropic properties:
the root of the sakau plant is the source of an intoxicating drink
in the islands of Micronesia in the western Pacific. This bitter
beverage numbs the mouth and the mind and has an overall
calming effect on the body. It is prepared by smashing the
plant's roots and then wrapping the pulp in hibiscus bark and
wringing the juice out into a cup. The resulting slimy liquid is
taken eagerly for its mild narcotic properties.

In 1768 the English botanist and explorer James Cook listed
this sakau plant as Piper methysticum, or "intoxicating pepper."
But to claim that the pepper itself contains a narcoticlike agent
may be stretching it, although the widespread evidence that
people get permanently hooked to peppers has led well-known
pepper botanists to speculate there might be something to it.
"We don't like to publicize that," said the late Roy Nakayama,
the New Mexico State University professor who developed
many varieties of chiles. "I say, gosh, let's not get people all riled
up, and then the federal government will have twice as much
work as they have now."

When I think of the pepper's violent temper, I wonder who was
the first man to have called its bluff. Humans, by nature,
instinctively avoid things that are irritants, because they are
usually harmful, even deadly. And hot pepper, on the very first

bite, sends that danger message loud and clear. How did the first man to bite the pungent fruit know that it was an empty threat? It may be that the first pepper a human bit into was mild and he eventually moved up on the Scoville scale to discover that the hottest of hot peppers not only didn't kill him but infused him with pleasant sensations.

On the other hand, it shouldn't be all that surprising that the pepper was found out. Consider the red-capped mushroom Amanita muscaria, a truly dangerous substance. Also known as Fly Agaric, it is hallucinogenic if taken in tiny amounts. Step over that precarious boundary and it brings about death. But somehow man learned that the poisonous mushroom taken in tiny amounts induced only a high. To this day some people in Finland and eastern Siberia eat tiny pellets of this mushroom and then drink their own urine to sustain their altered state of consciousness—instead of taking more pellets, which might kill them.

Researchers believe the pepper adopted pungency to deter marauding animals. In forests, animals avoid pepper plants; in laboratory experiments, monkeys, rats, and moose have been shown to scamper away when served their favorite foods laced with hot chiles. Prompted by such empirical evidence, researchers at the University of Pennsylvania's Monnell Institute, which is next door to Paul Rozin's department, are developing crop protectors made from the pepper's chemical. "So far it seems to have worked against deer, rabbit, and meadow voles," said Russell Mason, a researcher at the institute.

Though the repellent sounded promising, I wasn't so sure after talking to Russell Reidinger, director of the Denver Wildlife Research Center. He told me he had worked in the Philippines with a group of scientists from 1974 to 1978 to develop "a rodent-control mechanism." Rodents destroy hundreds of millions of dollars' worth of crops each year in that country. "We were investigating what kinds of crops rodents eat and were looking for ways to make repellents for them. One of the repellents we were thinking of was hot pepper," said Reidinger. "Then one day a co-worker came over with a grin and said our hot-pepper approach wasn't going to work. He showed me pepper crops that were rather extensively damaged by rats. We were quite surprised that rodents would attack these thick banana-shaped peppers, which were very, very hot. I couldn't touch it with my tongue. It cooled our interest in hot peppers."

Russell Mason is also making pepper-coated birdseed to keep squirrels and other backyard predators away from feeders; birds don't mind peppers. "Birds seem to eat these seeds without feeling any difference, but the squirrels scurry down the feeder with tails between their legs," Mason said. Birds, which have helped spread peppers from the Andes to other parts of the New World, are immune to capsaicin, the pepper's biting chemical. "Birds are completely insensitive," Mason said. "We have fed birds two percent capsaicin solution. That's just about the limit of solubility. It will kill you, but birds consume it willingly."

I told Mason that in "The Islands of the Bay of Bengal" written by A. Hume in 1874, I had come across an account of a ubiquitous dove in the Andaman and Nicobar islands that lived exclusively on the small and extremely pungent Nepal or "bird's-eye" chile, which grows abundantly on those islands. The locals thought the birds gorged on the hot peppers to spice their meat to discourage predators. According to Hume's account, one ornithologist who investigated the doves reported, however, that he ate several of the birds but "couldn't detect the slightest trace of this attributed pungency."

"Funny you should mention that," Mason said. "We are feeding chickens hot peppers and other spices to see if we can make preflavored poultry for the supermarket."

The thing about hot pepper is that even animals, who are supposed to be repelled by it, can't resist it once they discover the pleasant side of the pepper's bite. It seems all it takes is human mediation. Taking their cue from humans in Mexico's Yucatán province, goats and dogs and chickens have developed a taste for the habanero, the indigenous pepper that is so hot that even adept pepper eaters in the rest of Mexico find it intimidating. As a result, in Yucatán it is not uncommon to see pepper plants suspended from the ceiling in flowerpots. In India cats and dogs and even cows gladly devour spicy scraps, and I have seen dejected looks on their faces when they have been tossed only plain rice and lentil leftovers.

In one laboratory experiment conducted by Rozin, the University of Pennsylvania psychologist, chimpanzees were given identical-looking pungent and plain crackers. Initially the chimpanzees preferred the nonpungent, but after a few weeks they slowly tried the pungent ones and eventually developed a preference for them. That's why I doubted that Mason would succeed with his pepper-coated birdseed. Sooner or later the squirrels would notice that the birds were eating them with relish and then one seed at a time the squirrels themselves would develop a taste for the pepper-laced seeds. Perhaps the only way Mason could discourage the critters would be to first make them addicted to the pungency and then switch to normal, uncoated seeds. Deprived of the pepper, the squirrels would be overcome with withdrawal and dejection and leave the bland seeds all for the birds!

The same mediation that makes converts out of animals clearly also works on humans. Mexico is proof. In that country peppers often aren't cooked into the food—as is done in India, for instance—but rather served as a side dish, mostly in the form of salsa. Children can choose to take it or leave it. But they see adults seasoning foods with it, and sooner or later they do the same themselves. The children end up not simply liking the taste. They eventually find it indispensable.

That the uninitiated can be converted is a relief for the

pepper eater living in the West. As a social animal, he is often frustrated in the company of diners who have never eaten a peppery meal or don't much like the idea. Some have never before seen a hot pepper in their lives: Bill, a friend and Detroit attorney, once half-chewed a pod from a dish of fresh peppers on the dining table, then turned to me red-faced and in agony asked, "What's wrong with these pea pods?" How does the pepper eater persuade his dinner companions to consider Thai or Vietnamese when it comes to choosing a restaurant?

At home, too, when the pepper eater invites friends for dinner he has to deal with the problem as he stands behind skillets and saucepans in the kitchen and wonders if the guests are having a fine time. He takes a quick peek and sees them reposing, glasses in hand, awaiting the dishes that he has ostensibly declared will be Italian.

The guests are unaware that the host, having discovered the pepper, habitually tweaks every recipe that comes his way with this or that pepper. Habanero slithers into the pan where portabello mushrooms or squid are sautéing, or chile piquín or red Bhutanese climbs out of an airtight jar into the sauce for pasta, or slivers of serrano spike a starter dish of grilled pimiento and mozzarella cheese. The ensuing heat may not be everyone's idea of a good Italian meal, even that of Southern Italians who are accustomed to piquancy.

After the guests depart, the host looks in the kitchen sink to measure the general success of the evening. The plates are heaped high with food that was tossed and mashed to give the appearance that much of it had been consumed with relish. He knows better. While his own stomach is content, he feels sorry, even embarrassed, for the guests. To avoid similar situations in the future, he thinks of seeking out only like-palated friends as dinner companions. But keeping valued friends requires a bit of consideration, and, in the case of the pepper eater, this means assuming the role of a mediator.

One strategy that rarely works is blasting your subject with high levels of Scoville heat the first time. He is so overwhelmed, so much in agony, that he can't bear the thought of going through the experience again. (Although there might be exceptions. Bill, my Detroit friend, for instance. He had cursed and vowed never again to go anywhere near the "pea pod." Two summers later he was on the phone and wanted to know how to preserve fresh peppers for the winter. You see, he and his wife had planted a whole garden of them!) I usually resort to the Mexican strategy, offering hot peppers as a side dish or in a side dish, and leaving them to beckon the guests. When the pepper is added to the main course itself, I prepare the guests with tales of the pepper's mysterious and beneficial attributes and implore them with an evangelical pronouncement: "All it takes is an open mind."

The initiation exercise works if the uninitiated has an open mind and faith—the sort of frame of mind recommended for prompting God to reveal Himself. The pepper usually keeps its end of the deal. Sure, the first bite of the pepper initially causes sniffling and sweating and burning and other discomfort. But perseverance provokes a cloaked warmth—not a burning sensation but a soothing glow—that mushrooms to embrace the entire mouth. Somehow, so it feels, this engulfing energy whips the food into a texture with new contours and edges that enhances the mouth's enjoyment of the morsel. Saliva rushes from the deep wells of the tongue, cajoled by the pepper's heat, and sends the food merrily sliding down the throat. As the sensory pandemonium subsides in the mouth, it leaves in its wake a certain void, a yearning. The mouth—or is it the brain?—craves to repeat the experience. One reaches for another bite of the pepper. The assurance that the pepper won't burn a hole on the tongue or peel off the skin but instead will reward the pursuer with soothing sensations now encourages the mouth to go after the bite with greater vigor. Then somewhere along the way the pepper eater, feeling a mild euphoria, a subtle trance, finds himself hooked—the experts would say that the endorphin effect has kicked in at this point—and what was once repulsive is now sought with ever-increasing intensity.

Paul Rozin, the psychologist, describes this as a moment of "hedonistic shift."

Once initiated, the pepper eater unconsciously strives to build a rush. I talked about it with Andrew Weil, the expert on psychedelic plants. The "secret" of the pepper lover's tolerance, he said, is his knowledge that the sensation follows in the form of a wave that "builds to a terrifying peak, then subsides, leaving the body completely unharmed." The pepper eater thus glides along on that wave, in a vicious cycle of pain and endorphin-induced pleasure, in a technique he calls "mouth surfing."

It is a misperception that the pepper's chemical slowly desensitizes the mouth, and that it is this which allows the pepper eater to eat hotter and hotter. That is an argument often given by those who avoid hot peppers on the ground that the pungency would spoil their taste buds. If, indeed, the pepper desensitized the mouth, it would eliminate the very reason—the desire to feel the burn—that drives the pepper eater to yearn for the heat in the first place. The brain wouldn't have any reason to provide a shot of endorphin every time the pepper eater bites into a pepper. The regular ingestion merely increases the threshold for tolerance.

All psychological and mouth-feel and surfing theories aside, the spread of peppers has had something to do with the dietary principles of many cultures, including those of India and China. They emphasize balancing cold with hot—peppers being hot and yogurt and other dairy products being cold—a concept with roots in the medicinal practices of such cultures. Mysteriously, however, even in those countries that are so closely associated with chiles, there are huge regions that eschew pungency. In China only Szechwan and Hunan provinces have peppery foods, for instance. One explanation for this is that those provinces once traded silk for hot peppers and other spices from India, and the goods traveled overland on what came to be known as the Silk Road of Burma. Much of Europe still ignores the pepper, and that's baffling because its first stop after leaving South America was Europe; only Hungary has come to embrace the fruit. Anomalies exist even within South and Central America. Hondurans, for instance, aren't all that enamored of chiles, while their Guatemalan neighbors fuss over the flavor of jalapeños. Climates inhospitable to peppers may explain why some parts of the world have been slow to adopt the fruit. But then Europeans resorted to international adventure and piracy to procure black pepper from India, and all they have to do today is visit the ethnic grocer on their block for hot peppers.

Still, that a quarter of the world's population has become dependent on the pepper, many even addicted, is a remarkable following for a fruit that bites back with a vengeance. The English historian Edward Gibbon was perplexed that Romans had taken to a taste he called atrocious, that of the less pungent black pepper. This berry, indigenous to India, was crushed to preserve and spice meats, and it was even combined with Tokay wine to make love potions in Rome. "Pepper has nothing in it that can plead as a recommendation to either fruit or berry, its only desirable quality being a certain pungency, and yet it is for this that we import it all the way from India! Who was the first to make trial of it as an article of food?" Gibbon said of the black peppercorn in his eighteenth-century account of the Roman Empire.

Later, the searing South American pepper would be met with similar derision. The German traveler August Elbrich described his meal of meat and hot peppers on the Danube—before the Hungarians genetically emasculated the pungency from their paprika—as "glowing embers [and] worse." One English traveler temporarily paralyzed by the pepper's bite in South America described it as "a lash from Lucifer's forked tail." Even today many conjure up the image of speeding fire trucks when the hot pepper sets their mouths afire—"a five-alarmer," they say, as they hurriedly reach for a glass of water. The pepper is often described as stinging, irritating, biting,

Acknowledgments

This story of peppers was shaped, in large part, by a number of people whose names don't appear on the pages of this book. Holly Neumann, a writer and pepper devotee, read the manuscript in progress with unflagging enthusiasm and made invaluable suggestions. Martha Hernández Puga translated Spanish texts, and in Yucatán, Mexico, guided me through habanero pepper farms and Maya homes in what would become my most captivating encounter with the tempestuous fruit. Others recalled pepper lore, or drew some exotic facts to my attention, or brought back peppers from Ladakh and Belize and from the deserts of Arizona, or sauce from Jamaica and Hawaii and Morocco, or allowed me to observe their pepper habits at the dinner table, or simply endured my pepper talks. My thanks to them all: Dolly Barnes, John Bussey, Chuck Caulkins, Bill Cox III, Laraine Fletcher, Randall Fruehauf, Melinda Guiles, P. J. Johnson, Josefina Howard, James Marlas, Marta Martino, Abha Mehta, Jim Mehta, Peter Merner, Marie Nugent-Head, Vasil and Gina Pappas, Helen Runnells, Allen Scheuch, William and Kathy Schaefer, Richard Schweid, Fatima Shanaz, Joan Siefert, and Sarah Thurber. I am also grateful to Jean Andrews, a friend, Texas artist, and author of a scholarly book on peppers, for generously coming to my aid.

Index

A BOOK OF MIDDLE EASTERN FOOD
by Claudia Roden

More than 500 recipes from the subtle, spicy, varied cuisine of the Middle East, ranging from inexpensive but tasty peasant fare to elaborate banquet dishes, all translated into workable Western terms.

"Mrs. Roden is an inspiring guide.... Her recipes are mouth-watering and her directions clear and easy to follow. *A Book of Middle Eastern Food* is a landmark in the field of cookery."

—James Beard

Cooking/0-394-71948-4/$15.00

THE FOOD OF FRANCE
by Waverley Root

A compendium of recipes and advice on good eating, from peasant fare to haute cuisine, *The Food of France* is also full of fascinating excursions into history, language, nomenclature, architecture, and local customs.

"The most lucid and definitive book ever written in English on a cuisine that has flourished for centuries."

—Craig Claiborne, *The New York Times*

Food/Travel/0-679-73897-5/$13.00

THE FOOD OF ITALY
by Waverley Root

In summoning up the flavors of Italy, including its two hundred variations of the basic *ragù Bolognese*, Root has composed essential reading for the traveler as well as the cook, and conveys the mysterious and wonderful essence of all things Italian.

"Root has managed to capture not only the essence of the Italian table but also of the Italian soul."

—*Newsweek*

Food/Travel/0-679-73896-7/$15.00

AN INVITATION TO INDIAN COOKING
by Madhur Jaffrey

This quintessential guide, carefully worked out in American measurements and ingredients, demonstrates how subtle, varied, and exciting Indian cooking can be.

"The final word on the subject...perhaps the best Indian cookbook available in English."

—Craig Claiborne, *The New York Times*

Cooking/0-394-71191-2/$11.00

NATIVE HARVESTS
Recipes and Botanicals of the American Indian
by Barrie Kavasch

Hundreds of authentic recipes introducing this hearty and imaginative cuisine are in this book, including those for clover soup, purslane salad, meadow mushroom pie, stewed wild rabbit, and hazelnut cakes.

"The most intelligent and brilliantly researched book on the food of the American Indian."

—Craig Claiborne, *The New York Times*

Cooking/Botanical Guides/0-394-72811-4/$13.00

TASTES OF PARADISE
A Social History of Spices, Stimulants, and Intoxicants
by Wolfgang Schivelbusch

From beer to coffee, pepper to cigarettes, this beautifully illustrated book maps our ever-changing appetite for pleasure.

"Colorful anecdotes [and] carefully chosen illustrations enhance the book's charm. *Tastes of Paradise* is a well-spiced treat, a stimulating book replete with ideas."

—*The New York Times Book Review*

Social History/Food/0-679-74438-X/$13.00